Benj. F. (Benjamin F.) Babcock

The Presidential Favorites

A Political Handbook, Containing the Portraits of thirty American Statesmen

Benj. F. (Benjamin F.) Babcock

The Presidential Favorites
A Political Handbook, Containing the Portraits of thirty American Statesmen

ISBN/EAN: 9783744731515

Printed in Europe, USA, Canada, Australia, Japan

Cover: Foto ©Suzi / pixelio.de

More available books at **www.hansebooks.com**

THE

Presidential Favorites.

A POLITICAL HAND-BOOK,

CONTAINING THE PORTRAITS OF THIRTY

AMERICAN STATESMEN,

Together with their Biographies, and an Epitome of
Every National Political Convention ever
held in the United States.

ALSO THE STATUS OF THE DIFFERENT POLITICAL PARTIES
UPON THE QUESTIONS OF THE TARIFF AND
SILVER, AND A HISTORY OF THAT
METAL AS MONEY.

WITH OTHER INFORMATION INDISPENSABLE TO EVERY CITIZEN.

By BENJ. F. BABCOCK.

WASHINGTON, D. C.:
PUBLISHED BY
CAMPAIGN PUBLISHING COMPANY,
1896.

To the
Patriotic Impulse which
Prompts the Citizens of Our Country
to Acquaint Themselves with the Lives of Our Public Men
and Our National Politics,
The Author
Dedicates this Volume.

INDEX.

	PAGE
Title	1
Dedication	3
White House	5
Introduction	6
Grover Cleveland	7
Benjamin Harrison	11
Wm. C. Whitney	16
Levi P. Morton	21
Adlai E. Stevenson	26
Thomas B. Reed	30
David B. Hill	34
Wm. B. Allison	36
Jno. G. Carlisle	40
Matthew S. Quay	44
Wm. R. Morrison	50
Wm. McKinley, Jr	52
Claude Matthews	59
C. F. Manderson	63
Daniel W. Voorhees	68
Shelby M. Cullom	71
John W. Daniel	74
Russell Alexander Alger	77
H. Clay Evans	80
Wm. F. Vilas	84
Cushman K. Davis	87
Wm. L. Wilson	89
Henry M. Teller	92
Jno. T. Morgan	94
Stephen B. Elkins	96
Wm. M. Stewart	99
Jas. Donald Cameron	103
William V. Allen	106
Wharton Barker	108
W. O. Bradley	114
Epitome of American Politics, and Synopsis of Political Platforms, 1774 to 1896	117
Attitude of Parties, 1896, upon the Tariff and Silver Questions	138
History of Silver as Money	142
Amount of Gold and Silver in the Principal Nations of the World, with Per Capita Amount of Money in Circulation	145
Value of Foreign Coins in U. S. Currency	146
Electoral Votes for Presidents and Vice-Presidents, 1789 to 1892	147
Popular Vote for Presidential Candidates, from 1824 to 1892	150
Candidates for President and Vice-President since the Adoption of the Federal Constitution	153
Electoral Vote by States, 1872-1892	156
How President is Chosen, and the Law Governing the Counting of the Electoral Vote and Defining the Presidential Succession	156
Number of Congressmen from each State since Formation of Constitution	160
Governors of all States, Terms, Salaries, and State Capitals	161
Brief Sketches of the Presidents of the United States, When Born, Inaugurated, Term of Service, Died, etc	162
Vice-Presidents of the United States	164
Presidents Pro-tempore of the United States Senate	164
Speakers of the United States House of Representatives	165
Presidential Cabinet Officers	165
Justices of the Supreme Court	168
Signers of Declaration of Independence, Where Born, Delegated from, Died	169
Presidents of the Continental Congress, and Congress of the Confederation	170
Naturalization Laws of the United States	170
Constitution of the United States	172
Origin, Settlement and Population of United States and Territories	183
Population of United States, 1790-1890	185
White and Negro Population of the South by Decades, 1790-1890	186
Population of the United States according to Nationality	187
Number of Dwellings and Families in each of the States	188
Nationality of Inhabitants of Largest Cities, 1890	189
Requirements regarding the Registration of Voters	190
Woman Suffrage	190
The Ballot-box Reform Movement	191

INTRODUCTION.

IN writing the within pages, and compiling the statistics in this volume, the author and editor has been actuated by a desire to give only facts. There will not be found any fulsome praise or flattery in the sketches given of our public men.

The book is non-partisan, hence the author cannot indicate his choice. He believes the good sense of the American people will, as it has in the past, elevate to the Presidency and Vice-Presidency able and worthy men. There is little doubt but that the names and biographies of the men who will be nominated by the different political parties are here given.

May the men win who will best guide the ship of State, and most faithfully serve the interests of the people during the next four years.

The book is now launched upon the sea of public favor, and the author trusts it will merit the people's approval.

Grover Cleveland.

GROVER CLEVELAND.

THE present President of the United States was born in the county of Essex, State of New Jersey, March 18th, 1837. His ancestors came from Suffolk County, England, and settled in Massachusetts, early in the 17th century. Richard F., father of the President, was educated for the Presbyterian ministry, and in 1829 married Miss Neal, daughter of a Baltimore merchant, who was born in Ireland.

Grover was christened Stephen Grover after the minister who occupied the pulpit at Caldwell, N. J., where the President was born.

Grover Cleveland's educational opportunities were rather limited, consisting of a chance to attend the common schools and an academy at Clinton, Oneida County, New York, for a brief period. After leaving the academy he became a clerk for a year at one of the eleemosynary institutions of New York City; then he returned home, determined to go west to seek his fortune, and in May, 1855, with a companion, started for Cleveland, Ohio. Mr. Cleveland says he was attracted to that city because it had his name. On his way there he stopped at Buffalo, to visit an uncle, Mr. Lewis F. Allen, who used his best endeavors to dissuade his nephew from going farther. To make his arguments and entreaties effectual, he offered Grover a clerkship. As work was what young Cleveland desired, he of course wanted to stay, but declined to give positive answer until he consulted his young friend whom he had promised to accompany to Ohio. The young man promptly acceded to Mr. Cleveland's staying, saying he ought not to decline the proffered employment. Having determined upon the law as a profession, it was not long before he made arrangements to become a student in the office of Rogers, Bowen & Rogers. In 1859 he was admitted to the bar, passing most creditably a rigid examination. He continued with his preceptors four years, which gave him really eight years of thorough study and legal experience. He was then appointed Assistant District Attorney for the county of Erie, by C. C. Torrence, which position he filled for a period of three years. In 1865 he was nominated by the Democratic County Convention for District Attorney, to succeed Mr. Torrence, but was defeated by Hon. Lyman K. Bass.

Mr. Cleveland formed a law copartnership with the late I. V. Vanderpool, January 1st, 1866, which was continued until 1869. He then became a member of the firm of Laning, Cleveland & Folsom. In November, 1870, Mr. Cleveland was chosen Sheriff of Erie County, a position he creditably filled. After this service he became a member of the law firm of Bass, Cleveland & Bissell. This was the strongest and brainiest law firm in Western New York, and at once commanded a very lucrative practice. In 1881, Mr. Cleveland was chosen Mayor of Buffalo, though it was a Republican city, the State ticket of that party carrying the city by an average majority of 1,600 votes. Mr. Cleveland was elected Mayor by a very large majority, his fellow citizens feeling that he was the man needed to successfully stem the tide of ring rule and reckless expenditure. In the position of Mayor he attracted the particular attention, not only of his own constituency, but of the leading party managers of the State, notably, the late Samuel J. Tilden, and principally because of his vetoes of hasty and corrupt city legislation. Before his term of office expired as Mayor he was nominated for Governor, and elected over so able a man as the Hon. Charles J. Folger, Secretary of the Treasury of the United States, by the unprecedented plurality of nearly 200,000, and a majority over all of 151,742 votes.

The day he was elected he wrote his brother that he proposed " To make the matter a business engagement between the people of the State and myself, in which the obligation on my side is to perform the duties assigned me, with an eye single to the interests of my employers."

The result of this determination led the rank and file of his party to believe the "coming man" was Grover Cleveland, and hence the National Democratic Convention, which convened at Chicago, July 8th, 1884, nominated him, July 11th, for President, and he was elected, receiving of the popular vote 4,784,986, and a majority of 37 in the Electoral College. In his inaugural he declared his approval of the Monroe Doctrine, for strict economy in national expenditures, and gave recognition of the value of the Civil Service. The oath of office was administered by the late Chief Justice Morrison R. Waite. His Cabinet will be found in another portion of this book. During his first term as President, 1885-89, he vetoed 115 out of a total of 987 bills presented for his signature, 102 being private pension bills.

At the National Democratic Convention, in 1888, he was again nominated as President, but was defeated by Benjamin Harrison. At the expiration of his term, March 4th, 1889, he removed to New York City, which he had determined to make his home, and resumed the practice of the law, arguing cases only before the United States Supreme Court. While Mr. Cleveland had, because of the very positiveness of his character, excited the enmity of many leading men in his party, he retained a firm hold upon the regard of the masses, who believed that, while sometimes wrong, he was most generally right, and always honest, so that before the nominating days of 1892 it had become pre-determined that he should again be the Democratic standard bearer. He was nominated and elected over his old opponent, President Harrison. In the nominating convention Mr. Cleveland received 617 out of 908 votes; and in the Electoral College he had a majority of 110 votes over Harrison, Republican, and Weaver, Populist, and 132 over Harrison. The popular vote was 5,556,918 for Cleveland, 5,176,108 for Harrison, and 1,041,028 for Weaver.

His record as our present President is too recent to call for elaboration here. That he has excited the enmity of many of the leaders of his party by his attitude upon the silver question there is no denying; but that he believes he is right and doing for the best interests of his country no one, Republican or Democrat, denies. He is a man positively firm in the maintenance of his convictions, having a vast amount of the "by the eternal" of Gen. Jackson in his mental composition. He stands upon the money question for the payment of every dollar of the obligations of the United States in the best coin, which he believes to be gold.

On June 2d, 1886, he married Miss Frances Folsom, a daughter of his former law partner, Oscar Folsom, and is the father of three children, all girls; his wife has contributed in no small measure not only to his happiness, but personal popularity.

Benjamin Harrison.

BENJAMIN HARRISON.

GENERAL BENJAMIN HARRISON, of Indianapolis, was born at North Bend, Ohio, August 21st, 1833, at the house of his grandfather, President Harrison, who was a son of Benjamin Harrison, one of the signers of the Declaration of Independence from Virginia. His early education was received at home, from a tutor employed in the family, and at the age of fourteen he was sent to Cary's Academy, near Cincinnati, where he remained about two years. In the summer of 1850, he suffered the loss of his mother, and in the fall of the same year went to Miami University, Oxford, Ohio, then under the presidency of Rev. W. C. Anderson. Here he entered as a junior, and in June, 1852, graduated fourth in a class of sixteen. After a few months' vacation he commenced the study of law in the office of Storer & Gwynne, of Cincinnati, where he remained two years. In October, 1853, he married Miss Carrie L. Scott, daughter of Rev. J. W. Scott, D. D., of Oxford, Ohio. Two children of this marriage survive— Russell B. and Mamie S. Harrison. In March, 1854, Mr Harrison settled in Indianapolis, with a fortune of eight hundred dollars, inherited from the estate of a deceased aunt, Mrs. Gen. Findlay, of Cincinnati. Here he first entered the office of John H. Rea, Clerk of the District Court of the United States, and while there was invited by Major Jonathan W. Gordon, to assist in the prosecution of the "Point Lookout" burglary case. This was his first jury trial. Governor, David Wallace represented the defense. When Mr. Harrison sat down, after making his argument, and the Governor prepared to reply, he paid the young lawyer a graceful and well-merited compliment. Soon afterward he was invited to form a partnership with William Wallace, and accepted. This connection proved very pleasant, and the firm did a prosperous and successful business. Shortly after entering this partnership, Mr. Harrison was appointed by Judge Major to prosecute a case against a negro who was accused of putting poison in some coffee at the Ray House. He had but one night for preparation and no previous knowledge on the subject of poisons, but he sat up the greater part of the night, and, with the assistance of Dr. Parvin, acquired considerable information on toxicology, from several experiments for the detection of arsenic in the coffee exhibited by the doctor. The result was the conviction of the criminal. In 1860, his partner, Mr. Wallace, was elected Clerk of Marion County, and Mr. Harrison formed a law partnership with Mr. W. P. Fishback, which continued until he entered the army. In the fall of 1860, Mr. Harrison was elected Reporter of the Supreme Court of Indiana. During his term of office he published two volumes of reports (XV and XVI), and had nearly completed a third (XVII), when he entered the military service. A notable event in connection with the political canvass was his joint meeting with Governor Hendricks, at Rockville, Parke County, which was quite accidental, but in which the youthful orator acquitted himself in the most creditable manner. The joint debate is still remembered by all who heard it, and showed General Harrison to be an orator second in debate to none in the country. In July, 1862, Mr. Harrison felt it his duty to enter the army. Although a young man, holding a comfortable civil office, just starting in life, with a young wife and two little children, when Governor Morton in asking him to raise a regiment, said some one else could be found to lead it to the field, Mr. Harrison accepted the commission but refused the proposition, saying that if he persuaded a man to go to the field he would be found there with him. He raised and took the first company (A), of the 70th Indiana Regiment into camp, and in less than thirty days from the date of the first recruiting commission, was in Kentucky with one thousand and ten men. This was the first regiment in the field under that call. General Harrison continued in the army until the close of the war, when he was mustered out as a Brevet Brigadier-General. His regiment served in Kentucky and Tennessee, in the Army of the Cumberland, and was connected with a brigade commanded for a long time by General W. T. Ward, of Kentucky. In the Atlanta campaign, the brigade was attached as the First Brigade, to the Third Division of the Twentieth Army Corps, commanded by General Joe Hooker. After General Butterfield left the division, Colonel Harrison was assigned to the command of the brigade, and continued in that capacity until after the surrender of Atlanta. Being then temporarily detached for other duty, he was, after Sherman's army marched from Atlanta, assigned to command a provisional brigade, and with that took part in the battle of Nashville and the subsequent pursuit of Hood, to Tuscumbia, Ala. Being relieved at his own request, and ordered to join his brigade at Savannah, he would have joined them there, but on his way was prostrated by a severe fever, which confined him to his bed for several weeks. Before he was fully recovered he started for Savannah, and the army having moved, was assigned to command a camp in which the recruits and convalescents were gathered. When Sherman reached Raleigh, Colonel Harrison joined his brigade, and accompanied them to Washington. Meanwhile, in the fall of 1864, he was reëlected Reporter of the Supreme Court, and was offered a place in the law firm of Porter & Fishback, which then became Porter, Harrison & Fishback. After Mr. Fishback assumed the editorship of the *Journal*, General Harrison remained with Mr. Porter, in company with Judge Hines, the firm being Porter, Harrison & Hines. This firm was dissolved, and W. H. H. Miller became a member of the new partnership, under the firm name of Harrison, Hines & Miller, in which the General still continues. In 1876, General Harrison was the unanimous choice of the Republicans of Indiana for Governor, on the withdrawal of Godlove S. Orth. After a most exciting canvass he was defeated. Prior to the nominating convention he had declined, but on the withdrawal of Mr. Orth, felt it to be his duty to respond to the imperious call of the people from all parts of the State.

In 1880, he was Chairman of the Indiana delegation, at the Republican National Convention, when he cast the entire vote of the State for Garfield. The latter, when elected President, offered Mr. Harrison a seat in his Cabinet, but he preferred to become United States Senator, to which office he had been elected. As a Senator he at once commanded attention, and in recognition of his acknowledged ability was selected to serve on the more important committees.

In 1884, he was Delegate-at-Large to the Republican National Convention at Chicago, and in 1888, June 19th, was nominated in the same city, on the eighth ballot, for President, by the decisive vote of 544 delegates. The nomination was then made unanimous; for President, he received 233 electoral votes, against 168, cast for Grover Cleveland.

Early in his administration trouble arose between this country and Great Britain, over the Bering sea seal fisheries, but which were happily settled by a Board of Arbitration, James G. Blaine, being Secretary of State. Early efforts were also made for the holding of a Congress in Washington of the Central and South American States, and a Pan-American Congress was held in 1889-90, resulting in reciprocal relations as to trade and commerce.

During the first two years of his administration, six new stars were added to the American flag, the new States being North Dakota, South Dakota, Washington, Montana, Idaho and Wyoming.

Commissioners under the direction of the Secretary of the Interior, successfully purchased a vast amount of land from Indian tribes, with the result that Oklahoma was thrown open to settlement.

In the spring of 1891, a difficulty arose in Louisiana, between the city government and people of New Orleans on one side, and Italian residents on the other, which resulted in the killing of a number of Italians confined in prison upon the charge of murder.

The Italian government promptly made demand for redress and indemnity, in language peremptory in tone and almost offensive in manner. This demand was met courteously but firmly by the statement, that while the Government earnestly disapproved and denounced the action of the mob it could not recognize a national responsibility for its results, unless it could be shown that its action was the result of connivance on the part of the public authorities of New Orleans; and that the United States did not guarantee or become insurers of the lives of aliens; that the courts were open to them as well as to citizens.

The Italian Minister, Baron La Fava, withdrew, and the American Minister at Rome was given indefinite leave of absence. The matter was subsequently amicably adjusted.

Mr. Harrison did all in his power by suggestion and executive direction to strengthen the United States Navy, and widened and extended the Civil Service.

In 1891, he made an extended tour in the South, Southwest and to the Pacific coast. During this trip he made a great many speeches, and in so felicitous and happy a manner they not only pleased his auditors, but being reported in all the leading papers of the country, added lustre to his reputation as an exceedingly charming speaker, fertile in thought and expression. During his incumbency of the Presidency his beloved wife died, a victim to the social functions incumbent upon the wife of the Chief Magistrate of the nation. His two children survive, and his daughter, Mrs. McKee, is the mother of grandchildren who hold a very warm place in the ex-President's heart. He has declined to be considered an aspirant for the Presidency again, an act which only prevents his being a very formidable candidate; for Mr. Harrison is a man of sterling honesty, conscientious in the discharge of duty, and as a legislator, President and citizen, above reproach. For personal and political integrity no man stands higher in the United States, and he is looked to as a natural leader of the people.

He united with the Presbyterian Church at Oxford, Ohio, in 1850, and since 1860, has been a member of the First Presbyterian Church of Indianapolis.

WILLIAM COLLINS WHITNEY.

THIS gentleman, who was born July 5th, 1841, is a descendant in the eighth generation from John Whitney, one of the leaders of the English Puritans who settled in Watertown, Mass., near Boston, in 1635. His ancestors in the male line were men of exceptionally strong character, of indomitable will, with the courage of their convictions, and of prominence in the communities in which they lived. Among the number was Brigadier-General Josiah Whitney, of Harvard, Mass., who was active in the field during the Revolution, and a member of the convention which framed the Constitution for Massachusetts, as well as that greater assemblage which gave to us the Constitution of the United States.

William C. Whitney's father was Brigadier-General James Scolley Whitney, who, in 1854, was appointed by President Pierce, Superintendent of the United States Armory at Springfield, Mass., and in 1860, Collector of the Port of Boston, by President Buchanan. Upon his mother's side his ancestry goes back to William Bradford, Governor of Plymouth Colony.

Mr. Whitney was educated at Williston Seminary, East Hampton, Mass., at Yale College, where he graduated in 1863, and at Harvard Law School, which he left in 1864. Like many another New England lad, he chose to locate in New York City, and there commenced to practice law.

A young man to succeed in a great city, inviting as it does men of the keenest intellect, must have not only a well-equipped mind, but determination, sturdy honesty, energy, tact—and the last is far from the least. All this equipment Mr. Whitney possessed, and so it was not very long before he was known as a rising lawyer and safe counsellor.

He was a fearless lawyer, and in any case in which he was employed he gave all his time and talents to his clients. Added to this was a charming personality, which made friendships destined to be lasting. In 1871, in a critical period of New York City politics, he came into prominent mention by his activity in the formation of the Young Men's Democratic Club. In 1872, his scholarly abilities being recognized, he was made Inspector of Schools, and at the same time he became a recognized leader of the County Democracy. In 1875, he was appointed Corporation Counsel for the City of New York, an office of vast responsibility, and requiring not only knowledge of law but high executive ability. In fact, that department was wofully behind in its business, as over 3,800 suits were pending, involving more than $40,000,000. He at once reorganized the department, making four bureaus, and in two years more than doubled the annual amount of business disposed of, and at the same time lessened the expenses.

He resigned in 1882, in order to give proper attention to his personal affairs, having, in fact, retained office as a sense of duty and at great loss to himself.

When Grover Cleveland, in 1885, became President, he promptly named Mr. Whitney as Secretary of the Navy, and of all departments of the

William Collins Whitney.

Government, that was one that demanded new methods and the highest order of executive ability.

Mr. Cleveland evinced the highest wisdom in this selection, for when, four years later, Mr. Whitney gave place to another, he left a monument which will endure for ages, in a new navy created, which is, and always will be the pride of the Nation.

He prepared, in his first report to Congress, a plan for the reorganization of that department of the government business, and it was afterward claimed, and not denied, that by the results which followed its execution, for the first time in the history of the navy, it has been possible to prepare complete statements by classes of receipts and expenditures of supplies throughout the entire service, and of the total valuation of supplies on hand for issue at all shore stations. He then proceeded vigorously to build a new navy, with which his name is, and always must be, indissolubly associated. He aimed to restore the prestige of our country as a naval power, and to make it independent of the rest of the world for supplies in case of war. Determined that American labor, ingenuity, capital and skill should furnish the material for our naval establishment, he declined to place contracts abroad for forgings, guns or armor plate, and it was through his entreaties that the Bethlehem Iron Works was induced to expend over four millions of dollars for a plant that would turn out armor and guns equal, if not superior, to those manufactured for any European power. Later, the Carnegie Steel Company erected another plant at a cost of four to five millions of dollars, thus making it possible to complete battleships, cruisers and torpedo boats in as short time as any foreign nation, and at relatively the same cost. At the same time he induced private ship yards to undertake the building of naval vessels, with the result that at the present time the ship yards of Philadelphia, Newport News and San Francisco, can build ships that are acknowledged to be superior to those turned out by the great ship yards of Great Britain.

European powers have no longer a contempt for our navy; on the contrary, they hold it in wholesome respect.

In 1887 the real construction work of the rehabilitation of the navy was begun, and with such rapidity that in 1889, when Mr. Whitney left office, the vessels of the navy contracted for by him and completed, or in course of completion, consisted of five monitors, double-turreted; two new armor-clads, the dynamite cruiser Vesuvius, and five unarmored steel cruisers—the Newark, Charleston, Baltimore, Philadelphia and San Francisco.

The navy yards at Brooklyn and Norfolk, Va., had been put in shape to build steel war-ships and the navy yard at Washington, enabled to cast cannon of the largest caliber. He also contracted for a torpedo boat, and purchased the Stiletto for use in practice at the United States torpedo station.

Senator Preston B. Plumb, of Kansas, a strong Republican, but a shrewd observer of men and methods, said in the United States Senate, in February, 1889: "I am glad to say, in the closing hours of Mr. Whitney's administration, that the affairs of his department have been well administered. They have not only been well administered in the sense that everything has been honestly and faithfully done, but there has been a stimulus given, so far as it could be done by executive direction, to the best types of ships and the highest form of manufacture, and more than all that, to the encouragement of the inventive genius of our people and to the performance of all possible work, not in navy yards where they might be most surely made the instrument of political strength, but in private ship yards and manufactories, to the effect that we have got to-day enlisted in this good work of building the American navy, not only the Navy Department backed by Congress, but we have got the keen competition of American manufactories and the inventive genius of all our people, so that we may confidently expect not only the best results but great improvement each year."

"I am glad to say that during the past four years the Navy Department has been administered in a practical, level-headed, judicious way, and the result is such I am prepared to believe and say that within ten years we shall have the best navy in the world."

Returning to New York, Mr. Whitney devoted himself to his private affairs, but being consulted by his fellow-citizens upon all movements for his party or the public good; and believing the best interests of the country demanded the renomination and election of Mr. Cleveland again to the Presidency, he headed the movement to that end in the Democratic National Convention in 1892, and proved himself a born leader of men and an expert organizer of political forces. It is generally understood and believed that Mr. Cleveland would have appointed him to any office within his gift, but Mr. Whitney resolutely declined any appointment, declaring that he preferred the honorable distinction of a private citizen.

There is little doubt that Mr. Whitney could, if he desired, obtain the Democratic nomination for President, but he has definitely and positively refused to be a candidate, evidently preferring his present high place in the ranks, as the champion of Democratic principles and the highest political ideals, to any official position. He is an ardent believer in the probability of bimetalism being achieved through international agreement, and is giving much time and thought to that end.

In 1888 Yale bestowed upon Mr. Whitney the honorary title of LL.D.

Levi Parsons Morton.

LEVI PARSONS MORTON.

THIS gentleman, now occupying the Gubernational chair of the State of New York, was born at Shoreham, Vt., May 16th, 1824, and hence is in his 72d year. One unacquainted with this fact, looking at him physically and reading the product of his pen, or enjoying his conversation, would not imagine him to be over 60 years of age. His step is elastic, his eyes bright and his judgment as keen as that of any man of middle age. He is a direct descendant of George Morton, of York, England, who was financial agent of the colonists who came over in the Mayflower.

Three years afterward the good ship Anne landed George Morton at Plymouth, Mass., from whence he went to Middleboro, Plymouth county, where some of his descendants still live. John Morton, son of George Morton, was the first delegate to represent his town in the General Court of Plymouth Colony; elected first in 1670, he was again elected in 1672.

Levi P. Morton, the subject of this sketch, is the son of Rev. Daniel Oliver Morton and Lucretia Parsons Morton. His mother was a descendant of Cornet, Joseph Parsons, who was father of the first child born at Northampton, Mass., May 2d, 1655. His English title of Cornet denoted his position in a cavalry troop, it being the third officer in rank and bearer of the colors. Governor Morton received a public school and academic education; entered a country store at Enfield, Mass., at 15 years of age and commenced mercantile business as clerk in Concord, N. H., in 1841. From there he went into similar employment at Hanover, N. H., in 1843. He removed to Boston in 1850, and to New York in 1854, and was extensively engaged in mercantile business on his own account in both cities until 1863, when he entered upon his career as a banker, under the firm name of L. P. Morton & Co. So successful was this business, and such high rank in the financial world did his firm take, he not long afterward established a foreign branch under the name of L. P. Morton, Burns & Co. In 1869 these firms were succeeded by Morton, Bliss & Co., New York, and Morton, Rose & Co., London, England. Mr. George Bliss, who had been in the wholesale dry goods trade, and Sir John Rose, who was the Financial Minister of Canada, which position he gave up and went to London to conduct the business of the English branch, became the principal partners. Both of these great houses are still in existence and take rank among the great banking institutions of the world. In 1873 General Grant, then President of the United States, appointed Mr. Morton honorary commissioner to the Paris Exposition, and the Government made Morton, Rose & Co. financial agents of the United States abroad. In 1878 Mr. Morton was nominated by the Republicans for Congress; and although it was a strong Democratic district, and his competitor, B. H. Willis, the sitting member, was popular, he received 14,708 votes to 7,660 cast for Mr. Willis. In 1880 he was again elected by an increased vote over Jas. W. Gerard, Jr. In 1881 President Garfield nominated him as Minister to France, whereupon he resigned his seat in Congress to accept the appointment.

August 1st, 1881, he presented his credentials to President Jules Grevy, and though the United States has universally been represented at the French court by men of large learning, varied attainments and profound statesmanship, when Mr. Morton resigned after the inauguration of President Cleveland, it was the consensus of opinion in this country and abroad that no one had ever more fitly represented our country. A good business man, a polished gentleman, a student in the best sense of the word, discerning and tactful, he met the diplomats of Europe on an equal footing and gained advantages for his country which had been denied to his predecessors. Duty, to Mr. Morton, meant a watchful care of the political and business interests of the United States. Some of our products had been discriminated against, notably pork; but Mr. Morton succeeded in having the prohibition removed, the governmental decree being signed November 27th, 1883. The prohibition was subsequently renewed by the French legislative body. He also secured recognition of American corporations, drove the first rivet in the Bartholdi statue of "Liberty Enlightening the World," and on July 4th, 1884, accepted the completed work, on behalf of his Government.

This statue, probably the largest ever constructed, is erected on Bedlow's island in New York harbor, and is one of the notable sights of the Metropolis and greets the incoming traveler of the sea, with its torch of liberty in its uplifted arm. Returning to the United States, he devoted himself to his private affairs, until in 1888 he was nominated for Vice-President by the Republican National Convention assembled at Chicago, receiving 591 votes, against 234 votes for other candidates. In November he was elected to that exalted position, assuming the office March 4th, 1889.

As a presiding officer Mr. Morton was preëminently fair and just in his rulings, affable and courteous in his manner toward opponents and friends, and however high ran partisan discussion he did not fail to remember that he presided over Democrats as well as Republicans, and was bound to do justly by each. In this trying position he won the plaudits of all; and it is no exaggeration to say that no man ever sat in the Vice-President's chair who had warmer friends, or more of them, in the Senate of the United States.

On his retirement from the office he was the recipient of a testimonial dinner, tendered on the signed invitation of every member of the Senate; this great honor was unprecedented in the history of that illustrious body.

Mr. Morton's social life in the Capital was as popular as his official; and his estimable wife ably seconded every effort to make their entertainments not merely a social function but a pleasure for every guest.

After retiring from the Vice-Presidency, he removed to his beautiful home, Ellerslie, on the Hudson, and probably relinquished all idea of future political honors. In 1893 he went abroad, and while in Europe the sentiment in New York State in favor of his nomination became so strong it carried the leaders of his party before it, and at the State Convention, held at Saratoga, September 18th, 1894, he was unanimously nominated for Governor.

He accepted the honor, and was elected by the unprecedented majority of over 156,000 votes over David B. Hill, United States Senator and Ex-Governor. Mr. Hill had hitherto been invincible; and with his slogan, "I am a Democrat," had always rallied his party hosts to victory. In Mr. Morton he met his victor; and it is probably not too much to say, that the personal popularity of Levi P. Morton greatly aided in securing an overwhelming Republican majority in the legislature and the congressional representation of the State. Say what we will of the American public, we must admit that the man of sterling integrity, free from demagoguery, loyal to party and country, best succeeds in political life; the people may once in awhile be swept off their feet, so to speak, by passion or prejudice, but the returning wave of reason lands the real patriot and statesman in the position of leader. The people knew they could trust Levi P. Morton; they nominated him, voted for him, elected him. His term of office will expire on December 31st, 1896, but before that time it is not at all improbable that the mantle of the Presidency will fall upon his shoulders. Mr. Morton is a liberal, broad-minded man and charitable, though unostentatious in his giving. Perhaps the whole story is best told by saying he is respected by rich and poor, political friend and foe.

ADLAI EWING STEVENSON.

THE present Vice-President of the United States was born in Christian County, Ky., October 23d, 1835. He received his early education in the schools of the county, and, when qualified, entered Center College, Danville, Ky. When sixteen years of age he removed, with his father's family, to Bloomington, Ill., where he studied law and was admitted to the bar.

In 1859 he settled at Metamora, Ill., where he practiced law, attracting the attention of the people of the county by his assiduity and strict attention to his business. Here he lived ten years, acting as Mastery in Chancery four years, and as District Attorney four years.

It is only the truth to say that Mr. Stevenson proved himself, while at Metamora, an able lawyer, and had the confidence of all the people.

His conspicuous ability as a speaker, and devotion to Democratic principles, won for him the nomination for Presidential Elector in 1864, and in the campaign he made speeches in every county in the State, in the interest of General McClellan, for President.

At the expiration of his term as District Attorney, in 1869, he removed to Bloomington and formed a law partnership with J. S. Ewing. The firm soon enjoyed an extensive practice in the Federal and State Courts, and became recognized as one of the really great law firms of Central Illinois. In 1874, he was nominated by the Democrats for Congress; the district had been surely Republican by 3,000 majority, and his opponent was a noted orator and popular man, General McNulta. It seemed like a hopeless race, but Mr. Stevenson won out after an exciting canvass, during which personal antagonisms between the friends of the candidates manifested themselves in a degree unusual in Illinois. When the vote was counted Mr. Stevenson was found to be elected by 1,200 majority. His term in Congress was during the celebrated Hayes-Tilden contest for the Presidency, Mr. Stevenson believing then, as he believes now, that Mr. Tilden should have been seated.

In 1876 he was renominated, but was defeated. At expiration of his term he returned to Bloomington and resumed his law practice.

In 1884 he was a Delegate to the Democratic National Convention in Chicago, and upon the election of Mr. Cleveland to the Presidency, was appointed First Assistant Postmaster-General. In this position he had charge of all appointments, and while, of course, those who were deposed said it was because they were Republicans, Mr. Stevenson and his friends assert that his removals were for cause, and that he adhered strictly to the civil service law. When Mr. Harrison became President, March 4th, 1889, Mr. Stevenson returned to Illinois, taking at his old home an interest in Democratic politics, and aiding by his counsel and speeches that cause.

In 1892 Mr. Stevenson was a Delegate-at-Large from Illinois to the Democratic National Convention, and was there nominated for Vice-President. During the canvass that followed he made many speeches, and in November

Adlai E. Stevenson.

was elected for the term commencing March 4th, 1893, and ending March 4th, 1897.

Vice-President Stevenson is a Democrat of Democrats, and does not seek to conceal the fact, yet it is generally conceded that he is a fair-minded man, and not enough of a partisan to do an injustice to those who differ with him politically. As a presiding officer he gives satisfaction to Senators upon both sides of the Chamber. He has held one place in life by the grace of a Republican President, having been appointed by President Hayes, a member of the Board to inspect the United States Military Academy at West Point.

In 1866 he married a daughter of Rev. Dr. Lewis W. Green, President of Center College, Danville, Kentucky. He has now living three children, one son and two daughters. Since becoming Vice-President he has suffered the affliction imposed by the loss of a beloved daughter.

Mr. Stevenson is a man above reproach in all his dealings with his fellows, and no one can assail his character. He is a good husband, father, friend—a man of integrity and ability; what more need be said.

THOMAS BRACKETT REED.

THE present Speaker of the United States House of Representatives was born October 18th, 1839, in Portland, Maine. He attended the public schools of his native city until prepared to enter Bowdoin College, from which he graduated in 1860, winning first prize for excellence in English composition. During the greater part of the next four years he taught school and studied law. Before he was admitted to the bar, he was appointed Acting Assistant Paymaster, United States Navy, and assigned to duty on a small gunboat, ironically called a "tin clad," named the Sybil, which patroled the Tennessee, Cumberland and Mississippi rivers.

The Sybil's career as a war vessel was uneventful, and in 1865 Mr. Reed was discharged from service, fighting in the West having ceased. He returned to Portland, Maine, and soon thereafter was admitted to the practice of the law.

Young lawyers, especially those without influential and rich friends, figuratively speaking, have to do a deal of creeping before they can walk; in other words, have to wait a good while for clients with big fees. Mr. Reed, however, was fairly successful, and built his business upon the sure foundation of knowledge of the law, industry, integrity and devotion to his client's interests. In three years' time he had become so well known he was elected to the State Legislature, and in 1869 was reëlected. In 1870, political promotion came in his election to the State Senate, from which position he passed to that of Attorney-General of the State. In 1873 he became Solicitor of the city of Portland, filling the office so successfully as to induce his political friends to nominate and elect him to the Forty-fifth Congress.

While Mr. Reed is not given to the making of set speeches, and never talks for "buncombe," he came into prominence in the House and country early in his membership by a speech against the payment of damages arising during the war to William and Mary College of Virginia.

He took conspicuous part in the proceedings of the committee to investigate the election of President Hayes, and more firmly established himself as a sound lawyer and indefatigable worker.

That at least his constituents have high regard for his ability is evidenced by his having been continuously reëlected to Congress since 1876, and the further fact that the Fifty-first Congress elected him Speaker, and that no other Republican was mentioned or thought of for Speaker of this, the Fifty-fourth Congress. There is no doubt but that under our form of government the office of Speaker of the House of Representatives is the most important, after that of President, in our country. The President can, of course, suggest legislation, and can use the veto power; but the Speaker has it within his power, by the formation of committees and application of the rules, to influence always and generally modify legislation.

Mr. Reed was one of the members when the question of Congressional and National elections was under discussion, who upheld, in a speech, United

Thomas B. Reed.

States Marshals being appointed to be present at such elections. He has, in deference to his legal abilities, been Chairman of the Judiciary Committee of the House, and was Chairman of the Committee that distributed the balance of the Geneva award. He had become a recognized national leader before the Forty-ninth Congress convened, for in the Republican caucus he received the complimentary vote of his party for Speaker, and again in the Fiftieth Congress.

Mr. Reed evoked from the Democrats in the Fifty-first Congress a storm of angry protests because he counted members who were present on the floor and refused to vote as voting. The object in this was to prevent the defeat of legislation by filibustering, and if the rules adopted February 14th, 1890, were rigid and a new departure, they certainly were considered somewhat necessary, since in the Fifty-second Congress, which was Democratic, they were but slightly modified. In 1892 Mr. Reed was a delegate to the Republican National Convention, and received four votes for President.

He is an avowed candidate for the nomination this year, and at the time of this writing has secured many delegates.

Mr. Reed has achieved considerable celebrity by his writings upon political and economic subjects. His style is free from ambiguity; his command of language is comprehensive, and he is terse. He prefers cold, solid facts to visionary flights and flowers of rhetoric. He has usually made the higher magazines the vehicles for his essays, notably, the *Century*, *North-American Review*, etc. He is a protectionist and against the free coinage of silver, unless it can be done by international agreement. Mr. Reed is a large, heavy-set man, with a big head on good, square shoulders. He wears no beard and is partially bald.

He is of commanding presence and dignified in manner, though among his associates he relaxes and enjoys a good joke, which he can give or take as well as any other man.

A strict partisan, he has among his particular and warm personal friends a host of Democrats.

So far in public life, no breath of public or private scandal has assailed him, and no one doubts his ability or integrity.

DAVID BENNETT HILL.

THIS gentleman was born in Havana, Chemung County, New York, August 29th, 1843. He received his education in the common schools and academy of his native place, and after leaving school was obliged to hew his own way, not having the advantage of wealthy parents to push him along in the world. It is a rather remarkable fact that most of our eminent men have very early had to depend upon themselves, and have mapped out their own careers; so with the talented and senior Senator from the Empire State.

He early in life became a clerk in a lawyer's office in Havana, where he made the most of his advantages by storing his mind with legal lore. In 1863, he removed to Elmira, which has since been his home. There he studied law, and, in 1864, was admitted to the bar. The same year he was appointed City Attorney, which got him into politics, where he has been a power ever since.

From 1868 on, he was a Delegate to most of the State Conventions, and helped in no small measure to shape the policy of his party. He was chairman of the conventions of 1877 and 1881; a Delegate to the National Convention, 1876 and 1884, at the latter of which Mr. Cleveland, whom Mr. Hill had served with as Lieutenant-Governor, was nominated for the Presidency. It is a rather remarkable fact that both should have been Mayors of cities in the same year, and both been promoted, and practically because of the same manly qualities—fidelity to the people's trust and independence of character. In 1870 and 1871, Mr. Hill was sent to the Legislature; in 1882 made Mayor, and in the same year elected Lieutenant-Governor. When Mr. Cleveland resigned the Governorship, in consequence of his election as President, Mr. Hill became Governor; in 1885, was elected to that high office, and January 21st, 1891, was elected to the United States Senate.

As Governor, David B. Hill, made himself the leader of his party in the State, and there is probably no Democrat in New York, who has the masses of his party with him like the present Senator.

In 1894, Mr. Hill, much against his own wishes, was nominated for Governor again, and was defeated by Levi P. Morton. It is unnecessary here to dwell upon the causes of that defeat; sufficient it is to say that it does not reflect upon Mr. Hill. When the nomination was forced upon him, like a good soldier he obeyed and made a gallant fight. The conditions that existed in 1894, may never occur again, and the slogan of Mr. Hill, "I am a Democrat," may reverberate among the hills and valleys of New York once more, and be the battle cry of victory.

Senator Hill is a fluent and eloquent speaker, and does not hesitate to say what he believes. He commands in his speeches, not only the attention of the Senate, but of the country at large; "they always have meat," and are the result of careful thought and study. As a Senator, he is upon seven committees. He is a member of the Judiciary Committee, because of his high legal attainments, that he is a good lawyer is evidenced by the fact that he was President of the Bar Association of New York in 1886 and 1887. He is personally an affable, agreeable man; a man of excellent habits, and one who keeps himself well informed upon all current topics, as well as politics and statesmanship.

David Bennett Hill.

WILLIAM BOYD ALLISON

WAS born in Perry, Ohio, March 2d, 1829, his father, John Allison, having removed to that place in 1823, when twenty-five years of age. In the first quarter of this century Ohio was away out West, and most of the people who emigrated to the Western Reserve were no exception to the circumstance of being poor, and went west because land was cheap and fertile and to better their condition. The father of the subject of our sketch, was no exception to the above rule, and so William B., was bred like other country boys to hard work and plenty of it.

He was sent to the little district school house at an early age; but just as soon as he was big enough he was put to work, in the summer in the fields, and in the fall and winter did chores before and after school time. At school he was an apt scholar, especially in spelling and mathematics, and, after all, they are the foundation upon which, later, good scholarship is founded. Young Allison was fortunate in having as a teacher David Kimberly, afterward a bishop in the Methodist Church. He encouraged the youth, and, better yet, his father, and gave a good deal of personal attention to the boy's studies, outside of the school house, and bespoke for him a future if allowed to employ his talents. So it was that at the age of sixteen, John Allison sent his son to an academy at Wooster, Ohio, where he remained two years, making the most of his opportunity. Then for one year, through the influence of good friends he had made in Wooster, he attended Allegheny College, Meadville, Pennsylvania; but, as in those days there were no railroads in Ohio or Western Pennsylvania, he had to make the journey afoot, except at such times as an accommodating man, going his way, gave him a ride. At college he cooked his own meals and so lived very cheaply.

When he left college he returned to Wooster, Ohio, and entered the law office of Hemphill & Turner. Here he partly paid his way by outside work, and in two years' time was admitted to the bar and entered upon the practice of his profession. It was not a litigous community, and such clients as he got could not pay big fees; so he concluded, with Bishop Berkely, that "Westward the star of empire takes its way," and west he would go. It was a wise conclusion, but before going he just as wisely took along a young wife, the daughter of the Hon. Daniel Carter. As a brother of Mr. Allison had settled in Dubuque, he, after stopping a short time in Chicago, then a city of only 50,000 people, went to Dubuque, which has been his home ever since.

Before the bluffy city in Iowa, became Mr. Allison's home, he had been in a small way in politics. He was a Whig, and went as a Delegate, in 1855, to the State Convention that nominated Salmon P. Chase for Governor. In 1856 he supported the first Republican nominee for President, and before going to Iowa, had run for District Attorney in a Democratic county. "John Sherman, in his 'Recollections,' publishes a *fac-simile* of a letter which Mr. Allison wrote to him, under date of March 23d, 1861, congratulating him on his election to the Senate. In this Mr. Allison referred, facetiously, to his early defeat, as follows: ' Republics are not so ungrateful as I supposed when I was defeated for District Attorney.'

William B. Allison.

"As soon as he became a resident of Dubuque, he began to interest himself in Iowa politics. He had known Samuel J. Kirkwood in Ohio, and naturally became an adherent of the man since known in Iowa, as the War Governor. Mr. Allison was a Delegate to the State Convention which nominated Mr. Kirkwood in 1859. In 1860 he was honored by being sent as a Delegate to the National Republican Convention, the one which nominated Abraham Lincoln. He was selected to act as one of the Secretaries of that great gathering. His mastery of figures enabled him to play a rather interesting part in that Convention. He was the first to cast up the long column of votes and to announce to the presiding officer, sitting near him, that Lincoln had received the required number of votes and was therefore the nominee of the Convention.

"When Lincoln issued his second call for troops, during the summer of 1861, for 300,000 men, to serve for three years or during the war, Governor Kirkwood thought of the sincere and successful young man whom he had known in Ohio, as well as in Iowa. He placed Mr. Allison on his staff, with the rank of Lieutenant-Colonel, and gave him full authority to raise regiments in Northeastern Iowa and to equip them for service in the field. Mr. Allison entered on this work with great zeal. It was not an easy task. There were many difficulties to overcome, not least among which was the hostile attitude of those who opposed the war. He raised in all four regiments, two during the summer of 1861, and two during the early part of 1862."

Following his services in raising regiments, Mr. Allison suffered from a protracted sickness. He had hardly recovered from that when he received the nomination for Congress from the old Third District. His work in raising the regiments had made him known to the people of the various counties, and he went into the Convention with a good following, four other candidates contesting for the nomination. Up to 1860, Iowa was credited with only two Congressmen. The census of 1860, showed a remarkable increase in population, following the large foreign immigration to the State, as well as the immigration from the States farther east. By that census, Iowa became entitled to six Congressmen. The war Delegation in Congress from Iowa was one of great strength. Grimes and Harlan were in the Senate, and in the House were James F. Wilson, from the First District, Hiram Price from the Second, William B. Allison from the Third, A. W. Hubbard from the Fourth, J. B. Grinnell from the Fifth and John A. Kasson from the Sixth. They gave the young State immediate standing in the National Councils.

Mr. Allison was the first man who saw the importance and the justice of the soldiers in the field being allowed to vote; and there is no doubt but that their doing so saved a good many Congressmen to the Republican party, in a most critical period.

Mr. Allison took his seat in the House on the 3d of December, 1863. James G. Blaine and James A. Garfield took their seats in the same House for the first time. The three men always remained warm personal as well as political friends. He was reëlected three times, serving from 1863 to 1871. He declined a renomination in 1870, because he had contested with Judge Geo. G. Wright, of Des Moines, for a seat in the United States Senate. Though beaten, he had his ambitions centred on that body, and his friends also thought it was his place. Two years later, he defeated James Harlan for the Senate, and has served ever since, being elected five times, an honor almost unprecedented. In his second term in the House of Representatives he was placed on the Committee on Ways and Means, the most important committee of the Congress of the United States. As a member of the Ways and Means Committee, he opposed the Tariff Act of 1870, wherever it proposed to increase the duties then existing. It being a war tariff, he proposed that some of the duties should be lowered instead of raised, and in this he was supported by most of his Republican colleagues. In the following session the Dawes reduction, of ten per cent., horizontal, was carried through both Houses, thus vindicating Mr. Allison's judgment.

Mr. Allison has made a special study of our finances, and is accepted by Congress and the country as eminently sound, wise and conservative. He made two amendments to the Bland Silver Bill, which sought to bring about free and unlimited coinage. The bill had passed the House; Mr. Allison believed it was fraught with danger; his amendments completely changed the effects of the bill; it turned its influence in exactly the opposite direction. The two important features of the amendments were the coinage of silver on Government account, and the committal of the Government to the policy of the use of both gold and silver as coinage metals, looking to an ultimate international agreement as to a ratio of coinage. In recognition of his eminent service to finances, Mr. Allison was sent, in 1892, to Brussels as the Chairman of the American Delegates to the International Monetary Conference held in that city. Mr. Allison acquitted himself there with great credit, and maintained ably the American contention for the use of both metals, gaining the respect and the admiration of the Delegates from the other countries.

Mr. Allison is not a high protective tariff man; but he has stood all the time for the idea of protection to American industries and adequate revenue for the economical administration of the Government. In closing a debate on the Tariff Bill of 1883, he said: "If we are to have a fair bill we must have some relation to the people who consume in this country. * * I have acted upon that principle, serving and endeavoring to protect fairly every industry in this country in every vote I have cast."

Mr. Allison was a candidate for the Presidency in 1888, but failing to get the nomination his strength was thrown to Mr. Harrison, who was nominated and elected. He has been twice offered a position in the Cabinet, once by Garfield and once by Harrison. James G. Blaine felt that Mr. Allison ought to take the Treasury portfolio, and so wrote to Mr. Garfield. For over thirty years he has been a power in our politics; in it all he has maintained a safe, conservative attitude. He is an intellectual man, the peer of any one in the Senate. His temperament, his habits of thought and study, make him a statesman, rather than a brilliant politician. This year he is again an avowed candidate for the Republican nomination; and if nominated and elected, he will undoubtedly give the country a capable, honest administration. Senator Allison's first wife died in Dubuque, in 1860. In 1873 he re-married, choosing Miss Mary Neally, the step-daughter of ex-Governor and ex-United States Senator, Grimes. She was almost an invalid when he married her, she having contracted the Roman fever abroad and from which she never fully recovered. He has survived her; and it was because of her sickness, and the duty of devotion to her, that he refused the Secretaryship of the Treasury, proffered by President Garfield.

JOHN GRIFFIN CARLISLE.

THE subject of this sketch was born in Kenton county, Ky., September 5th, 1835. His father was a farmer in rather limited circumstances, and had a large family, rendering it necessary that his son John should labor at farming during the working season, limiting his chance for schooling to the winter months. The character of the man was in the boy, however, and he made the most of his opportunities in the public schools of the neighborhood, and at home read with avidity in the evenings such books as came to his hand. After leaving school he was obliged to give himself entirely to farm work during the day; but such was his thirst for knowledge, tired though he was, he sat up late at night studying and reading. From the earliest he was ambitious to get an education; he wanted to know as much as the great men he read about, and realized that this could not be accomplished except through persistent application to books.

With a retentive memory, natural ability and a sound body, he became proficient in knowledge of those subjects to which he could gain access, and judging by the character of his speeches and addresses, he must have had access to some of the English classics, for no man in public life uses purer english, or is less verbose. His sentences are always composed of words which exactly convey his meaning. When seventeen years of age, he began to teach school in a small country district. At this time he became ambitious to be a lawyer, and after school hours read law. Just as soon as possible he removed to Covington, Ky., just opposite Cincinnati, Ohio, where he taught school, and afterward entered the law office of Hon. J. W. Stevenson, late United States Senator, and W. B. Kinkead, afterward prominent in law and politics. In 1858, Mr. Carlisle was admitted to the bar. When a short time afterward he made his maiden speech in the Covington Court House, as an attorney, in a case which even his best friends considered hopeless, he surprised spectators, judge and jury, by his presentation of it and his mastery of the law affecting it. When he arose to speak he did not exhibit any of the nervousness usual with actors, clergymen and lawyers, when they first face an audience, that they feel will be critical.

The confidence born of the knowledge that one knows what he is talking about, Mr. Carlisle had; and beginning his address in a quiet, dignified manner, using plain but well chosen words, he gradually warmed up and surprised every one by his forceful manner, well modulated voice, concise and logical argument.

When he finished, many crowded around and congratulated him; and even the judge predicted for him a brilliant future in the law. This proved true, for within two years, it is said, he had the largest practice in the county, and the news had floated across the Ohio, to her metropolis, that John G. Carlisle was a safe man to intrust with the most difficult cases in the courts of Kentucky.

John G. Carlisle.

The distinguishing characteristics of Mr. Carlisle were then, as now, simplicity, earnestness, orderly arrangement of facts, use of language plain and simple, not liable to be mis-construed, for he is never ambiguous, quick comprehension of the facts in a case, and their logical array. He never uses twenty words when five will do as well, and he prefers calm, dispassionate oratory, to rhetorical display or word painting. Mr. Carlisle is always believed when he says a thing is so; political and legal opponents may differ from him in his conclusions, but never in the honesty of his judgment.

Besides this, he is always judicially fair, affable and just. As a Speaker of the House of Representatives, he had the sincere friendship and warm admiration of his political foes as well as political friends.

The writer, in 1884, at Chicago, was told by a leading Republican member of Congress that, barring his politics, he would as soon have Mr. Carlisle for Speaker as James G. Blaine, he was so fair in his rulings.

His natural ability and charming personality early made him friends in his party who were ready to push him forward, politically, so that before he had practiced law a year, he was elected a member of the Kentucky legislature and served from 1859 to 1861.

In 1864 he was nominated for Presidential Elector, but declined to run. In 1867 he was sent to the State Senate, and in 1868 made his first appearance in national politics, as Delegate-at-Large from Kentucky, to the Democratic National Convention, held in New York, and which nominated Horatio Seymour for President and Geo. H. Pendleton for Vice-President.

In 1869 he was reëlected State Senator, but before the expiration of the term was nominated for Lieutenant-Governor, whereupon he resigned as Senator and was elected, serving until 1877. In 1876 he was chosen alternate Presidential Elector-at-Large, and upon expiration of his term as Lieutenant-Governor was chosen to represent his district in the United States House of Representatives. He was reëlected six times to Congress, serving one-half the time as Speaker. He became a member of the Committee on Ways and Means in the inception of his Congressional career, a distinction only accorded to those who are acknowledged as being peculiarly qualified for service on the leading committee of the house.

He soon attracted the attention of the country by a very able speech on revenue reform, a subject to which he has devoted exhaustive study; in fact, he regards this subject, finances and the revival of our merchant marine, as among the most important intelligent legislation. He is flippantly spoken of as a free trader, which is not true; but he does not believe in a tariff which builds up trusts and monopolies, and enriches the few at the expense of the many. He rather believes in a tariff so adjusted as to be equitable and not burdensome; providing sufficient revenue for the economical administration of the government.

In December, 1883, he was elected Speaker over Samuel J. Randall, the most formidable opponent in his party and an extreme protectionist. It was a battle royal, within party lines, between high tariff and revenue reform. He gave such satisfaction as Speaker he was easily reëlected in 1885 and 1887. As a parliamentarian it is enough to say he ranks with Blaine and Henry Clay, his mastery of the rules being perfect.

In the Forty-sixth Congress he made a profound impression by his support of what was known as the Carlisle internal revenue bill, defending it with such vigor that its most determined opponent had praise for the man, if not for the measure.

The three per cent. bond bill he successfully carried through the House, though it was opposed by the Secretary of the Treasury; it also passed the Senate, but was vetoed by President Hayes.

In all of Mr. Carlisle's discussions of public questions he has taken the broad view of the interests of the people at large, believing that "he serves his party best who serves his country best."

When James B. Beck, United States Senator from Kentucky, died, Mr. Carlisle was chosen to fill the unexpired term, but resigned to accept the portfolio of Secretary of the Treasury, when Mr. Cleveland was inaugurated, March 4th, 1893. There has been a great deal of discussion as to Mr. Carlisle's attitude on the silver question, it being contended on the one hand by certain people in his party that he had become a "gold bug," and on the other that he was at heart a bi-metalist.

The writer has no knowledge upon the subject not possessed by the country, and does not speak by authority; but from an acquaintance with the man, begun in 1872, he has no hesitation in saying that Mr. Carlisle would like to see gold and silver on a parity and circulating side by side as money. Mr. Carlisle is a perfectly honest man; a man of sterling integrity, and therefore believes that any kind of dollar issued by the United States should be as good as any other kind of dollar.

As Secretary of the Treasury, he has administered the law as he found it; his personal preferences have had nothing to do with the matter. Should he be elected President of the United States, he will administer the law as he finds it, without fear or favor, and undoubtedly obey the will of the people, as expressed in well considered legislation. That he will aid in every practical endeavor to restore silver to a parity with gold upon some agreed ratio that can be maintained, there is no doubt.

January 15th, 1857, Mr. Carlisle married Miss Mary Jane Goodson daughter of Major John A. Goodson, of Covington, Ky. In every sense of the word she has been his helpmate, and his home life has been most happy.

The surviving children are Wm. Kinkead and Lilbon Logan, both men of prominence in the law. The former practices in Chicago, and was counsel to the Columbian Exposition; the latter is now Chief Clerk of the Treasury Department.

MATTHEW STANLEY QUAY.

MATTHEW STANLEY QUAY, the Junior Senator from Pennsylvania, like the present President, Grover Cleveland, is the son of a minister of the gospel. It is not asserting a truth too broadly to say that Mr. Quay is the most astute politician in this country, the best controller and manipulator of large bodies of men, and the man of all men who correctly interprets public opinion and molds the sentiment of the masses to his own views. Far-seeing, vigilant, determined, calm and unruffled amidst the angry moods of political tempests, he is like the trained navigator on the stormy deep who skilfully pilots his craft to port, a captain never wrecked, saving not only himself but his political friends.

Men like to obey his political mandates, not merely because he is a master of the art, but because those to whom he professes friendship know they can depend upon that faithful quality in every emergency.

In estimating a man's character and determining its true quality, cognizance must be had of his home life; his every-day standing with his immediate neighborhood. If his home has an atmosphere of love, his wife being his truest companion, and his children believe he is the best father and friend in the world, while his neighbors, rich and poor, Christian and sinner, political friend or foe, sincerely admire his neighborly qualities, and believe his word is as good as his bond, it may be depended upon that such a man is true and honest in whatever sphere of life his work lies.

The writer, before attempting this sketch, visited Beaver and talked with many of his neighbors who had known him for years, and whether Democrat or Republican, was questioned, the replies were: Mr. Quay is an honest man, a good friend and neighbor, and loves and is beloved by his family.

In 1710, three brothers from the Isle of Man, off the coast of England, came to America and settled in Canada. Believing that Pennsylvania was a better field than Canada, in 1715 one of the brothers settled in what is now Chester county. From this brother sprang the Quay family in the State of Pennsylvania.

Joseph Quay, the grandfather of the Senator, was the eldest son of the man bearing the same name, who, in the early part of the eighteenth century, first made his home in the Keystone State.

It is a matter of record that this second Joseph Quay, was a strong man intellectually and physically, combined with qualities of bravery that led him to serve his country in the Revolutionary War and that of 1812, he being among the first to enlist. He married the daughter of a gentleman named Anderson, of Scotch-Irish descent, and to this couple was born Anderson Beeton Quay, who naturally became a Presbyterian minister, and who for many years of his life ministered to congregations in Western Pennsylvania. Matthew Stanley Quay was born in Dillsburg, York county, September 30th, 1833, and the foundation of his education was laid at the

Matthew Stanley Quay.

academies of Beaver and Indiana, from whence he entered Jefferson College, graduating with distinction at the age of seventeen. When Mr. Quay was six years old his parents moved to Pittsburg and afterward to Beaver, his present home.

Graduating in 1850, he traveled, taught school, lectured and then studied law in the office of the present Chief Justice of the Supreme Court, Hon. James Sterrett. With literary inclinations, he soon after graduating resolved to establish a Union paper in Louisiana; but his mother persuaded him to abandon the idea. Anti-slavery agitation was then at its height, and it is more than probable that had he persisted in the idea, his press would have been destroyed and himself subjected to personal indignities.

Before he finished his law studies he was seized with the "Southern fever," and located in Texas. There he lectured for awhile, then went to teaching school in Colorado township.

At that time the Indians were troublesome, forcing him to close his school. Money was a scarce article, but with what little he had he bought a rifle and a pony, and started for Austin to join a regiment of mountain rangers, organized for service against the Indians. Reaching the Capital, he found that the Legislature had failed to pass the bill for the organization of the regiment and its payment.

Colonel Glenn, in his admirable sketch of the Senator, says: "This was his first experience in the uncertainties of legislation. He has had many since, but none more serious to him." Selling his outfit, he returned to his home in Beaver county, and resumed the study of law with R. P. Roberts, and was admitted to the Bar in 1854, ten days after he had reached the age of twenty-one. The following year he was appointed Prothonotary of Beaver county, to which office he was elected in 1856 and again in 1859. The war of the Rebellion coming on, he resigned his office and enlisted in 1861, in Company F, Eleventh Pennsylvania Reserves, but was soon made First Lieutenant.

Before the Reserves were ordered into active service, Governor Curtin, recognizing his ability, appointed him Commissary General upon his staff with the rank of Lieutenant-Colonel, and he was called to Harrisburg, where his great capacity for handling men, meeting the emergencies that arose and surmounting the obstacles presented, together with his capacity for work and mastery of the details of organization for active service of the troops, won the encomiums of officers and men and the esteem of the authorities.

Camp Curtin, in those days, had centered upon it the eyes of the State, and it is safe to say that no man connected with organizing and sending forward troops that there rendezvoused was more popular or labored harder for the public weal.

When the military staff was abolished, Governor Curtin wisely appointed the young man from Beaver his Private Secretary. But Mr. Quay desired to be at the front, the place of danger being to his mind the place of duty; so when the One Hundred and Thirty-Fourth Pennsylvania Infantry needed a Colonel, he was appointed and assumed command early in August, 1862, and on the 30th of that month made a forced march to the front. Colonel Quay in those days was a rather frail, delicate man, and he had overtaxed his physical ability. He was seized with a severe illness, from which he arose too soon and joined his regiment.

Eminent surgeons foreseeing that he could not possibly stand the exposure incident to camp life, urged, and insisted upon, his resigning. It was reluctantly accepted, and he was on the eve of leaving for home when it was decided by General Burnside to fight the battle of Fredericksburg.

No longer an officer in the army, and, of course, unable to command his regiment, he volunteered as an aid upon the staff of General Tyler.

In General Tyler's official report of the fight, he thus speaks of Colonel Quay's services:

"Colonel M. S. Quay, late of the One Hundred and Thirty-fourth, was upon my staff as a voluntary aide-de-camp, and to him I am greatly indebted. Notwithstanding his enfeebled health, he was in the saddle early and late, ever prompt and efficient, and especially so during the engagement."

"It is told of him that when he went into the fight he was all ready to start home, and that his men had sent considerable money by him to friends and kindred in Pennsylvania; but so intent was he upon going into the fight with the regiment, his health had forced him to leave just upon the eve of the battle, that when General Tyler accepted his services as a staff officer he forgot money and all else, and went into the action with it upon his person."

That Colonel Quay proved his personal courage upon the battlefield is proven by the unusual distinction of a Congressional medal. Upon his return to Harrisburg, Governor Curtin appointed him Military State Agent at Washington, a position unusually hard to fill, owing to its great responsibility and labor.

When Governor Curtin, early in the Rebellion, said, "that no soldier of Pennsylvania killed in battle should be buried off her soil," he meant it, and thereupon devised a plan for the watchful care of the sick and wounded and the forwarding of the dead to their late homes. The State Agent at Washington, therefore, had his hands full, as the saying goes, for he had a general care of all the soldiers of the State in the camp, field and hospitals.

There are thousands of old soldiers in the State who will never forget his watchful care, his kindness and his sympathy; all this work, full of detail, Colonel Quay performed while in feeble health.

In 1863 the office of Military Secretary was created, and Governor Curtin appointed him to that position, realizing fully the untiring energy and intelligence of his former Private Secretary. In addition to the duties of that position, Colonel Quay assumed those of Superintendent of Transportation and Telegraph, made vacant by the death of Colonel Sees.

In 1864, Washington and Beaver counties elected him to the Legislature, and in 1865 he resigned as Military Secretary and was made Chairman of the Committee on Ways and Means, an unusual honor to bestow upon a new member. During that session the law was passed that exempted real estate from taxation for State purposes. Many other acts of importance bore the impress of his intelligent action.

Governor Curtin always admitted that Colonel Quay was an invaluable aid to him as Governor, and as a soldier and civilian he won distinction, and in those troublous days he was known as a bold fighter and a faithful friend.

In 1868, as Secretary of the Republican State Committee, he displayed those qualities of organization that have since made him the greatest political general of the century.

Colonel Quay always had a taste for journalism, and in 1869 established a paper named the Beaver *Radical*.

He gave no notice of its appearance, and at its first issue did not have a single subscriber; but he conducted it with such ability it soon had a State reputation and a large patronage. Editor Quay was a success and his editorial opinions were quoted far and wide.

When General John F. Hartranft was nominated for Governor it was made a signal for the enemy to assault the whole line; and if Colonel Quay had not come to the rescue, and by matchless organization and generalship put the Republican forces in fighting shape, it is exceedingly doubtful whether the Republicans could have carried the State.

Hartranft, elected, he appointed Quay Secretary of State, which office he held until appointed Recorder of the City of Philadelphia. After he resigned that office Governor Hoyt appointed him Secretary of State again. He was Chairman of the Republican State Committee in 1878–79, Delegate-at-Large to the National Republican Conventions in 1872, 1876, 1880, 1884 and 1892.

In 1885 the Democrats and disaffected Republicans determined to down the Colonel and relegate him to private life. He accepted the gauge of battle, went before the people and was elected State Treasurer by over 50,000 majority, the largest ever given up to that time. While State Treasurer he was elected by the Legislature of 1887, United States Senator to succeed Hon. John I. Mitchell. At the expiration of that term he was reëlected to serve the term 1893–99.

In 1888 Senator Quay was Chairman of the Republican National Committee and ex-officio Chairman of the Executive Committee.

In that campaign he exhibited phenomenal powers of leadership and won recognition as the most astute, clear-headed and withal boldest, political leader in the Union. As a political leader Senator Quay is as astute, calm and determined as the late S. J. Tilden, with vastly greater audacity and courage. No Rubicon halts this political Cæsar. He comes, he looks, he conquers.

There is hardly an intelligent man in the country who will not say that Matthew S. Quay won the battle for Benjamin Harrison.

When he retired from the National Republican Committee the following resolution was passed:

Resolved, That we accept against our own judgment and much doubt as to the wisdom and expediency of it for the party's interests, the action of Senator Quay in his resignation as Chairman and member of the National Committee. In submitting to it, we desire to express, from our own knowledge of the facts of preëminent service to the party, our sense of deep obligation under which he has placed the Republican party, and the cause of good government and patriotism. He undertook the leadership of a doubtful contest at a time when the Republican party was disheartened and the Democratic party confident, in the power of supreme control in the government of the nation, when the odds of the contest were against our party, and by his matchless power, his unequaled skill in resources and his genius to command victory, won for his party an unprecedented victory in the face of expected defeat. We know, as no one else can know, that the contest which he waged was one of as much honor and fair methods, as it was of invincible power and triumphant victory, and that it was won largely by the power of his superior generalship and unfailing strength as a political leader.

Hon. J. S. Clarkson, of Iowa, who was elected Chairman to succeed Senator Quay, on November 23, 1891, made eulogistic speech, which deserves and will always receive conspicuous space in the annals of political history.

In it he not only bore testimony to Senator Quay's matchless leadership, but to the manly and fair way he fought his political battles; in effect saying, that which all well-posted public men know, that while a great tactician he is not a trickster; not only a politician but a diplomat and a statesman.

Of his work in the Senate the public know. He largely helped to make the McKinley tariff bill a law; and when, in 1894, the Democratic majority in the House and Senate, tried to force through the Wilson bill, he effectually blocked its passage by his famous speech, commenced on the 14th of April and concluded June 16th. By this, he forced amendments which in a measure protected the manufacturing interests of Pennsylvania and other States. Had the Democratic Senators persisted in passing the bill as it left the House, Senator Quay, under the rules of the Senate, would have talked to the end of the session. He took the leading part in the legislation which led to the closing of the World's Fair on Sunday, and has uniformly advocated morality in political action.

In the summer of 1895, he fought a political fight within his own party, and despite the fact that the State Administration and the leading politicians of the great cities of his State were against him, he routed the combined forces, "foot, horse and dragoon." He appealed to the people, to the rank and file of the party, and as always before, they rallied to his banner, on which defeat had never been inscribed. This last victory attracted the attention of the whole country, as no other State battle ever did; and as in it he declared for clean, good government, especially for municipalities against rings and the corrupt use of money in politics, he has the sentiment of the best people with him.

Senator Quay lives in a fairly commodious, red brick house, in the quiet borough of Beaver, surrounded by his wife and five children. His life at home is unostentatious, and all his social relations are of the pleasantest character.

He is a member of the Grand Army of the Republic and the Loyal Legion.

A man who has been in as many political battles as he has, who never refuses to fight when forced, has of necessity more or less political enemies inside, as well as outside of his party.

He pays no attention to vituperation, but calmly and fearlessly goes his way, serene in the consciousness that time will vindicate and justify his action.

WILLIAM RALLS MORRISON.

MR. MORRISON was born in Monroe county, Ill., September 14th, 1825. He received his early education in the neighboring schools, and entered McKendree College, where he graduated in the classical course. He then studied law, was admitted to the bar, and practiced his profession, obtaining a fairly lucrative practice. In a short time, 1852, he was elected Clerk of the Circuit Court of Monroe county, serving until 1856. From 1857 to 1860, he served in the Legislature of the State, the last term, 1859-60, as Speaker of the House. When the war came on he organized the Forty-ninth Illinois, Infantry Volunteers, having had service as a soldier in the Mexican War. At Fort Donaldson, he was wounded, and while still in command of his regiment, was nominated by the Democrats of his district and elected to the Thirty-eighth Congress, 1863 to 1865. He was defeated for the Thirty-ninth and Fortieth Congresses, but was again chosen in 1873, serving continuously until 1887. In 1886, he was an unsuccessful candidate for reëlection. He was a Delegate to the National Union Convention in 1866 and to the Democratic Convention in 1868. Mr. Morrison, has been known for years as a pronounced "free trader." He has made special study of the tariff question, and in 1884, while Chairman of the Committee on Ways and Means, introduced a tariff measure, which made a horizontal reduction of all duties upon imports, excepting some articles, which were to be free. The bill came within four votes of passing the House of Representatives. He was very instrumental in making John G. Carlisle, Speaker of the House, in the Forty-eighth Congress; and during his entire term of service never omitted an opportunity to press tariff reform. In the Democratic National Convention of 1884, Mr. Morrison was Chairman of the Committee on Resolutions.

When he retired from Congress, President Cleveland appointed him a member of the "Inter-State Commerce Commission," upon which he is still serving.

It is generally understood that the Illinois delegation will press him before the Democratic National Convention for the nomination for President of the United States.

He is, and always has been, a bi-metalist, but from recent interviews, it would seem that he believes, free coinage of silver can only be successfully brought about by international agreement, or, in other words, that the commercial nations must agree upon a ratio, in order to keep the metals at parity.

He is a common, plain man, accessible to all, of good ability, and clean as to his character and public service; he has many of the elements of popular strength.

Wm. R. Morrison.

WILLIAM McKINLEY.

WILLIAM McKINLEY was born on January 29th, 1843, at Niles, Trumbull County, O., where his father was interested in one of the early iron furnaces of that section. He was educated in the common schools and at the Poland Academy, and in 1860, at the age of seventeen, entered Allegheny College. Taking sick early in the term, he returned home, and that winter, following the example of so many great Americans, taught a country school near Poland. His duties ended in April, 1861, and it was his intention to go back to Allegheny College that fall. But while this young country boy had been teaching his little school, great and portentious events were transpiring. Secession was trying to dismember the Union. The young teacher had scarcely laid aside his books when the roll of Sumter's guns summoned the people to arms. A new school opened its doors to the youth of the North—the grim school of war.

Abraham Lincoln called for soldiers to defend the Union and the flag. Ohio's response was a ready one. In June the Twenty-third Regiment of Ohio Volunteers was organized at Columbus. Its first Colonel was William S. Rosecrans, afterward Major-General and Commander of the Department of the Cumberland. Its Lieutenant-Colonel was Stanley Matthews, who became United States Senator and Justice of the Supreme Court. Its Major was Rutherford B. Hayes, later thrice Governor of Ohio, and President of the United States. There were famous names on the roster of the Twenty-third Ohio Volunteers, and there marched in the ranks of Company E, knapsack on his back and musket on his shoulder, an eighteen-year-old private, in a new suit of blue, whose name was William McKinley.

The regiment was hurriedly mustered in and trained, and sent to West Virginia. For fourteen months the young soldier served in the ranks—one of hundreds of thousands of privates who marched and toiled and fought and made the Major-Generals famous. But they saved the Union. Every duty of a private soldier William McKinley performed. He shouldered the musket and carried the knapsack, and in camp and on the march, on picket and in battle, bore his part.

In West Virginia, the Twenty-third fought under Rosecrans and McClellan. Private McKinley, saw his first battle when Rosecrans defeated Floyd, at Carnifex Ferry. After the West Virginia campaign the regiment joined the Army of the Potomac and fought under McClellan. At Antietam and South Mountain, the young soldier saw war in its grimmest aspect. After Antietam, he was promoted to Second-Lieutenant, and exchanged the musket for the sword. Just previous to this promotion, however, he had been made Commissary-Sergeant.

Remembering the oft-published item that he resembles Napoleon, the Governor one day said to an interviewer: "I never was a corporal;" he does not seem to think highly of Napoleonic resemblances.

Subsequent promotion came—to First Lieutenant and Captain—and he served on the brigade and division staff of General R. B. Hayes, part of the

William McKinley.

time as Aide-de-Camp. Then he was detailed as Acting, Assistant Adjutant-General, on the staff of General George Crook, and was with Sheridan, in his great campaign through the Shenandoah Valley. He was at Winchester, Cedar Creek, Fisher's Hill, Opequan, Kernstown, Cloyd Mountain and Berryville, and all the other battles and skirmishes of that eventful time.

Did he do any fighting? Well, we have General Sheridan's testimony on that point. He found the young Major rallying the troops at Cedar Creek, the morning of his famous ride from Winchester, and tells of it in his Memoirs. Then his horse was shot under him at Berryville. One of the most cherished of his possessions is a document, worn and time-stained now. It is his commission as Brevet Major of the United States Volunteers, given in 1864, " for gallant and meritorious services at the battles of Opequan, Cedar Creek and Fisher's Hill," and it is signed "A. Lincoln."

Mr. McKinley remained in the army until after Appomattox, when he was mustered out and returned to the duties of civil life. It is but fair to say, however, that he returned reluctantly; he had imbibed a liking for army life, and but for his father's persuasions he would have taken a commission in the regular army.

He studied law with Charles E. Glidden and David Wilson, of Mahoning county, took a course at the Albany (N. Y.) Law School, and in 1867, was admitted to the bar, and located at Canton, Stark county, since his home. Two years later he ran for Prosecuting Attorney of the county. Stark county was Democratic, but McKinley was elected and served two years. He ran for reëlection, but fell short by forty-five votes when his State ticket was beaten over six hundred. Meanwhile he became active in politics. He took the stump for his party, and soon made himself a power among the people. In 1876, he was proposed as a candidate for Congress. The sitting Congressman, L. D. Woodworth, of Mahoning, Judge Frease and several other Republicans, three of them from his own county, were opponents for the nomination. In Stark county, delegates to the Congressional convention were elected by a popular vote; McKinley carried every township in the county but one, and that had but a single delegate. In the other counties he was almost equally successful, and the primaries gave him a majority of all the delegates in the district. He was nominated on the first ballot over all the other candidates. For fourteen years he represented the district of which Stark county was a part—not the same district, for the Democrats did not relish the prominent part he was playing in Congress, and "gerrymandered" him three times. They began early at it, too, for in 1878, he was put into a district that had 1,800 Democratic majority. McKinley carried it by 1,300 votes. In 1884, they tried a similar "gerrymander," but McKinley was not to be downed, and made 1,500 Democratic majority 1,530 the other way. Finally in 1890, the year he had placed upon the statute books of the Nation, the famous "McKinley bill," partisan intolerance had its most iniquitous expression. Stark county was put in a district with Wayne, Medina and Holmes. One year before, these counties had given Campbell, Democrat, 3,900 majority for Governor. McKinley made the fight, and against ex-Lieut. Gov. Warwick, a prominent and popular Democrat. Not, perhaps, since Abraham Lincoln contested Illinois for the Senatorship, against Stephen A. Douglas, has there been—in one sense—a local political struggle which the whole country watched with such intense interest. It was indeed a battle royal. Some curious schemes were resorted to by his opponents. The cry that the McKinley bill had raised the prices of necessaries was harped upon incessantly. It is even said that in Holmes county, a Democratic stronghold, the Democrats sent men, purporting to be tin peddlers, into the country districts for the express purpose of intentionally deceiving the farmers. These offered ordinary tin drinking cups at one dollar a piece. When the people remonstrated, the answer was: "the McKinley bill has put so heavy a duty on tin plate that the prices of tinware have gone away up."

Despite the heavy odds against him, and such electioneering methods as these, Major McKinley was beaten by a beggarly 303 votes. And that on the fullest vote ever cast in the district. He polled 2,500 more votes than had been given Harrison in 1888. This defeat in 1890, took him out of Congress. It made him Governor of Ohio in 1891.

It is unnecessary to dwell upon Major McKinley's record in Congress. The people know it. He was active and prominent from the very first. When James A. Garfield became President, Major McKinley took his place on the Ways and Means Committee. In the Fifty-first Congress, Speaker Reed, made him its Chairman, and he framed the famous tariff bill that bears his name, and led the fight that resulted in its passage. During those fourteen years in the House the name of William McKinley, of Ohio, became known to the whole people.

Possibly no measure passed by Congress has been the subject of so much discussion and so widely varying opinions, as has the McKinley tariff bill. Its friends have sung its praises; its enemies have been loud in their denunciations.

A famous feature of this bill was the "Reciprocity Clause." The credit for this important clause has been accorded (and in large measure most justly) to James G. Blaine. But an oft-repeated charge has been that McKinley opposed the reciprocity feature. Nothing is farther from the truth. As evidence of this, the following extracts from an authorized interview with William E. Curtis, Secretary of the Bureau of American Republics, are to the point. Mr. Curtis was for many years close to Mr. Blaine, and this interview was published a year and a half before that lamented statesman's death. It appeared in the *Massillon Independent* of August 19th, 1891, Mr. Curtis being then a visitor to that city. After stating that Mr. Blaine opposed any disturbance of the duties on South American products, to which the Ways and Means Committee did not agree, Mr. Curtis said:

"When Mr. Blaine found that it was proposed to remove the duty on sugar, he sent me to Mr. McKinley with a proposition which he wanted added to the bill as an amendment. It afterward became known as the Hale amendment. It provided that the President should be authorized to take off the duty on sugar whenever the sugar producing nations removed their duties on our farm products and certain other articles.

"Mr. McKinley presented this amendment to the Committee on Ways and Means. It was not adopted. Mr. McKinley voted for it the first time it was presented. Then a second proposition containing some modifications was presented, and Mr. McKinley voted for that, as he voted for the Blaine reciprocity amendment every time it was submitted, in whatever form.

"It has been currently reported that Mr. Blaine denounced the McKinley bill with such vigor that he smashed his hat. Mr. Blaine's opposition to the bill was because of the free sugar clause. He criticised the refusal of Congress to take advantage of conditions which he thought were favorable to our trade. They proposed to throw away the duty on sugar when he wanted them to trade with it.

"When what was known as the Aldrich amendment was adopted, Mr. Blaine was perfectly satisfied, and there is nothing in the current tales that he is unfriendly to Major McKinley. On the contrary, he is one of his warmest friends. Had it not been for Mr. McKinley and Senator Aldrich, of Rhode Island, the reciprocity clause in the tariff act would never have been adopted."

Samuel J. Randall, of Pennsylvania, was Speaker when Major McKinley entered Congress, and they became warm friends. There was one memorable scene in the Fiftieth Congress in which both figured. It occurred on May 1st, 1888, the day on which the general debate closed on the Mills bill. Mr. Randall opposed this measure, and incurred the displeasure of the free trade element, headed by Mr. Mills, of Texas. He took the floor to speak against the bill. In feeble health, his voice at times almost inaudible, the great leader labored under much disadvantage in this, his last fight for protection. Before he was through his time expired; amid cries of "go on," Mr. Randall asked for an extension, but Mr. Mills walked to the front and said: "I object!" The cry was repeated by many Democratic members.

It was a sad sight to witness this great Democratic leader, thus silenced upon a momentous question by his own party friends. There was an exciting scene. Amid it all the Chairman announced that Mr. McKinley, of Ohio, had the floor. The latter was to close the debate on the Republican side. His desk was piled with memoranda and statistics.

"Mr. Speaker!" he cried, and his voice stilled the din about him to silence, "I yield to the gentleman from Pennsylvania out of my time all that he may need to finish his speech on this bill."

In 1891, Major McKinley was unanimously nominated for Governor. He made the contest against Governor James E. Campbell, and was elected by a plurality of over 21,000. Two years later he was again unanimously nominated, and it was then that he received the highest vote ever cast for any candidate in Ohio. He defeated "Larry" Neal, his Democratic opponent, by the unparalleled majority of 80,995 votes.

Meanwhile he had been otherwise prominent in public affairs. In 1884, as Delegate-at-Large from Ohio to the Republican National Convention, he supported James G. Blaine for President. He was again Delegate-at-Large in 1888, this time advocating the nomination of John Sherman. It was a long and exciting contest. The convention was in session over a week. Mr. Blaine, then in Europe, was ardently supported by many, despite his celebrated "Florence letter," declining to be a candidate. There grew up a strong feeling for McKinley. Many of the leaders favored his nomination as the best solution of the difficulty. Senator Quay, of Pennsylvania, said:

"If Major McKinley comes into the fight, I think our delegation would rally more enthusiastically around him than any other man. He is up to the Pennsylvania idea of a man, and the delegation I think, will be for him."

On Saturday, June 22d, every Republican member of the House then in Washington, joined in a telegram to Chicago, saying that the best interests of the party demanded the nomination of Major McKinley. That same day, while the balloting was going on, Connecticut cast a vote for McKinley. He rose in the midst of the roll call and said Ohio had sent him there to support John Sherman and his heart and judgment accorded with his instructions. He could not remain silent with honor, nor consistent with the credit of Ohio, honorable fidelity to John Sherman, or with his own views of personal integrity, "consent or seem to consent to be a candidate."

"I would not respect myself," said he, "if I could find it in my heart to do, or to say, or to permit it to be done, that which would even be ground for any one to suspect that I wavered in my loyalty to Ohio, or my devotion to the chief of her choice, and the chief of mine. I do not request, I demand that no delegate who would not cast a reflection upon me, shall cast a ballot for me."

It is probably the truth to say that Major McKinley's fidelity to John Sherman lost him the Presidency, since the Republican candidate was elected.

Four years later, in 1892, at the Minneapolis Convention, Major McKinley was made permanent Chairman. Here, when Blaine's friends saw that their candidate could not be nominated, they attempted to stampede the convention to Major McKinley. This he resisted, urging that he was not a candidate and would not consent to a nomination. That, of course, settled the matter, and Mr. Harrison was nominated.

No man in the United States is a better campaigner than Major McKinley. His services are always in request, and he has made as many as seventeen short speeches in one day. He is quick at repartee, as a gentleman at New Orleans found out when he fired the question at him: "What about the Force Bill?" "We are more interested, just now," replied the Major, "in the Board Bill." He made one tour, taking in eighteen States, from Minnesota in the North, to Louisiana in the South, and from Kansas in the West, to New York in the East. He agreed to make forty-six speeches, and he did, and three hundred and twenty-five to boot.

He speaks slowly at first, in low, measured tones, but gradually warming up, his voice becomes stronger and is heard by all in his audience. He is epigrammatic at times; always logical, clear and concise in statement.

"Capital won't work without profit any more than the laborer will work without wages. Yet capital can wait on its dividends, but the workingman can't wait on his dinner."

"The capital of the workingman is his strong right arm and the deftness and skill of his brain, and if they are unused for a month, or three months or six months, that much of the workingman's capital has gone forever. What we want to-day is to keep that capital invested. You can't do it if you give Europe a part of our work to do."

"Diminution of domestic production means diminution of the demand for American labor. There is nothing cheap to the American that comes from Europe if it enforces idleness at home."

"The dearest things to any people are idleness and poverty."

These are a few of his short, pithy statements, easily comprehended and remembered.

Major McKinley does not use intoxicating liquors, but he does smoke good cigars. In religion, he and his wife, who has been an invalid for years, are Methodists. They never had but two children, and they died in infancy. He is a most devoted husband, and to him his wife is still sweetheart.

No one has ever impugned Major McKinley's motives, or cast a doubt upon his integrity; and the writer thinks it one of the proud things an American can say about our most prominent men in all parties, they are honest in their convictions, honest in their personal dealings, staunch Americans and liberty loving.*

---

*The editor of this book acknowledges his indebtedness to Mr. Henry Hall, of the *Press* for a large share of this sketch.

Claude Matthews.

CLAUDE MATTHEWS.

PLUCK, integrity, tact—a trinity of words that give expression to the character of every successful man, in either political or commercial life. Lacking either one of these, failure is almost certain to follow the best directed efforts. Tact is the open eye, the receptive ear, the taste that judges, that indefinable something that puts the man in bond of sympathy with his fellows.

Your cold, distant man, however learned, is like a piece of steel never touched by the electric wand; your tactful man is the magnetic iron that attaches, draws. Usually the man that is in touch with the people, is of the people. He has not lived in any realm apart; he has been companion, counsellor, friend, with those who toil in the industries that give vigor to national life, and by their manifold development make a people great.

Such a man is the subject of our sketch, and the man who reads the news of the day, need not be told that it is no eulogy to say, that Claude Matthews, Governor of Indiana, knows not only how, but when to do the right thing. Like all free-thinking men, he is a partisan; but he never forgets that as the Chief Executive of a great State, he governs Republicans, Populists and Democrats, and he deals justly by all.

Born in Kentucky, fifty years ago, he is now in the full vigor of manhood. He was educated at Center College, that State, after having the usual trials in getting a common school education.

Soon after graduating, he removed to Indiana, and was wedded to the daughter, and only child, of ex-U. S. Senator James Whitcomb, one of Indiana's well-known and early statesmen. Governor Matthews, settled upon a farm in Vermillion county, and has been, and is now, a practical farmer, giving great attention to breeding of blooded cattle, Jerseys and Shorthorns. In fact, he has been active in the organizations in the United States and Canada, which have grown up to foster the development of these breeds.

Living in a district giving a large Republican majority, his party, the Democratic, selected him as a candidate for the Legislature. He entered the canvass to win, and overcame a majority of 300, being elected by a majority of 250 votes. In 1890, the Democratic party in casting about for men who could carry the State, selected Claude Matthews to head their ticket as Secretary of State. The nomination was given him almost without solicitation on his part, the delegates feeling that they must select their strongest man. In 1892, a candidate for Governor was to be selected, and with singular unanimity, the convention concluded that the tried Secretary of State, should be the man to head the ticket.

All students of American politics are aware that in Indiana, of all States, the game of politics is played for all it is worth. It is a see-saw game, "sometimes up and sometimes down," neither party having anything like certainty, until, in fact, it has become a proverb, "as goes the State of Indiana, so goes the Union." Claude Matthews carried the State, and by a majority large enough to fasten the attention of the country upon him as a man truly popular with the people.

In fact, his majority for Governor was the largest ever given any candidate. Poll Indiana to-day, it is safe to say that without regard to party, the *people* Republicans, Democrats, or what not, will subscribe to this declaration: He has been an ideal ruler; firm in his convictions, not obstinate, devoted to duty, calm and resolute. He is not a narrow-minded man; he looks at all sides of a question and gives every one a hearing. He is liberal in his views, and looks beyond the matter of persons to the great arena where the consensus of opinion must be the ultimate arbiter.

Although a farmer, he possesses the judicial mind, calm, sober and reflective; but he never gets out of touch with the people—the common Sam, Bob, or Tom, of every-day life. He has grown up in the world, with the people whose aggregate wisdom constitutes the whole; whose judgment as expressed at the polls, is the final verdict from which no appeal can be taken.

Not born with a "silver spoon in his mouth," he has worked in the planting and the harvest, and hence knows that it is incumbent upon our legislators to study economy in expenditures to the end that taxation may not become onerous.

Without being a high tariff man he would so adjust imposts that sufficient revenue shall be provided for the economical administration of the Government. Like all fair-minded citizens, he does not believe in taxing, directly or indirectly, the many for the advantage of the few. Monopolies and trusts, he believes, to be "Canada thistles" in our free soil, to be uprooted and destroyed.

It is very safe to say that if Governor Matthews is elevated to the Chief Magistracy of this Nation, watchful care will be taken that expenditures are kept well within receipts, and that Wall street gamblers do not reap a harvest by illegitimate gains from the United States Treasury.

He is a firm believer that this is a nation "by the people, for the people," and the greatest and best upon earth. Like every patriot, its honor is his individual care, and so far as he can, he jealously guards it. To attain the highest office, Governor Matthews will not descend to devious ways; he has made his record to be read of all men, and he points to it with pride. His promise is to *all* people that if nominated and elected President of this great country he will administer the high office for the benefit of the citizens at large, and strive to keep our credit and honor untarnished. He comes of a stock noted for devotion to principle—the Scotch-Irish—and for being hardy and fearless; his immediate ancestors, both maternal and paternal, were noted as soldiers and statesmen, so that he has by birthright a place as a leader.

From a recent article printed in a leading Western newspaper, I quote the following:

"Governor Matthews is a man of broad views. He could not be called a one-idea man from any possible standpoint. In the administration of the public affairs with which he has been intrusted, he has shown at all times the broadest liberality consistent with the public good, and the highest type of moral courage. It has never occurred to him, and never would occur to him, that there was anything for a public official to do but his whole duty under any circumstance.

"Governor Matthews, has many qualities which especially fit him for a Presidential candidate as well as for the Presidency. He is essentially a man of the people. His Democracy is of the warp-and-woof of his character. His knowledge of men comes from his close contact with men. It may be truly said of him that from his very earliest boyhood he has touched elbows with the world. His manners are dignified and engaging. He believes in the fullest possible discussion of all questions affecting his party and his country, and is ready at all times to give the fullest audience to questions concerning party and public welfare, whether the views expressed agree with his own or not.

"Governor Matthews' family consists of himself, his wife and two children. His oldest child is the wife of Cortez Ewing, a prominent attorney in a neighboring city. The Governor's youngest child, and the only one remaining at home with her parents, is Miss Helen Matthews, a young lady of rare beauty and accomplishments. Governor Matthews is very domestic in his tastes, and spends with his family all of his time that is not necessarily devoted to his business affairs. His country place in Vermillion county is one of the handsomest estates in Indiana, and is known far and wide as 'Hazel Bluff Farm.' The place is well stocked, and he goes out there frequently to see how the trotters, and the shorthorns, and the colts, and the calves, and the lambs, are getting along. He is fond of life on the farm, and says he will be glad when he is through with politics, so that he can go back to 'Hazel Bluff' and take things easy."

It is generally conceded, that the Central West will furnish the Democratic candidate for President. Indiana will enthusiastically support Governor Matthews. They say no man has ever been elected President, since Indiana became a State, who has not got her electoral vote, and they declare that he can carry the State against any antagonist.

Having excited no jealousies in his party, it is believed his name will be a tower of strength in all the doubtful States, and that, therefore, it is political wisdom to give him the nomination.

The writer of this article makes no claim to being a prophet, but he does think that he can pretty accurately judge public men by their official acts, and has no hesitancy in saying that if Claude Matthews becomes President no emergency will arise that will not find him equal to the occasion.

C. F. Manderson.

GENERAL CHARLES FREDERICK MANDERSON.

CHARLES FREDERICK MANDERSON was born of Scotch-Irish ancestry in Philadelphia, Pa., February 9th, 1837, and received his education in the schools of his native city. At the age of 19 he removed to Canton, Stark county, Ohio, where he studied law and was admitted to the bar in 1859. In the spring of 1860 he was elected City Solicitor of Canton, Ohio, and was reëlected the next year.

On the day of the receipt of the news of the firing on Fort Sumpter he enlisted as a private with Captain James Wallace of the Canton Zouaves, an independent company in which he had been a corporal. Receiving permission from Governor Dennison, with Samuel Beatty, an old Mexican soldier, then sheriff of Stark County, to raise a company of infantry, they recruited a full company in one day in April, 1861, Manderson being elected and commissioned First Lieutenant. In May, 1861, Beatty, the Captain, being made Colonel of the 19th Ohio Infantry, Manderson became Captain of Company "A" of that Regiment. He took his command into Western Virginia among the first troops occupying that section, and the 19th Ohio became a part of the Brigade commanded by General Rosecrans in General McClellan's Army of Occupation of West Virginia. The Regiment participated with great credit in the first field battle of the war on the 11th day of July, 1861. Captain Manderson received special mention in the official reports of this battle. In August, 1861, he reënlisted his Company for three years, or during the war, and in this service he rose through the grades of Major, Lieutenant-Colonel and Colonel of the 19th Ohio Infantry, and on January 1st, 1864, over 400 of the survivors of his Regiment reënlisted with him as veteran volunteers. The battle of Shiloh, during which Captain Manderson acted as Lieutenant-Colonel, caused his promotion to the rank of Major, and he was mentioned in the reports of General Boyle and General Crittenden, for distinguished gallantry and exceptional service. General Boyle says in his report:

"Captain Manderson deported himself with cool nerve and courage and personally captured a prisoner."

He was in command of the 19th Ohio Infantry in all its engagements up to and including the battle of Lovejoy's Station on September 2d, 1864. At the battle of Stone's River, or Murfreesboro, the Regiment lost in killed and wounded 213 men out of 449 taken into the engagement, or 44 per cent. It won distinguished renown and exceptional mention for its participation in this great battle, and the official reports gave particular credit to its charge in the cedars which checked the enemy's advance upon our right and restored the line of battle to one that could be maintained. General Fred Knefler, who commanded the 79th Indiana, said in his official report:

"It may not be improper to remark that the behavior of my regiment, which had but few opportunities for drill, and had not been long in the field, may be attributed in a great measure to the splendid conduct of the 19th

Ohio, Major Manderson commanding, the effect of whose example was not lost upon the officers and soldiers of my regiment."

General Grider, commanding the Brigade, says:

"The command was splendidly led by its officers, among whom was Major Manderson, who exhibited the utmost coolness and daring."

During its three years and its veteran service, the 19th Ohio Infantry participated in the following campaigns and battles: Shiloh, Siege of Corinth, Action near Farmington, Movement from Battle Creek, Tenn., to Louisville, Ky., Perryville Campaign, Crab Orchard, Stone's River, Murfreesboro, Tullahoma Campaign, Liberty Gap, Chickamauga, Siege of Chattanooga, Orchard Knob, Mission Ridge, Knoxville Campaign, Atlanta Campaign, Cassville, Dallas, New Hope Church, Pickett's Mills, Ackworth Station, Pine Knob, Kulp's Farm, Kenesaw, Affair near Marietta, Crossing the Chattahootchie River, Peach Tree Creek, Siege of Atlanta, Ezra Chapel, Jonesboro, Lovejoy's Station, Franklin, Nashville and pursuit of Hood's Army.

The Brigade Commander says of the battle of New Hope Church in his official report:

"The second line, commanded by Colonel Manderson, and composed of the 19th Ohio, the 79th Indiana and the 9th Kentucky, advanced in splendid style through a terrific fire. Officers and soldiers acted most gallantly, the regiments of the second line particularly, which advanced in admirable order over very difficult ground and determinedly maintained their ground against very superior numbers. Conspicuous for gallantry and deserving of special mention is Colonel C. F. Manderson, of the 19th Ohio."

While leading his demi-brigade composed of the 19th Ohio, the 9th Kentucky and the 79th Indiana, in a charge upon the enemy's works at Lovejoy's Station, Ga., on September 2d, 1864, in which the front line of works was taken and held, he was severely wounded in the spine and right side.

General Knefler, commanding the Brigade, says officially:

"I cannot say too much of Colonel Manderson, who was severely wounded and always conspicuous for gallantry and skill."

General Wood, who commanded the Division, says of the charge upon the enemy's works:

"It was gallantly made, and we lost some valuable officers, among them Colonel Manderson."

The ball being unextracted, and much disability arising therefrom, he was compelled to resign the service from wounds, in April, 1865, the war in the West having practically closed. Previous to his resignation he was breveted Brigadier-General of Volunteers, U. S. A., to date March 13th, 1865, "for long, faithful, gallant and meritorious services during the War of the Rebellion." This distinction came to him on the recommendation of army commanders in the field and not by political influence.

Returning to Canton, Ohio, he resumed the practice of law, and was twice elected District Attorney of Stark County, declining a nomination for a third term. In 1867 he came within one vote of receiving the Republican nomination for Congress in a district in Ohio, then conceded to be Republican by several thousand majority.

In November, 1869, he removed to Omaha, Neb., where he still resides, and where he quickly became prominent in legal and political affairs. He was a member of the Nebraska State Constitutional Convention of 1871 and also that of 1874, being elected without opposition by the nominations of both political parties. He served as City Attorney of Omaha, Neb., for over six years, obtaining signal success in the trial of important municipal cases and achieving high rank as a lawyer. For many years he has been an active comrade in the Grand Army of the Republic, and for three years was Commander of the Military Order of the Loyal Legion of the District of Columbia. He was elected United States Senator as a Republican to succeed Alvin Saunders, his term commencing March 4th, 1883. He was reëlected to the Senate in 1888 without opposition, and with exceptional and unprecedented marks of approval from the Legislature of Nebraska. His term expired March 3d, 1895, and he declined to be a candidate for a third term, announcing publicly his intention to retire from public life. In the Senate he was Chairman of the Joint Committee on Printing and an active member of the following committees: Claims, Private Land Claims, Territories, Indian Affairs, Military Affairs and Rules. Many valuable reports have been made by him from these committees, and he has been a shaping and directing force in the way of legislation of value relating to Claims, the establishment of the Private Land Claims Court, the Government of the Territories, the admission of new States, pensions to soldiers, aid to soldiers' homes, laws for the better organization and improvement of the discipline of the United States Army, and for the improvement and better methods for the printing of the Government.

In the second session of the Fifty-first Congress, he was elected by the United States Senate as its President *pro tempore* without opposition, it having been declared by the Senate, after full debate, to be a continuing office. This unanimous election to the Presidency of the Senate was without a precedent, and was the highest compliment that could be paid by that august body to one of its members. In March, 1893, the political complexion of the Senate having changed, he resigned the Presidency of the Senate, and was succeeded by Hon. Isham G. Harris, of Tennessee. General Manderson retired from the Senate March 3d, 1895, and being tendered the position of General Solicitor of the Burlington System of Railroads west of the Missouri River, entered upon the duties of the place on April 1st, 1895, continuing his residence at Omaha, Neb.

The preceding, which we quote from a recent publication, illustrates one characteristic of General Manderson, namely, that whatever he undertakes he proposes to carry to a finish. He enlisted in the war of the rebellion at the very first, and he continued in it until a wound absolutely disabled him, the bullet which caused it being still in his body. Fortunately, the messenger came after, or at least, about the time the real fighting had been done; so that it may be said he was in the war from start to finish.

The wound which disabled him was so severe the surgeons were almost hopeless of his recovery, and it is a fact that his lower limbs were paralyzed for over two months.

When Corporal Tanner was Commissioner of Pensions, in looking over the records, he found the case of General Manderson, and, from the description of the wound he received, concluded that he was entitled to the allowance for full disability instead of half, which he was getting. He thereupon put General Manderson on the pension roll for $30.00 per month instead of

$15.00. General Manderson knew nothing of this, being absent in Alaska at the time, and never asked that it should be done. In fact, as soon as he knew it had been done, he wrote the Commissioner that it should not be without a medical examination, and demanded that a medical commission be appointed to examine him. Meantime Senator Manderson's political enemies took the matter up, and asserted that full disability had been allowed from time of receiving the wound, and that he had received a check for some thousands of dollars of back pension, all of which was distinctly untrue. Of course the lie " flew on the wings of Mercury and the truth followed after on leaden shoes." The discussion resulted, however, in great good, as it invited the attention of the country to the pension system, Mr. Manderson maintaining that every wounded or disabled soldier, be he millionaire or pauper, was entitled to a pension as a right. It stands to reason that if a rich man is debarred from receiving a pension because he is wealthy, the poor man can be upon some pretext that can be trumped up. In this Republic, equity demands that every man shall stand before the law on the same plane with every other man ; there must be no discrimination. It also evolved the idea, which is now sturdily maintained, that the pensioner has a vested right which cannot be disturbed at the whim or caprice of those in authority.

Every veteran soldier owes General Manderson a debt of gratitude for his sturdy defense of their interests. It is not amiss to say in this connection that while Senator, Mr. Manderson handled over 45,000 pension cases, a " thank you job gladly performed," which cost the Senator over $500 per annum for postage, clerk hire, etc. After the death of General Logan this business seemed to drift his way, showing that the old soldiers recognized him as their especial friend—and he is and was.

General Manderson's sturdy independence of character and absolute integrity has never been questioned. He has always kept in touch with the people, and as their servant in the Senate served their every interest with fidelity. He is a sound thinker, a pleasing speaker, and is self-reliant, as becomes all citizens of a republic. In 1865, he married Rebecca S., daughter of Hon. James D. Brown, of Canton, Ohio.

DANIEL WOLSEY VOORHEES.

VERY few men in public life are better known to the public at large than Senator Voorhees, who was born in Butler county, Ohio, September 26th, 1827. His ancestors came from Holland, and were early settlers in New Jersey, the original name being Van Voorhees.

The Senator is proud of his ancestry, and often dwells upon the genius and valor of the people of the Dutch Republic, in its historic days. Soon after the Revolution, his grandfather removed to Kentucky, where he married a Miss Van Arsdale, whose father fought with Daniel Boone, against the Indians at Blue Lick, Ky. Senator Voorhees' father, Stephen Voorhees, was born in Kentucky, but removed early in life to Ohio, where he married Rachel Elliott, of Irish ancestry and a native of Maryland. She was a woman of large intellectual endowments and great strength of character. In 1827, when Daniel was but two months old, his parents removed to Indiana, and purchased land in Fountain county. Daniel grew to manhood on the farm and had his full share of the hard work incident to a pioneer farmer's life, and he says he liked it and became thoroughly interested in rural matters. Readers of his speeches will note that he often illustrates them with scenes and incidents of his farm life.

To obtain an education, he attended the common school fall and winter, and read such books as he could get, in the evenings. By close application he had become so proficient, when eighteen years years of age, he entered Indiana Asbury (now De Pauw) University, where he graduated in 1849. At the University he displayed great mental abilities and rare oratorical powers. He studied law at Crawfordsville, and in 1851 commenced to practice at Covington, Ind., the seat of justice of Fountain county. While at Covington, young Voorhees delivered a Fourth of July oration, which was listened to by United States Senator Hannegan, of Indiana, himself one of the great orators of his time. Mr. Voorhees' speech so captivated the Senator, he at once proposed that they form a law partnership, which was accepted in April, 1852. The next year, 1853, Mr. Voorhees, in defending a criminal, found himself confronted by ex-Governor Wright, but he so far held his own as to establish his reputation as a criminal lawyer of rare ability. In 1856, the Democrats nominated him for Congress, but he was defeated. Soon after he removed to Terre Haute, which has ever since been his home, and where he gained the *sobriquet* of the "Tall Sycamore of the Wabash." From 1858 to 1861, he was United States District Attorney for Indiana. In 1859, at the earnest, personal request of Gov. Ashbel P. Willard, of Indiana, he went to Charlestown, Va., to defend John E. Cook, brother-in-law of the Governor, and one of the associates of John Brown in the raid upon Harper's Ferry His able defense of his client and remarkably eloquent speech to the court and jury, on that occasion, was published all over this country and translated into several languages; from that day Daniel W. Voorhees, was a National character. In 1860, he was elected to Congress, and reëlected in 1862 and 1864. In 1866, his seat was successfully contested by Henry D. Washburn; but in 1868, he was again victorious, and

D. W. Voorhees.

was reëlected in 1870 and 1872. From 1872 to 1877, he practiced law, and was more than ordinarily successful, being attorney in many very important cases.

When Oliver P. Morton died, a vacancy in the United States Senate, from Indiana occurred, and Mr. Voorhees was appointed. He was subsequently elected by the Legislature for the term, and reëlected in 1885 and 1891.

Senator Voorhees is a strong partisan, and at times delivers and receives heavy blows; but being a man of generous impulses, he usually gains the personal good-will of his political opponents.

He is a man of most decided convictions and sturdy independence of character. His opinions are not for sale and he is honest to the core.

Even those who differ from him politically, admit that he intends in all matters of legislation, vital to the interests of the people, to do exactly right.

He has been an impelling and a shaping force in his party for many years, and has had a wonderful hold upon the masses in his State.

S. M. Cullom.

SHELBY MOORE CULLOM.

LIKE Abraham Lincoln, who was his friend and neighbor, this gentleman was born in Kentucky, at Monticello, November 22d, 1829. His father was the Hon. R. N. Cullom, a farmer, as have been a host of Southern legislators and statesmen.

In 1830, Shelby's father removed to Illinois, and as the boy grew toward manhood, he had to do his share of a farmer's work. Having early formed a purpose to devote himself to the law, he devoted two years to study at Rock River Seminary, Mount Morris, Ill., teaching school part of the time to help defray his expenses.

In 1853, he entered the law office of Stuart & Edwards, at Springfield, Ill., which has ever since been his home. In 1855, he began practice, and was immediately brought into contact with such legal giants, as Stephen T. Logan, John T. Stuart, Abraham Lincoln, B. S. Edwards, John A. McClernand and others not unknown throughout the State.

Mr. Cullom's arguments in the Circuit Court, bespoke habits of close application, and were concise and logical. Within a short time he had a good practice and a reputation of earnest devotion to his clients' interests.

The civil war caused a large amount of litigation, and soon Mr. Cullom found himself in receipt of $20,000 income per year. Though with such a practice, he had already entered the arena of politics, having been elected, in 1856, to the Illinois House of Representatives. He identified himself with the new Republican party, and was reëlected in 1860, in a Democratic district. There being a Republican majority in the House, he was elected Speaker, at that time the youngest man ever chosen in the State.

In 1862, President Lincoln appointed him, with Governor Boutwell, of Massachusetts, and Charles A. Dana, Commissioners to examine and pass upon the accounts of United States Quartermasters and Disbursing Officers. In 1864, he was elected to Congress by 1,785 majority over his old preceptor, Hon. John T. Stuart. He became an active and aggressive member of the House, and heartily favored the thirteenth, fourteenth and fifteenth amendments to the Constitution of the United States.

He was Chairman of the Committee on Territories, and recognized the necessity of dealing severely with polygamy. He was reëlected in 1866 and 1868, and added to the reputation he had already made, of being thoroughly posted upon all the subjects he discussed or considered in committee.

In 1872, he was again sent to the State Legislature, and again made Speaker. He was reëlected in 1874. In 1876, the Centennial year, he was chosen Governor of his State, and so well did he perform his duties, he was reëlected, an honor that had never been conferred upon any one in the history of the State. He was watchful of the people's interests, kept down expenditures, and had a vigilant eye upon the various State institutions; his ambition was, if he could, to extinguish the State debt. In 1883, the Legislature chose him United States Senator, and reëlected him in

1889 and 1895. He is a most influential member of that body, serves on many committees, and never favors hasty or ill-advised legislation.

Like the late President Lincoln, Mr. Cullom is a very convincing speaker, using language that any one can understand, and is apt in illustration. He does not indulge in rhetorical display, but goes at the pith of the subject, and gets the attention of his auditors by the simplicity of his speech, the force of his argument and the logical array of his facts and figures.

It is understood that he is a candidate for the Republican nomination for President, and will have the support of the delegation from his State ; and it may be, that unless some one is nominated on a very early ballot, the shifting of votes may give him the prize.

He is a self-made man, and has won the confidence of his people by the rugged honesty of his character, as well as by his abilities.

JOHN WARWICK DANIEL.

THIS gentleman, now United States Senator from Virginia, was born at Lynchburg, Campbell County, Virginia, September 5th, 1842. His father was William Daniel, Jr., a learned lawyer, brilliant advocate and able jurist, for many years Judge of the Supreme Court of Appeals, of Virginia. His grandfather was William Daniel, Sr., long distinguished as a Judge of the General Court. Judge Peter V. Daniel, of the United States Supreme Court, was his kinsman, as was also Raleigh T. Daniel, an eminent lawyer of Richmond, who was Attorney-General of the State. It is undoubtedly from the father's side that the subject of this sketch inherits his judicial mind and forensic ability.

John W. Daniel, was educated at Lynchburg College and at Dr. Gessner Harrison's University School. While at the latter, the Civil War broke out, and with the ardor of youth that believes in the justness of his cause, he threw aside his books and enlisted as a private soldier, and soon became a Second Lieutenant in Stonewall (Gen'l Thomas J.) Jackson's Brigade. He was wounded twice at the first battle of Manassas (Bull Run), the very first conflict of great importance between the Federal and Confederate armies.

Later he became Adjutant of the 11th Virginia Infantry, and in action at Boonsboro, near Antietam, was again wounded. The Confederate Government, recognizing his ability and fighting qualities, promoted him to the rank of Major, and appointed him Adjutant-General on General Jubal Early's Staff. May 6th, 1864, in the desperate battles in the Wilderness, he was permanently crippled, illustrating that bullets, like death, choose "a shining mark."

He studied law at the University of Virginia in 1865-66, was admitted to practice, and has been a practitioner ever since. He has contributed to our jurisprudence a learned volume, entitled "Daniel on Attachments," and another, on "Negotiable Instruments," has passed through four editions and is considered the leading authority on that subject, being frequently quoted by the highest tribunals of Great Britain and the United States, and is used as a text-book in some of the Universities and Colleges.

When twenty-seven years of age, he entered politics, serving in 1869-70, and 1871-72, in the Virginia House of Delegates. Here Mr. Daniel made a great reputation as a ready and eloquent speaker, concise and logical. From this on he became, not a merely a local political power, but an influence for good in the State; and nothing was more certain than, that if he lived, he would receive from his Commonwealth the highest political honor it could bestow. From 1875 to 1881, he served in the State Senate; in 1876 was Elector-at-Large on the Tilden and Hendricks ticket, and Delegate-at-Large to the National Democratic Conventions of 1880, 1888 and 1892.

In 1881 he was defeated for Governor by W. E. Cameron, Readjuster, a party that derived all its strength from issues growing out of the readjustment of the State debt; a measure deemed necessary principally because of the division of the State, by the creation of West Virginia, during the

John W. Daniel.

war. He was elected a member of Congress, and served from 1885 to 1887, attracting the attention of the Nation, and preparing the way for his elevation to the United States Senate, the doors of which he entered as a member March 4th, 1887. He served his constituents so faithfully, he was unanimously reëlected in December, 1891, to serve from 1893 to 1899.

Mr. Daniel is really recognized as one of the most eloquent men in the country; a man of sterling integrity, rare good judgment, calm and fearless in the expression of his views, and at the same time one of those men who give due weight and courtesy to the opinions of their opponents.

A thorough Democrat, he holds to the fundamental doctrines of his party; but in divided issues he ranges himself according to his individual convictions. It is an acknowledged fact that both the great parties are divided upon the issue of bi-metalism and mono-metalism. He believes in a sound currency; that every dollar the poor man carries should be as good as any other dollar; but so believing, the writer understands that Mr. Daniel believes it is not necessary to put all our currency upon a gold basis, but that silver should be restored to all its old time functions as money, and that it can be retained on a parity with gold. However, this is not *ex-cathedra*.

Mr. Daniel is an affable man, who does not lift himself up above his fellows, and is easily approached by all. His courtesy of manner is not affected; his politeness extends to the poor as well as the rich, the humble as to the proud. On all National questions he ranges himself on the side of the loftiest patriotism,—his motto being, "the greatest good to the greatest number." That he will be a power in National politics in the years to come, his friends and opponents, both alike, believe.

Russell A. Alger.

RUSSELL ALEXANDER ALGER.

THE subject of our sketch, was born in Lafayette, Medina county, Ohio, February 27th, 1836. His ancestors came to this country early in its history; John Alger, his grandfather, participated in many battles of the Revolutionary War, and was a sturdy patriot, as well as valiant soldier.

Russell, is the son of Russell and Caroline Moulton Alger, so that there is united in his veins the blood of both English and Scotch ancestry; a mixture which insures stability of character, tenacity of purpose and vigor of mind. Mr. Alger's father emigrated to the Western Reserve, Ohio, in 1820, and like most pioneers of that time, cultivated the soil; dying in 1848 (his mother having died in 1847), he left his son an orphan at the age of twelve, with a younger brother and sister dependent upon him for support. In 1848-49, he worked for his board and clothing, being allowed to attend school three months each year. In 1850, at fourteen years of age, he commenced to work by the month as a farm hand, for $3.00 per month; the next year he got $4.00 per month at first, and $5.00 thereafter for six months. Out of this he clothed himself and helped his brother and sister, finding for them places where they could work for their board. In 1851, his wages were $6.00 per month; 1852, $8.00; 1853, $10; 1854, $12.00; 1855 and 1856, $15.00, and in 1859, $20.00. He attended fall and winter terms at Richfield Academy, sawing wood noon times, and working morning and evenings, for his board. As can be imagined, he was a very busy young man, and his path in pursuit of knowledge rather thorny; but he never despaired, he kept his eye upon the top of the ladder; climb it he must, climb it he would, and as the sequel has shown, climb it he did. The last two years he taught school during the winter months.

In 1857, he began to study law with Wolcott & Upson, in Akron, Ohio, and in 1859, was admitted to practice by the Supreme Court. He soon found employment in the law office of Otis, Coffinbury & Wyman, at Cleveland, but was forced by the state of his health to abandon office confinement. In 1860, he went to Grand Rapids, Mich., and embarked in the lumber business in a very limited way. War clouds soon began to float across the sky, and all thoughts of peaceful pursuits were dispelled, when the call to arms came in 1861. He enlisted as a private in the Second Michigan Cavalry, soon became Captain, and April 25th, 1862, Major. This regiment had for its Colonel, that intrepid leader, Phil. Sheridan.

At Boonesville, Miss., July 1st, 1862, with ninety picked men, he attacked the enemy's rear, routing them, though he was wounded and taken prisoner. He escaped the same day, and October 16th was made Lieutenant-Colonel of the Sixth Michigan Cavalry, and February 28th, 1863, became Colonel of the Fifth Michigan Cavalry. June 28th of the same year his regiment was the first to enter Gettysburg, where, July 1st-3d, the bloodiest battle of the war was fought. He was specially mentioned in General Custer's report of cavalry operations. While in pursuit of the enemy, July 8th, he was again, and severely, wounded at Boonesborough, Md.

When Sheridan made his famous campaign in the Shenandoah Valley, in 1864, Colonel Alger, by a brilliant charge at Trevillian Station, captured over 800 Confederates, June 11th, 1864. The same day he was breveted Brigadier and Major-General of Volunteers.

His war experience over, General Alger returned to Michigan and entered the lumber business at Detroit.

He was soon made president of two great lumber companies, employing over 1,000 men and cutting over 140,000,000 feet of timber annually. He also became actively interested in other business and a director in several companies. He, however, has never been a speculator, believing that a man should engage in pursuits that tend to develop the resources of the country and is of value to the world at large as well as himself. He also carefully avoids litigation, proving the fairness of his dealings and his desire to be just to all.

In 1884, he was Delegate to the Republican National Convention, and was soon thereafter, elected Governor of Michigan. He declined renomination as Governor, and in 1888, at the earnest solicitation of numerous friends in his own and other States, became a candidate for the Presidency, and in the Republican National Convention, received 142 votes for that high office, 100 of the votes staying by him to the last. In the same campaign he was chosen Republican Elector-at-Large.

In 1889, he received at Milwaukee, what he probably regards as the greatest honor of his life, namely, the Commander-in-Chiefship of the Grand Army of the Republic. He is also a member of the Loyal Legion, and is noted for his regard for all the veterans of the war, in which he was so conspicuous a figure.

As a boy, so as a man, he finds no idle time; and remembering the hardships of his early days, he takes special interest in boys, especially the newsboys. It was the "newsies" of Detroit who originated the cry heard at the convention in Chicago, "He's all right;" others have appropriated it, but it belongs to General Alger.

In April, 1861, he was married to Annette Henry, daughter of one of Grand Rapids leading citizens. Nine children have been born to them, five of whom are now living.

His home life has been most pleasant, and he and his family enjoy the respect of all the citizens of Detroit, where, from the very nature of things, they are best known. General Alger is a philanthropist, but not ostentatious in his charities. He has made a fortune by strict attention to legitimate business; not by reaping what others have sown.

H. CLAY EVANS.

H. CLAY EVANS, was born in 1843, in Juniata county, Pa. The family moved to Wisconsin, then a territory, in 1846, and became farmers, living there until 1859. H. Clay, then a boy of sixteen, became a clerk in the Register's office of Grant county. He next clerked in a store at Lancaster, where he remained until he enlisted in the 41st Wisconsin Infantry Volunteers.

He went to Tennessee, in the early part of 1864, and was mustered out of service in October of that year. He then went to Chattanooga and accepted a position as civilian in the army. Chattanooga, at that time, was the depot for military supplies for the army south and east of there, and had 17,000 civilian employés. Mr. Evans served in responsible positions in the Quartermaster's department, and was afterward appointed agent by the Secretary of War, and though only twenty-one years of age, closed up the depot, by shipping away all the supplies of regular army pattern and selling the balance, which amounted to millions of dollars.

Mr. Evans held a responsible position in connection with the United States service, from 1865 to 1867, in the removal of the Union dead from the battlefields and burying grounds, to the established National cemeteries at Chattanooga, Knoxville and Marietta. This service required the greatest of care and involved the expenditure of large sums of money.

In 1869, Mr. Evans went to Fort Brown, Texas, as chief clerk for the subdistrict of the Rio Grande, which office had charge of the building of permanent barracks along the frontier, for the United States army, at a cost of millions of dollars. In 1870, he returned to Chattanooga, where he already had property interests, and engaged in business. He established the Chattanooga Car Wheel Foundry. In 1872, he accepted a position with the receivers of the Alabama and Chattanooga Railway Company as general book-keeper, where he remained until 1874, when he resigned to accept the position of superintendent of the Roane Iron Company, at Rockwood, where they operated coal mines, ore mines and blast furnaces. He remained until 1875, when he resigned and returned to Chattanooga. A few days afterward, he was appointed by the Chancery Court, receiver of the Webster & Marks Foundry and Machine shop, then the largest one in the South. Afterward he was elected secretary and treasurer of the Roane Iron Company, at Chattanooga, and subsequently became vice-president and general manager of their rolling mills and of their furnaces and mines, at Rockwood.

In this capacity he served until January, 1884, when he resigned and became cashier of the First National Bank of Chattanooga. This place he resigned in August, 1884, and that fall was nominated by acclamation, and made the race, for Congress, in the Third District of Tennessee, against the Hon. John R. Neil and 3,000 Democratic majority, and was defeated by only 67 votes.

In 1885, he took charge of the Chattanooga Car Foundry Co., and in 1886, purchased the property and has been sole proprietor of that business ever since. Mr. Evans has also many other business interests in Chattanooga,

H. Clay Evans.

and other places in Tennessee. He has been for twenty-five years actively engaged in the up-building of Chattanooga, and belongs to that active, energetic, stirring business element which has done so much to develop the natural resources of Tennessee.

Mr. Evans is one of the original school commissioners that established the public schools of Chattanooga, in 1872. He was afterward President of the Board of School Commissioners. At first, he and his associates borrowed money on their own individual credit, to run the schools, and to this first board is largely due the present efficient public school system of that city.

Mr. Evans' first official appearance was in 1873, when he was elected Alderman.

In 1880, he was again elected Alderman, and devoted himself particularly to the city's financial affairs, with the result that its paper, which was worth only fifty cents on the dollar, speedily rose to par. He was reëlected and afterward was Mayor of the city for two terms.

In 1888, the Republicans again nominated him for Congress, and he defeated Hon. C. F. Bates by 288 votes.

The Democrats undertook to prevent his being seated by amended returns from Rhea and Meigs counties, and Governor Taylor, upon representation of politicians, signed the certificate of election for Mr. Bates, without seeing the returns, but refused to deliver the certificate that night.

Mr. Evans, being advised by wire of what was being done, hastened to Nashville, arriving early the next morning, and, appearing before the Governor, warned him that the move was a flagrant attempt to steal his seat. Although of opposite political faith, Governor Taylor was a fair man, and after investigating the matter, gave his decision that Mr. Evans was entitled to the certificate. Then his opponents, through Chancellor Allison, secured an injunction, restraining the Governor from granting the certificate. Upon a hearing, however, the Chancellor decided he had no jurisdiction, whereupon an appeal was taken to the Supreme Court, where the final decision was in Mr. Evans' favor.

In 1890, the Republicans renominated him for Congress, but the district had been gerrymandered, so as to give it was thought, at least 1,500 Democratic majority; but when the votes were counted Mr. Evans was defeated by only 523 votes.

In 1891, the district was again gerrymandered, so as to have 2,700 apparent Democratic majority; and again Mr. Evans ran and was defeated by only 919 votes, while President Cleveland had nearly 2,700 majority.

In Congress, Mr. Evans was a valuable working member, and was made a member of the Committees on Post Offices and Post Roads, Banking and Currency, and Patents; and Chairman of Sub-Committees on Extension of Patents and Postal Telegraphy.

To Mr. Evans' efforts, very largely, was due the passage of the anti-lottery law, which was the death of the Louisiana State Lottery, the most corrupt and corrupting in its influences, of any class or species of gambling. The better element of Louisiana's people were anxious to rid the State of the disgrace, and United States Senator White, of Louisiana (now assistant Justice the U. S. Supreme Court), took occasion to call upon Mr. Evans in and cordially thank him on behalf of the people of Louisiana, for his in this matter.

During Mr. Evans' term of service in the Fifty-third Congress, he contributed most largely to the passage of the law authorizing the "Chickamauga and Chattanooga, National Military Park," and securing of an appropriation for the purchase of 6,000 acres of land, necessary for that purpose. This Park will be, when completed, one of the greatest object lessons in the world, for students of military affairs.

He also did much work in the Committee on Post Offices and Post Roads, of the Fifty-first Congress, toward establishing a postal savings system throughout the United States, and this bill was favorably reported by the general committee.

He was appointed First Assistant Postmaster-General, by President Harrison, succeeding Gen. Whitfield, closing up the business for that bureau for that administration, and at the urgent request of the succeeding Postmaster-General, remained and served in same capacity for nearly three months under the Democrotic administration.

In 1894, the Republican Convention in Tennessee, nominated him for Governor, and at the count of the votes it was found that 105,134 had been cast for Mr. Evans, and 104,350 for Mr. Turney, the Democratic nominee. This would elect Mr. Evans by 784 votes. The legislature being Democratic, they, in canvassing the returns, threw out enough to seat Mr. Turney. This together with his previous running record, and his well-known ability, has brought Mr. Evans forward as a formidable candidate for the Vice-Presidency.

Mr. Evans has held many positions of honor and trust, disbursing millions of dollars, and he has never held one of any kind, but that it was carried out faithfully to the letter as well as in spirit.

WILLIAM FREEMAN VILAS.

POSTMASTER-GENERAL, Secretary of the Interior and United States Senator; these the positions which the subject of this sketch has filled acceptably to the people of this country. He was born July 9th, 1840, near a mountain-top in the town of Chelsea, in Vermont, on a farm which his father and grandfather had wrested from the forest sides of Mount Sterling. Mr. Vilas' father was named Levi B. and his mother was Esther G. (Smilie) Vilas. His grandfather emigrated to Vermont, from Connecticut, and was one of those sturdy men who, while cultivating a sterile soil, helped to make New England famous. His grandfather on his mother's side was Nathan Smilie, noted as an acute man, broad and wise in mind, and a leader in his party in the State and for many years in its Legislature.

Levi B. Vilas, born and bred in a farm house on that mountain side, early thirsted for knowledge, and with indomitable purpose, set out at the age of sixteen, to trudge to Randolph, sixty miles away, where there was a school in which he could satisfy his ambition. Here he laid the foundation upon which was built a brilliant career as lawyer, legislator and citizen. Having won a comfortable independence, he resolved to remove to Madison, Wis., and there educate his five sons, all of whom took degrees at the State University.

William F. Vilas took his degree in the regular classical course in 1858, and though exceedingly studious, was not averse to taking a share in the college sports. Leaving the University in 1859, he took a course of instruction in a commercial school, meantime studying law. He then attended the Albany Law School, graduating in May, 1860, and was admitted to the bar of New York State. Returning to Wisconsin, he was admitted to practice in the Supreme Court, and at twenty years of age argued his first case. On the 9th of July, he formed a law partnership with Charles T. Wakely, to which early in 1862, Eleazer Wakely was added as senior partner. Mr. Vilas had drilled with Colonel Ellsworth, then Captain of the Madison Zouaves, and in July, 1862, tendered his services to Governor Salomon, who accepted them; whereupon he raised Company A, of the 23d Wisconsin Infantry Volunteers. He was sent in September to Covington, Ky., and thence to Memphis, to join Sherman in an expedition to Vicksburg. While at Memphis, Captain Vilas nearly lost his life from an attack of typhoid fever; but luckily, having a cousin in the city, he was carefully nursed, and in a few weeks was convalescent, whereupon he rejoined his regiment and participated in the Vicksburg campaign. While at Milliken's Bend, he was promoted to Major and Lieutenant-Colonel. He participated in the battles at Port Gibson, Champion Hill, Black River Bridge and at the assault upon Vicksburg, commanding the regiment. The day following the surrender, he marched with Sherman in pursuit of Johnston. Soon afterward he returned to Vicksburg and was sent in command of his regiment to Carrollton, near New Orleans, La. Here the command remained several weeks in idleness; Having received word from home that his father was likely to lose his

William F. Vilas.

estate, owing to litigation, he resigned and returned to Madison. He settled down in 1865, to the practice of the law again, in which he very shortly made his mark.

From 1872 to 1881, his partner was Edwin E. Bryant, later Dean of the Law Faculty, of the State University. Before this partnership expired, Mr. Vilas had accumulated a large fortune, and was recognized in the Northwest as one of the soundest lawyers of the country.

In 1868, upon the opening of the law school of the University, Mr. Vilas was chosen as one of the professors, and regularly lectured for seventeen years. He was also a regent of the University from 1880 to 1885.

Ever since 1860, he has taken part on the stump in every political campaign as a Democrat, and has done as much as any other man to keep his party in fighting trim, while for many years in a hopeless minority. He was a Delegate to the Democratic National Conventions of 1876, 1880 and 1884, being permanent Chairman of the last named, and made the address of notification of nomination, to Cleveland and Hendricks. In 1884, Mr. Vilas was elected to the State Legislature, and while there was appointed Postmaster-General by President Cleveland.

When Mr. Lamar, Secretary of the Interior, was made a Justice of the Supreme Court, he was transferred to the Interior Department, which position he occupied from January 16th, 1888, to March 6th, 1889.

While Postmaster-General, he refused to expend the appropriation of the Forty-eighth Congress for subsidizing the ocean mail service. His action, of course, met with severe criticism, but the succeeding Congress sustained him in his position.

After his retirement as Secretary of the Interior, he returned home and resumed his law practice; but the State campaign of 1890, once again allured him to the stump, from which he made speeches daily for three weeks. The result of the campaign was a Democratic Legislature, after thirty-five years of waiting, and William F. Vilas was elected to the United States Senate, for the term commencing March 4th, 1891, and ending March 3d, 1897. He has a national reputation as an orator, and his speech to the toast, "Our First Commander," at the meeting of the Army of the Tennessee, at Chicago in 1879, is an American classic.

Mr. Vilas is a man of large intellect, great capacity for facts, a logical mind to array them, so they will *tell* when he faces an audience; and that manner which arrests and then commands attention.

He is a man of good presence, affable, sociable and democratic in his ways; as courteous to the poor as to the rich; a good citizen, neighbor, friend. Say what we may of our public men as to their political action, this country has yet to produce a prominent man who is a "snob."

Mr. Vilas evidently believes he is a man of the people, and when he is elected to a high office, he is not above being their servant. He does his duty as he sees it, and is above resorting to tricks or devious ways; a man of honor, strict integrity and great ability.

Cushman K. Davis.

CUSHMAN K. DAVIS.

SENATOR DAVIS was born in the town of Henderson, Jefferson county, N. Y., June 16th, 1838. His parents were in comfortable circumstances, and resolved that he should have a thorough education. He laid the foundation for it in the common schools; and when far enough advanced, entered the University of Michigan, at Ann Arbor, where he graduated in June, 1857. Mr. Davis was an apt scholar, quick to learn, with a most retentive memory, and an inclination for the study of philosophy, the classics and the languages. His speeches reveal the tendency of his mind, and are worthy models for those who would study the niceties of language.

After graduating, he studied law, and was admitted to the bar. He removed to Wisconsin and served as First Lieutenant in the Twenty-eighth Wisconsin Infantry Volunteers from 1862 to 1864. After the war he emigrated to Minnesota, settling in St. Paul, and was elected to the Minnesota Legislature in 1867. He was United States District Attorney, 1868 to 1873, and Governor of Minnesota in 1874 and 1875. Senator Davis is, without a shadow of doubt, one of the best lawyers in the Northwest, and it is said that by strict attention to practice he can easily earn $50,000 per annum.

He early took a leading place at the bar in Minnesota, and at the same time a prominent place in politics. He is not only a forceful, convincing and logical speaker, but an eloquent one, swaying his audience by his fervid speech.

The Legislature of Minnesota elected him United States Senator, to succeed Hon. S. J. R. McMillan, and he took his seat March 4th, 1887. He was reëlected for the term 1893 to 1899. In politics Mr. Davis is a Republican, and one of deep convictions. He is a student now, as he has been during his past years, and hence is not a narrow, bigoted partisan. He realizes full well that in this great, progressive nation, new issues are constantly being made and new ideas evolved. He is always ready to meet them, as he keeps abreast of the times; and he possesses that philosophic, judicial and trained mind that leads to just decisions upon all governmental and political subjects; and having made his conclusions, he has the ability to maintain them.

William L. Wilson.

WILLIAM LYNE WILSON.

THIS distinguished gentleman was born near Middleway, Jefferson county, Virginia (now West Virginia), May 3d, 1843, and after a preparatory schooling, entered Columbian College (now University), Washington, where he graduated in 1860, when only seventeen years of age.

Leaving Washington, he entered the University of Virginia, and left it to enter the Confederate army.

Mr. Wilson as a scholar, was evidently drawn to *Belles-lettres* and philology, as we find him at the early age of twenty-four years, professor of the Latin language and Literature, in Columbian University, which professorship he occupied from 1867 until 1871.

Previous to this he had studied law and been admitted to the bar. While a professor, he made exhaustive study of political economy and politics, and is to-day, probably the best posted public man in the country upon the science of government, the history of our government, and that of other nations. Mr. Wilson's mind is analytical and philosophic; and his mastery of languages and his diction enable him to charm readers as well as hearers.

He resigned his professorship to practice law, and as is not unusual with men of his talents, he soon became entangled in politics, and in 1880 was Elector-at-Large on the Hancock ticket. In 1882, was chosen President of the State University. While occupying this position, he was elected to the United States House of Representatives, and reëlected five consecutive terms.

Mr. Wilson's record in the House is as well known as that of any contemporaneous statesman of the period. Being placed upon the Committee upon Ways and Means, he quickly became a guiding force in all economic legislation, and soon, as chairman of that committee, the leader of his party upon the floor of the House.

He introduced and carried through the House the bill for repeal of the Sherman law. He mainly prepared and introduced the tariff bill, which, taking his name, became the subject of more praise on the one hand and more condemnation on the other, than any measure that has been presented to Congress in very many years.

He passed it through the House, after a stormy debate; but when it reached the Senate, it was amended and changed in many particulars, as the McKinley bill had likewise been in the previous Congress.

Upon the subject of the tariff, Mr. Wilson has most pronounced views, and has done much to educate his party to his way of thinking. In everything he does, he displays the trained mind, the thoughtful man, the concise and the logical thinker. He is never verbose; he knows what to say and in just how few words to say it. As they say upon the stage, "he never plays to the galleries;" he realizes that this matter of government affects nearly seventy millions of people, and he believes his views, if given effect, would lift the burden of indirect taxation.

He has been a hard worker, and in the last session of Congress his health gave way under the strain.

After the adjournment of Congress he rapidly recuperated; and when Hon. Wilson S. Bissell resigned his position as Postmaster-General, President Cleveland promptly tendered the portfolio to Mr. Wilson. He accepted, and entered upon the duties of his office in April, 1895. He has conducted the business of his department wisely and economically, and has received praise from some of his political opponents in Congress.

Mr. Wilson is a graceful speaker, but is better known as a worker. A man of integrity, indomitable purpose, great ability, it remains with the future to disclose what higher position he will take with the people of this country.

He is a member of several learned societies, a regent of the Smithsonian Institution, and a trustee of the John F. Slater fund, and has received the degree of LL.D. from several colleges and universities, among the number, Columbian University, and the University of Mississippi, and Tulare University, New Orleans.

He was Permanent President of the National Democratic Convention, at Chicago, in 1892, a graceful recognition on the part of his political associates, of his leadership in the House and championship of revenue reform, called for in previous national platforms of his party.

HENRY M. TELLER.

THIS gentleman was born in Allegheny county, New York, May 23d, 1830. His ancestors came to this country from Holland, settling in New York State. His father was a farmer in comfortable circumstances, and gave him an excellent education. After his student days were over, he studied law, and was admitted to the bar in New York State. In 1858, he removed to Illinois, and practiced for three years in that State. In 1861, he emigrated to Colorado, settling in Central City, then one of the principal mining towns of the Territory. He was not long in gaining a large and lucrative practice, to which he applied himself assiduously, though often asked to take a hand in politics. He refused to become a candidate for any office, until in 1876, Colorado became the Centennial State, when he entered the lists and was chosen United States Senator. He drew the short term, ending March 3d, 1877, but the Legislature again elected him for the term ending March 3d, 1883. In April, 1882, he was asked to take a seat in the Cabinet, as Secretary of the Interior, by President Arthur. He was averse to leaving the Senate, and so said, but the political and personal pressure became so great he reluctantly consented, and served until March 3d, 1885, when he again took a seat in the Senate, having been elected to succeed Hon. Nathaniel P. Hill. His administration of the Interior Department, the most complex of any Department of our Government, met with Congressional and public approval, and materially added to his reputation, establishing him as a fine executive officer. In 1891, Mr. Teller was re-elected United States Senator, without opposition in his own party. As a Senator, he has materially aided in the legislation of the period, being Chairman of the Committee on Pensions, Patents, Mines and Mining, and a member of the Committee on Claims. While a Republican, Mr. Teller differs with many of his party upon the silver question. He believes in the free coinage of silver, at an established ratio of sixteen to one. He is a moderate tariff man, believing the duties on imports should be adjusted to the needs of the treasury for the economical administration of the Government; that it should be incidentally a protection to American labor and manufactures, but should not create trusts or monopolies.

Mr. Teller is an affable gentleman, easily approached, and thoroughly a man of the people. He is a good speaker, and can maintain his end of the argument at all times.

H. M. Teller.

JOHN TYLER MORGAN.

HON. JOHN T. MORGAN, now United States Senator from Alabama, was born in Athens, Tennessee, June 20th, 1824. His family moved to Alabama in 1833, and were among the pioneers in that section of the State. His father, George Morgan, was of the same Welsh stock as the famous Revolutionary hero, General Morgan, and the daring Confederate Cavalry leader, John H. Morgan.

He received an academic education, and became a good Latin scholar before he was nine years old. In 1845, he was admitted to the bar, and practiced his profession until he became a United States Senator. During these years of active practice of his profession, he gained the reputation of being one of the very best and a leading member of the Southern bar.

In 1860, Senator Morgan was a Breckinridge and Lane Elector-at-Large; and in 1861, a member of the Alabama Secession Convention. When the war broke out, he enlisted as a private soldier, and served successively as private, Major, Lieutenant-Colonel, and Brigadier-General of Infantry, resigning the latter position to rejoin his regiment, the Colonel of which had been killed in battle. Subsequently, he acted as Brigadier-General of Cavalry until the close of the war.

He was a gallant soldier, and participated in the great campaigns of the west, doing his duty fearlessly, and stimulating his men by his personal bearing when under fire.

After the war he returned to his home and resumed the practice of law, and in 1874 was chosen Elector-at-Large on the Tilden and Hendricks ticket. The same year he was elected United States Senator, and reëlected in 1882, 1888 and 1894. His great strength with his people, and their estimation of his character, is best shown by his successive reëlections to the Senate, without his ever having asked for a vote. Senator Morgan is recognized as a man very learned in the law; especially so in Constitutional and International law. For this reason he was selected, with Justice John M. Harlan, as an Arbitrator for the United States, before the Bering Sea Tribunal. In that august body, he was found able to cope with the distinguished jurists and diplomats of England, France, Canada, Italy and Sweden and Norway.

He is a skilful pleader and a most successful advocate; is ready in debate, fluent in speech, a close student, and has a vast fund of knowledge to draw upon; in fact, his versatility seems unbounded, for he is equally at home when pleading a common law case, a point of Constitutional law or an intricate and tangled case of international law. He is, in matters relating to foreign affairs, considered by the Senators upon both sides of the house an authority.

In the reorganization of the Senate Committees, during the present Congress, he was Chairman of the Committee upon Foreign Relations and can ill afford to spare him from its councils.

J. T. Morgan.

STEPHEN BENTON ELKINS.

THIS trusted friend of the late James G. Blaine, and Republican Senator from West Virginia, was born in Perry county, Ohio, September 26th, 1841. His ancestors were Virginians, and his grandfather a man of considerable wealth and prominence, and a slave owner. He sympathized, however, with President Jefferson's emancipation scheme, and, in consequence, removed to Ohio, and bought a large amount of land in the southern part of the State. Among other property, he owned 3,000 acres in the Hocking Valley, now worth probably $2,000,000. It is in the very heart of the coal measures which have made the valley famous; it was sold by the senior Mr. Elkins for "little or nothing." The present Mr. Elkins was born near where General Phil. Sheridan and General Jerry Rusk saw the light. His parents subsequently removed to Missouri, where he received his education in the public schools until far enough advanced to be sent to the University of Missouri, where he graduated in 1860; having chosen the law as his profession, he studied and was admitted to the bar in 1863. The same year, "Westward ho!" captivated his imagination, and he crossed the plains, then a formidable undertaking, for there is a vast deal of difference between going in a prairie schooner, drawn by oxen or mules, and a Pullman sleeper, especially when one might encounter Indians bent upon a "scalp raising expedition;" *en route* he studied Spanish, and soon after reaching New Mexico was proficient in the language. There he practiced his profession with great success and profit, being employed specially in the Maxwell land grant case.

Though he has not been of late years actually engaged in the practice of the law, he stands well with that learned profession. In 1866, he was elected to the Legislature, and shortly afterward was made Attorney-General of New Mexico. In 1868, President Johnson appointed him United States District Attorney, in which position he won lasting reputation by the strict enforcement of the laws, especially that one, providing that there shall not be slavery or involuntary servitude in the territories or District of Columbia; by his efforts several thousand peons or slaves held by the Mexicans, were set at liberty. He was the first to put the act into effective operation.

In 1873, he was elected Delegate in Congress from New Mexico, beating his opponent, a native Mexican, by 4,000 votes. He was nominated and elected to the next Congress, though traveling in Europe at the time.

During his first term he was made a member of the Republican National Committee, and served thereon twelve consecutive years. In Congress he was noted for his industry, ability and support of important measures. He made an earnest and impassioned speech for the admission of New Mexico into the Union; it attracted general attention and established him as an ardent, logical, reasoner and debater. He secured the passage of an enabling act in the House by a two-thirds vote; it also passed the Senate, but with an amendment to which the House would not agree. In the House Mr. Elkins became the trusted personal friend of James G. Blaine, whose nomination for President in 1884 he did much to secure. In 1888, he was very instrumental in the nomination of Benjamin Harrison for President, and by

Stephen B. Elkins.

his success became ranked as one of the most sagacious, skilful, and forceful leaders of his party in the Nation.

Though Mr. Elkins has done much hard work in politics, it is perhaps, his minor rôle, as he has been *par excellence* the man of business; not merely the accumulator of money, but the sagacious, clear-headed man who has gone into the rugged fastnesses of nature, and from the stored rock and minerals lying inert and worthless, has wrested fortune to his own and his fellows good. Stephen B. Elkins, the politician, the statesman; Stephen B. Elkins, the developer of hidden resources; the employer of labor; the builder of highways and the founder of communities; the one a political man and the other a business man, successful in either rôle; of which shall the most praise be said? His rare organizing and executive abilities have left their impress upon a State and given to geography a name to perpetuate him. While in New Mexico, he was, for years, the President of the First National Bank of Santa Fé, and so successful was his management he became known among the financiers of Philadelphia and New York. In the territory he became an extensive land owner, and also a mine owner in Colorado; but his latest and greatest adventures have been among the mountains whose peaks cast shadows into the Potomac, up whose valleys nearly one hundred and fifty years ago the Father of His Country wended his way, compass in hand. First known, overlooked, neglected, it was reserved for this man who had worked in the shadows of the Continental divide, to come, to see, to conquer.

Through the serried hills his railroads run, bearing to market the black diamonds. A town snuggles by the base of an everlasting hill, and they call it by his name. Off on a lofty crest his mansion overlooks the leaping river and the narrow valley, through which the iron horse drags his load to the markets of the world.

In all that Mr. Elkins does he is practical; wealth with him means employment of men; the opening up of waste places; the diffusion of modern intelligence. In thinking and writing of Mr. Elkin's mastery of the forces of nature we have lost sight of his political record. In December, 1891, he became Secretary of War, and so administered his office as to win the encomiums of even his political foes. He has the rare gift of seeing a thing at once; knowing how and when to direct; hence is an executive officer.

In 1888, he delivered a very thoughtful, eloquent and forcible address before the University of West Virginia upon the subject of "American Civilization." It was patriotic; it was eloquent; it was learned. His manners are pleasing and popular; in his tastes he is scholarly and refined. He realizes, the writer thinks, that to remain a scholar one must always be a scholar. The world moves; the thought of the world progresses; new issues are constantly arising, and the man who keeps up with "the procession" must study; hence Mr. Elkins is a student. He is seldom seen at clubs or hotels; he is domestic, either at home with his family, or in his library, or abroad on business. He is a large man, over six feet high, with well rounded figure, full, broad chest, and large head on powerful shoulders. He is a linguist; Greek, Latin, Spanish and French are to him open books; he need not ask the translator to tell him what the thinkers of other countries say. In 1894, the State of West Virginia, largely through his endeavors became Republican, and when the Legislature met they chose Mr. Elkins as United States Senator, to succeed Hon. Johnson N. Camden. His term will expire March 3d, 1901.

W. M. Stewart.

WILLIAM MORRIS STEWART.

ONE of the first men that strangers, visiting the Senate of the United States, ask to have pointed out, is the senior Senator from Nevada, because his sturdy defense of silver has made him one of the most-talked-about men in the United States. He was born in Lyons, Wayne county, N. Y., August 9th, 1827, but when he was six years old his family removed to Trumbull county, Ohio, where he attended the common schools and Farmington Academy. Returning to Lyons, he prepared for college in the Union School, and through his own exertions and the aid of Mr. James C. Smith, a young lawyer, who afterward became a Judge of the Supreme Court of New York, entered Yale College, where he remained until 1850, when he went to California by way of the Isthmus of Panama. From the age of thirteen, Mr. Stewart had to support himself by manual labor and teaching school. He early determined to obtain an education and study law, and he had to overcome many obstacles in order to succeed in his purpose. Arriving in San Francisco, May 7th, 1850, he resolved to engage in mining, in order to obtain funds to tide him over until he could engage in the practice of his contemplated profession. For two years he prospected, mined and built canals, constructing one which was twenty miles in length, and is still in use in Nevada county, Cal. It was surveyed by him in 1851, and constructed along the mountain sides by the aid of rude levels made by himself. Early in 1852, he commenced to study law, and was admitted to practice the following fall. He was appointed District Attorney of Nevada county, and in 1853, was elected to the same office, and in 1854, was appointed Attorney-General of California, serving for six months; certainly a wonderful record for a lawyer who was almost self-taught in the science, and had practiced less than two years.

In 1855, Mr. Stewart married Annie E. Foote, daughter of Hon. Henry S. Foote, the Mississippi Senator and statesman, then a citizen of the Golden State. From 1855 to 1860, he was a leader at a bar famous for the ability of its members, and rapidly acquired not only money, but fame as a practitioner. Upon the discovery of the famous Comstock lode, in 1860, he removed to Virginia City, Nev., where he was immediately retained by the original lode claimants. The Comstock lode, some miles in length, was indicated on the surface by croppings several hundred feet in width. The first locators, according to rules and regulations which they made, claimed the same with all its dips, spurs and angles. A population of 15,000 soon gathered, and thousands of claims were located parallel to the original ones, under the assumption that the Comstock was a system of parallel veins, and not a single lode. Mr. Stewart contended from the first for the latter idea, his view being termed the "one lode theory." The result was the most important mining litigation in history, and Mr. Stewart won the battle, the title of the original locators being judicially confirmed; he, very naturally, became an authority in mining law, and his services were in great demand.

Being a Union man and a Republican, he took part in the contest to determine whether Utah and California should remain loyal to the Union or not, for there was a powerful faction, headed by Dr. Gwin and others, seeking their secession. These were exciting times, and Mr. Stewart was induced to serve a year in the territorial council assisting in the organization of the territorial government, framed in 1861, and was a member of the Constitutional Convention of 1863. The next year Nevada was admitted as a State into the Union, and Mr. Stewart was elected the first Senator, his colleague, Gov. James W. Nye, being elected the next day. He served five years, and was reëlected in 1869, but his fortune having become impaired, he declined a reëlection for the term 1875 to 1881. Those years, eleven in number, of his first service in the United States Senate, embraces a large part of the most notable portion of American political, financial and economic history.

An active supporter of the war legislation, he, before the Fourteenth Amendment was adopted, prepared a plan of reconstruction, which provided for universal amnesty and suffrage. By this plan the Southern States could have prevented suffrage restrictions, because of participation in the Rebellion, and voters of the same class that supported secession could have brought their States back into the Union, simply by providing that thereafter there should be no restriction of the right of suffrage on account of race, color or previous condition of servitude; it was not adopted. When General Grant was elected President, Mr. Stewart, as a member of the Judiciary Committee, wrote, reported and secured the adoption of the Fifteenth Amendment to the Constitution, being aided therein by the influence of the President. He is the author of our mining laws, recognizing and continuing all local mining regulations then in existence. These have grown into a system of common law, admirably adapted to the use of our mining communities. From 1848 to 1866, all locators were trespassers; but Senator Stewart contended that non-action had created equities that rested upon the broad principles of natural right; the view prevailed.

On retiring from the Senate in 1875, he resumed practice and set about restoring his fortune; in this he was successful, and so, when called upon in 1886 to again become a Senator, he accepted, and since has been reëlected for the term ending in 1899. He has devoted a great deal of study and time to the cause of the remonetization of silver and its free coinage, and to irrigation. These two subjects he regards as of greatest importance, the one affording sufficient currency to do the business of the country, the other successfully applied, furnishing homes to hundreds of thousands of people and causing the desert to blossom and bear fruit.

He is independent sometimes of party behests, for when in the Fifty-first Congress the Republican party became committed to the Federal Elections bill, he opposed it. He is like a large share of the Western statesmen, a tariff man only as it is necessary to provide revenue for the expenses of the Government and the protection of American labor. He believes that the strictest economy should be practiced, and is against paternalism, trusts and monopolies.

Mr. Stewart wears a flowing beard, which is now white; has a florid complexion, keen, blue eyes, and is massive of frame and above the average stature. He is of striking appearance, and with age, has rounded out sufficiently to give him a finely proportioned form. He makes no claim to being an orator, but is a most effective and convincing speaker. He is a man of full, active brain, a good judge of men, a constant reader, ready of speech, choice in his language, and of open courage. He has a mellow, strong voice, and is peculiarly effective in off-hand debate, as his sentences are pointed, incisive and often axiomatic. Courteous in manner, he is democratic in habits and sympathies, and has great kindness of heart.

Don Cameron.

JAMES DONALD CAMERON.

THE present senior Senator from Pennsylvania, was born at Middletown, Dauphin county, Pa., May 14th, 1833. He is a son of the late Hon. Simon Cameron, who was Secretary of War, Minister to Russia, and for nearly twenty years United States Senator.

The subject of this sketch, after the necessary preparatory schooling, entered Princeton College, where he graduated in 1852, when but nineteen years of age. This fact proves that he must have been studious and industrious in his early life, as he has been in his later years.

After graduation, he entered the Middletown Bank (now National Bank of Middletown) as a clerk; but displaying aptitude for finances, was soon promoted to Cashier, and then to President.

Early in life he was very successful in several business enterprises, and laid the foundation for a large fortune. In 1863, he was elected President of the Northern Central Railway, which, in very large measure, owed its existence to the foresight, energy and wealth of his distinguished father. This position he relinquished in 1874, when the Pennsylvania Railroad, came into possession of the property. In May, 1876, General Grant made him Secretary of War, which position he held until the close of the administration.

Mr. Cameron was a delegate to the Republican National Conventions, of 1868 and 1876. In the latter convention he was very influential, and the leaders of the party, recognizing his abilities as an organizer, made him Chairman of the National Committee. He was again a delegate in 1880. Meantime his father resigned his seat in the United States Senate, and he was elected to succeed him, taking his seat October 15th, 1877, when only forty-four years of age. It is rarely the case in our history, that a son succeeds his father in that august body; and it is a remarkable coincidence that both father and son should also have been Secretary of War. Mr. Cameron has been reëlected to the Senate three times since, his present term expiring March 3d, 1897. In an open letter he has declined to again become a candidate.

He is not an oratorical member of the Senate, though he says tersely and well, that which he delivers. He is rather a working member, and does his full share of committee duties. During his service as a Senator, he has been a member of the Committee on Coast Defences, to inquire into all claims of the United States against Nicaragua, on the committee upon the five civilized tribes of Indians, Military Affairs, Chairman of Committee upon Naval Affairs, and active upon other committees appointed upon special subjects.

He has large interests in various enterprises in Pennsylvania and owns many valuable farms in Dauphin and Cumberland counties. He has a magnificent home in Harrisburg, fronting on the Susquehanna River, and a nice residence on Lafayette Square, Washington, D. C.

Although a wealthy man, a capitalist, a lender, rather than a borrower, he has by vote and speech, signified his belief in bi-metalism. He wants to see silver circulating side by side with gold, and he has not hesitated to say so.

Mr. Cameron has been twice happily married, his first wife being Miss Mary McCormick, a representative of a prominent Pennsylvania family. She died in 1874, and four years afterward he married Elizabeth Sherman, daughter of Judge Sherman and niece of the late General Sherman and Senator John Sherman, of Ohio.

Mr. Cameron is independent in his thought and sturdy in his convictions. No one can accuse him of moral cowardice or venality. He is a kind father and a loving husband; a good type of the best American citizen.

WILLIAM VINCENT ALLEN.

MR. ALLEN was born at Midway, Madison county, Ohio, January 28th, 1847. When only ten years of age his parents removed to Iowa, where he attended the common schools and later, for a time, the Upper Iowa University, at Fayette, but did not graduate. Like most country lads, Mr. Allen had to work in his boyhood days, early acquiring the knowledge that he must be the architect of his own fortune. When nothing but a boy, the war of the Rebellion came on, stirring his patriotic impulses to such a degree we find him within a uniform of blue, carrying a gun in the ranks of Company G, 32d Iowa Infantry Volunteers. He did a soldier's full duty until the war closed, the last five months being upon the staff of General Jas. I. Gilbert. Returning home, he read law at West Union, and was admitted to the bar in 1869. For twelve years he practiced his profession in Iowa, then removed to Nebraska, where, after making his reputation in a new field as a true and able counsellor, he was elected by the people, Judge of the District Court, Ninth Judicial Circuit.

Mr. Allen has always preferred to be known as a man of the people; his sympathies go out to the men who fight the battles of life and conquer difficulties by the force of their unaided exertions; that clear the wilderness by their brawn and direct the destinies of the new communities by their brain. When the old parties, in his judgment, failed to give relief from onerous taxation to the people, and would not accord sufficient currency to meet the requirements of business, he joined the new People's party, and was the President of the Nebraska Populist Convention, of 1892. February 7th, 1893, the party having a majority in the Legislature, he was elected United States Senator, to succeed Hon. A. G. Paddock, Republican. In the Senate, Mr. Allen has made a reputation as a fearless advocate of the free coinage of silver, at a ratio of sixteen to one. He is a good speaker, not afraid of a controversy with any Senator, and perfectly fearless in his advocacy of what he believes is best for his constituents and the country.

W. V. Allen.

WHARTON BARKER.

WHARTON BARKER, son of Abraham and Sarah Wharton Barker, was born in Philadelphia May 1st, 1846. He is the grandson of Jacob Barker, the distinguished banker, merchant and statesman, who took an active part in public affairs and business from 1800 to 1868. Jacob Barker was born on Swan Island, Maine, in 1779, and died in Philadelphia in 1872. He was a warm, personal friend of Alexander Hamilton, DeWitt Clinton, James Madison, Andrew Jackson and other leading men of the day. He took the United States war loan of 1814 ($10,000,000) and supported President Madison with earnestness throughout the war. Although a citizen of Louisiana, he was always a consistent anti-slavery man. Jacob Barker and Benjamin Franklin were cousins.

Mr. Abraham Barker, one of the most respected citizens of Philadelphia, has been a banker since 1837, and is still in full vigor of both mind and body. He is one of the charter members of the Union League of Philadelphia; and during the war of 1860-65 was very active in all work looking to the advancement of the cause of the Union, notably the work incident to putting in the field thirteen thousand colored soldiers. He believes that the cause of the great ruin and bankruptcy that is now seen on all sides is due to the demonetization of silver, and he is an ardent and effective co worker with his son in the effort to reëstablish bimetalism. He is a man of strong convictions and of great energy.

Wharton Barker is related on the Barker side to the Folgers, Hazards and Rodmans, and on the Wharton side to the Fishers, Rodmans and Redwoods, all distinguished families in New England and Pennsylvania from Colonial days to this time.

In early childhood Wharton Barker was delicate, and could not attend school until his twelfth year. He was educated at the Latin School of Charles Short and at the University of Pennsylvania, where he took the degree of Bachelor of Arts in 1866 and of Master of Arts in 1869. He is one of the Trustees of the University of Pennsylvania, having been elected in 1880, and was Treasurer from 1881 to 1890. In 1863 he, as a volunteer, had temporary command for three months of a company of the Third United States Colored Troops. He took an active part from the day he graduated at college in discussion of public affairs, and soon began to do political work. That he might have a means to discuss public questions to a larger audience than he could reach by tracts, he established in January, 1870, *The Penn Monthly*, a high-class magazine, devoted to literature, arts, science and politics, and continued its publication until the end of the year 1881. That he might have a still broader field and more frequent opportunity to make his views known, he established *The American*, a weekly national journal, and began its publication October 16, 1880. *The American* is now recognized as the highest authority, and the editorials are frequently used on the floor of the Senate and House of Representatives of the United States; are reprinted in many newspapers in all sections of the country, and frequently made the basis of discussion by editors of the

Wharton Barker.

metropolitan press. Editorials from *The American* are translated and reprinted almost weekly in *L' Economiste Europeen*, of Paris, a paper edited by the distinguished French economist, Edmond Thery.

Wharton Barker was much opposed to the nomination of General Grant for the Presidency for a third term, and took an active part in the movement that ended in his defeat at Chicago in 1880. He did not believe his work at that convention ended with the defeat of the General; he thought he still had a duty to perform; that he should present a candidate who could be elected. He brought out General Garfield, a man who he thought represented the interests of the people. Judge Samuel W. Pennypacker, of Philadelphia, said at a memorial meeting of the Historical Society of Pennsylvania, held shortly after the death of President Garfield, "no party convention ever had it in its power to affect more seriously the institutions of the country than that which assembled in Chicago in 1880 to nominate a candidate for the Presidency. A few months earlier the selection of ex-President Grant had seemed inevitable. For two years a banker in Philadelphia (Mr. Wharton Barker), with a taste for higher politics, had been urging the nomination of Mr. Garfield in the columns of the *Penn Monthly*, and making combinations looking to that result. On the first ballot Mr. Garfield had but one vote, that of a friend of the Philadelphia banker. On the thirty-sixth ballot he was nominated."

In 1881 he, with Charles Wolfe and George E. Mapes, organized the revolt in the Legislature of Pennsylvania against the Quay-Cameron candidate for the United States Senate, that after a struggle of six weeks resulted in defeat of their candidate, Mr. Oliver, and in the election of Mr. Mitchell. In 1882 he organized the Independent Republican revolution against Quay and Cameron's dictation of the nomination of General Beaver and others for State offices. In 1884, he made an effort to nominate for President General Harrison, believing he was the only available Republican candidate; but failing in that, he gave Mr. Blaine earnest support. March 29, 1884, General Harrison wrote Wharton Barker: "I ought to have acknowledged yours of the 26th inst. sooner. But I have no information that would be of interest or use to you. I do not think there is any danger of any body crossing your plans, for I really think you are so far in the advance as to be almost lonesome. * * * Again, June 12, 1884, General Harrison, writing at length on the result at the convention, said, among other things, "I think you know that I had much less enthusiasm and confidence than you; possibly because I know your candidate better than you did."

Mr. Blaine wrote Wharton Barker June 14, 1884: "I wish you would pack your grip-sack and come down here for a day or two, coming directly to my house. I have so many things to say to you that it is discouraging to begin on paper. If you gain no other pleasure from the trip I promise you a sight of the beautiful island where your eminent grandfather was born in 1778 (I think), in the midst of the great struggle. It is but fifteen miles from my door. Come as early next week as your convenience will allow. The committee to advise me of my nomination will be here on the 20th, a good time for you to come. I refrain from giving thanks or suggesting plans. Hope to cover all points in our conference."

Defeat of Blaine did not discourage Wharton Barker. He was convinced General Harrison could have been elected, and he went to work making combinations that resulted in the nomination of Harrison in 1888, in face of the opposition of politicians of the Quay-Sherman class.

The extracts we have given from the letters of two as distinguished men as Blaine and Harrison are introduced to show that, statesmen as they were and practical politicians, they wished Mr. Barker's advice and the fruit of his judgment. They recognized that he was correct in his conclusions; a good judge of men and measures, and fearless in the execution of that which he deems to be right.

How fearless may perhaps be best illustrated by the statement that when General Harrison made his alliance with Senator Quay and Mr. John Wanamaker, disgusting all the Independent Republicans, and working on lines the gold cliques advocated, Wharton Barker went on with his contention in *The American*, criticising the administration, urging the adoption of an American policy, and the election of able and independent men to public office.

In another portion of this work will be found the platform of the American League, adopted January 2, 1894. It was written by Mr. Barker. There seems to be no doubt now but that it will be the basis upon which bimetalists will rest their request for the support of the American people in the present campaign.

In 1883, and until the assembly of the National Convention at Chicago in 1884, he opposed the nomination of Mr. Blaine, on the ground that he was not the best candidate, and that his election would be jeopardized by the vehement opposition to him that existed in his own party throughout the country. When, however, he had been nominated, and the choice lay between him and Mr. Cleveland, who represented the principles against which he had contended for so long, Wharton Barker gave him an ardent and hopeful support, bringing to him the aggressive support of Irish Americans in New York and in other States.

In 1885, 1886 and 1887 he supported the policy of the Republican party in Congress, suggesting from time to time measures which, in the Chicago platform of 1888, in the Senate tariff bill of that year, and in the McKinley bill of 1890, are nearly all embodied—the abolition of the sugar duties, as no longer a protective but simply a revenue measure, accompanied with the insistance (in which, for a long time, he stood substantially alone) that in return for the opening of our markets to the sugar producing countries we should have an adequate return.

Upon this point, indeed, reciprocity in trade relations, Wharton Barker outlined a definite and broad policy. In October, 1881, he proposed the creation of a Zollverein system with Canada, and this policy, since known as "Commercial Union" and "Unrestricted Reciprocity," was steadily advocated and explained by him, until—in the absence of any such, or, indeed, any statesmanlike adjustment of the differences between the two countries—our relations with Canada became so irritated as to make the subject for the time an unpractical one. In 1883, six years before the clauses in the McKinley bill gave the plan of reciprocity Congressional approval, Wharton Barker, in *The American*, and in an open letter addressed to Senator Morrill, had pointed out the trade which we should secure from the West Indies and Central and South America through the concession to them of a removal of the sugar duties.

In 1887 and 1888, Wharton Barker again urged the nomination of General Harrison; again opposed that of Mr. Blaine and Senator Sherman, and when General Harrison was selected he supported him earnestly for election. During his administration Mr. Barker spoke with uniform terms of praise of those acts which were dignified and consistent with the principles declared for and by him; on the other hand, he was compelled to condemn the many lapses from that line by which he surrendered so much to unworthy party managers and to the money cliques of the country; and in the near relation which these circumstances had to the politics of Pennsylvania, he led the Independent Republicans in their support of the Democratic candidate for Governor in 1890, considering that this was the obvious duty of all citizens who cherished a just measure of personal self-respect and a clear apprehension of public duty.

Wharton Barker has made no professions of that cosmopolitan magnanimity which is said to lift a man above the narrow bounds of patriotic feeling. He has believed in our country first of all, in her greatness, her future, her essential moral soundness, and her capacity to outgrow or to reform what is wrong in her policy and her character. On purely political questions he has in general acted with the Republican party, but he has never hesitated to criticise its faults and shortcomings. Consequently with these general principles he has been at all times earnestly American. He has defended the policy of protection; he has insisted on a just manliness of national character; he has supported an adequate navy, and coast and harbor defences; he has condemned a servile attitude toward foreign powers; he has advocated the encouragement of our ocean commerce by national aid; and following out logically this policy of a dignified self-assertion in the American nation he has insisted on the national rights of other countries as well. He has upheld the cause of oppressed nationalities everywhere, and whenever a people called to be a nation is struggling with the yoke imposed by an alien power. Throughout the entire period of his taking part in public affairs he has never abated his advocacy of the right of the people of Ireland to such self-government as would express their just national aspirations.

Wharton Barker has maintained the policy of protection from early life. He has always demanded an intelligent, a broad-minded, a scientific application of the protective principle to the external revenue system of the country. This principle demands that when the inflow of foreign products is discouraged and checked, domestic production shall be freely competitive, and he has never hesitated to denounce domestic "Trusts," which were designed or were likely to create monopolies, and thus destroy at home the very benefit which protection along the frontier line is intended to secure. He has endeavored, at the same time, to broaden and to deepen the public conviction upon this subject, to show that it is a national question, not a class question; that protective duties are not imposed for the sake of manufacturers, but for the public advantage of diversified industries and industrial independence, and for the maintenance of comfort and intelligence amongst the working people. He has never been a ranter in behalf of indiscriminate protection; on the other hand, he has never regarded the policy of free trade as other than a surrender to competitive foreign nations and as an acceptance for our people of their wages and social conditions.

He became an advocate of bimetalism soon after the demonetization of silver in 1873. He spoke and wrote against the policy of gold monometalism at all times when the question of reëstablishment of bimetalism was under discussion. For the last three years he has been acknowledged as the highest authority on the question. His discussion has been scientific as well as practical.

So much for his political work and position. In business he has been active from the day he went into the office of Barker Brothers & Co. He soon became a partner of his father; the business increased rapidly and his reputation extended to all parts of the world. In 1878 he was made financial agent of the Russian Government in connection with the building of the four cruisers, Europe, Asia, Africa and Zabieca, a work done so well that the Czar Alexander II conferred upon him the Order of St. Stanislaus, a distinction rarely conferred upon a foreigner. In the summer of 1879 he went to Russia at the request of men in high authority, to consider a proposition for the development of the coal and iron of the Donetz region. After a survey of the country north of the sea of Azof, by competent American engineers sent out by Mr. Barker, he made proposals for great works to be undertaken under Imperial concessions that involved an expenditure of ten million dollars. Prince Sergius Dolgorouki, then Minister of the Public Domain and Master of Ceremonies at the Court, sent a cable to Mr. Barker three days before the death of the Emperor to prepare to go to Russia, for the Czar and Grand Council of the Empire had decided to grant the concessions asked for. After the death of the Emperor this great work was dropped. Mr. Barker has been to Russia four times, last in 1894, each time going upon important business.

He is a member of the American Philosophical Society, the Academy of Natural Sciences, the Historical Society of Pennsylvania, and the American Academy of Political and Social Science. He was the first President of the Penn Club, and is now a member of the Union League and the Manufacturers' Club.

Wharton Barker married Margaret Corlies Baker, of New York, in 1867. They have three sons, Samuel, Rodman and Folgar Barker, all grown men.

There are few more active men, and almost none who have worked upon so many lines, to wit: business, politics, letters, and always with force. Should the new party see fit to nominate him for President, and the American people should ratify the nomination by election, the Nation would have as its Chief Executive a man of integrity, rare ability from long discussion of public affairs and acquaintance with statesmen, not only of the new but the old world. Above all else they would have an American of Americans, devoted to the development of the country's resources and our independence of the dictation of foreign capitalists, and those of our own land who foster National indebtedness which the people must pay by the issue of bonds to meet current governmental expenditures.

WILLIAM O'CONNELL BRADLEY.

WILLIAM O'CONNELL BRADLEY was born March 18th, 1847, in Garrard county, Kentucky, near the town of Lancaster. His father, Hon. Robert M. Bradley, was perhaps the ablest and most successful land lawyer that ever lived in Kentucky, and was one of the most ardent and efficient promoters of popular education in the State.

Gov. Bradley's mother was a Miss Ellen Totten, the daughter of a sturdy, intelligent farmer of Garrard county, a very strong-minded woman and a devout believer in the faith of Alexander Campbell, the founder of the Christian Church, of which she was a member.

William spent his boyhood days at Somerset, where his parents had removed. The Civil War wrecked his father financially, and his education was necessarily cut short at the age of fourteen. Twice he ran away and joined the Union army, but his father secured his release on each occasion and returned him home. He manifested a strong disposition to study law, and so well qualified was he at the age of seventeen, that the Kentucky Legislature passed a special act to license him to practice, for at that time the Statute forbade any person under the age of twenty-one to practice.

He first entered politics in 1869, and has been at the front of all the political battles in the State since that time, save 1891, when he was confined by dangerous illness in a Louisville hospital. He was elected Prosecuting Attorney in 1870, of Garrard county, over an opponent of fine legal attainments and great personal popularity. In 1872 and 1876, he was nominated for Congress against Milton J. Durham, but was defeated by greatly reduced majorities after brilliant canvasses. He declined the nomination for Attorney-General in 1879, on account of ill-health, and in 1880, was a Delegate to the Chicago National Convention and seconded the nomination of General Grant. In 1884, was a member of the National Republican Committee, Delegate-at-Large and Chairman of the Kentucky delegation at the Chicago Convention, and delivered the speech which defeated the proposition from Massachusetts and Indiana, to curtail the representation from the South ; at the close of his speech the vast audience arose and repeatedly cheered him.

In 1884, President Arthur selected him to prosecute the "Star Route" cases, but the Attorney-General refusing to allow a full and impartial prosecution, he withdrew. Twice before he was of eligible age he was nominated by his party for United States Senator.

In 1887, he made the race for Governor as the Republican nominee, and whittled a Democratic majority of 45,000 down to less than 17,000. It was in this memorable campaign that he made the terrific attack upon the Democratic State officials, charging corruption at Frankfort, and which resulted in an examination of the books, and in finding State Treasurer Dick Tate, a defaulter for $247,000, and in foreign lands.

In 1895, he was again unanimously nominated for Governor, met the Democratic candidate, Hardin, in joint debate, and carried the State by 9,000, electing a full set of Republican State officials.

Governor Bradley is a typical Kentuckian, plain and unassuming, and filled with that unostentatious hospitality that has made Kentuckians so

W. O. Bradley.

popular the world over. He is as brave as a lion ; nothing can daunt or disconcert him. In native wit, eloquence and magnetic power over a jury or an audience, few men equal him at the bar or on the stump ; a splendid story-teller, full stocked and with always a new one ; a disposition that is as sunny as a summer's day, and a heart so big that it overflows with genuine love for his fellowman. No man was ever more devoted to his friends, and no man ever had more devoted friends than he. A Republican, inflexible and incorruptible, a patriot of the highest type, he is every inch an American citizen. He came up through poverty and privations himself, and knows and appreciates the difficulties of the poor, and what it is to labor for his bread. He is a friend to every one who wants to do right ; liberal to his party, to the deserving poor, his friends, to every one, and only unmindful of himself. Kentucky is proud of him, and well may the nation be, for there are few abler, better or truer men than William O. Bradley, the first Republican Governor of Kentucky.

Governor Bradley is an indefatigable worker and a methodical one. Probably one of the best campaigners in the country to-day. Physically, mentally, and in every way a *giant*, his name will be presented at the St. Louis Convention, June 16th, for the Presidential nomination, and Kentuckians of his political faith believe he can be nominated and elected.*

* The editor acknowledges his indebtedness to Mr. E. C. Linney of Louisville, Ky., for most of above sketch.

EPITOME OF AMERICAN POLITICS,

From the Foundation of the Government, Together with Date and Place of Assemblage of Every Important National Political Convention Held in the United States.

IT may be said that previous to 1776, parties, strictly speaking, had no place in our history. People previous to that time were Whig or Tory, just as they had happened to be in the mother country, or as their sympathies had grown in consequence of parental training. When, on the 7th of June, 1776, Richard Henry Lee, of Virginia, moved the Declaration in these words : " *Resolved*, That these United Colonies are, and of right ought to be free and independent States ; that they are absolved from all allegiance to the British Crown, and that all political connection between them and the State of Great Britain is, and ought to be, totally dissolved," and when, on the 4th of July, the Declaration of Independence was adopted, parties took shape, and Whig and Tory assumed a new meaning. Having taken the initiatory steps for independence, it was of course necessary for the separate States to delegate to some central government the power necessary to bring about unity of action.

As early as June 11th, 1776, a committee was appointed to prepare the form of a Colonial Confederation, and one member from each Colony was appointed to the task. They submitted a report, which was laid aside the 20th of August, 1776, taken up April 7th, 1777, debated from time to time until November 15th of the same year, when the report was agreed to. It had then to be submitted to the several States, which was done, the Legislatures being advised to authorize their Delegates in Congress to ratify the same. On the 26th of June, 1778, the Articles of Confederation were ordered to be engrossed ready for the signatures of the Delegates.

July 9th, New Hampshire, Massachusetts Bay, Rhode Island, Connecticut, New York, Pennsylvania, Virginia and South Carolina signed ; Georgia, July 21st ; North Carolina, July 24th : New Jersey, November 26th ; and Delaware, February 22d, 1779. Maryland refused to ratify until the conflicting claims of the Union and the States to the Crown lands should be adjusted. The lands in dispute were ceded to the Union, and Maryland signed March 1st, 1781.

On the 22d of March, Congress assembled under its new powers, and continued to act for the Confederacy, until March 4th, 1789, when the Federal Constitution took effect.

The Federal Constitution is the result of the labors of a Convention which convened at Philadelphia in May, 1787. At that time it had become evident that the old Confederation had outlived its usefulness, the days of peace trying it more severely than the days of war, when a common danger united the people and made them less captious and exacting in regard to legislation.

The Confederation at this time had no credit ; the Revolutionary soldiers were unpaid ; no provision was made for the payment of interest on the public debt, and, as Cooper justly observes, "it was a failure from the disappointed hopes of many who thought freedom did not need to face responsibilities." When the Convention met, a large share of the Delegates wished to retain the Articles of Confederation, amending them so as to give Congress additional powers, instead of forming a Constitution. A long discussion followed, and a very able one, the result being our Constitution, embodying a division of legislative, judicial and executive powers. It was adopted by the several States, so that the machinery of our Federal Government was set in motion by the inauguration of Washington, as President, April 30th, 1789.

PARTIES.

When in the struggle for independence, the Whigs were of course in a majority. In fact, those of the old Tories who would not become Whigs found it best to emigrate or keep still enough to have their sentiments forgotten or unnoticed. When the question of the Union came up, the Whigs naturally divided upon the question of State rights, the smaller and largest of the States being the most strenuous that no central government should usurp their powers. The class of thinkers who held with greatest tenacity to the extreme idea of State rights, were called Particularists.

"Those who argued that local self-government was inadequate to the establishment and perpetuation of political freedom, and that it afforded little or no power to successfully resist invasion," were called strong Government Whigs. Some of them wanted a government patterned after England, but Republican in name and spirit. The essential differences, if they can be reduced to two sentences, were these: The Particularist Whigs desired a government republican in form and democratic in spirit, with rights of local self-government and State rights ever uppermost. The Strong-Government Whigs desired a government republican in form, with checks upon the impulses or passions of the people; liberty sternly regulated by law, and that law strengthened and confirmed by central authority, the authority of the National Government to be final in appeals. ("Cooper's American Politics," book 1, p. 5.)

The trouble with the Confederacy was this: It was not respected by the people; the States did not acknowledge its power; in fact, it had no power, it was a rope of sand. If it made a requisition the States disregarded it; it could not regulate foreign commerce; foreign nations refused to bind themselves by commercial treaties with such an inoperative power; there was open and constant jealousies and business rivalries between the States; it was "a house divided against itself, and it could not stand." Wisely, and with the prescience for which we cannot give the memory of the Delegates too much honor, they framed the Constitution of the United States; they took the parts and welded them into a harmonious whole.

The act providing for its submission provided that when ratified by nine of the thirteen States, it should be binding upon those ratifying the same. Now, amendments to the Constitution, when adopted by three-fourths of all the States, are binding upon all. When the Constitution was submitted the Strong-Government Whigs became known as the Federals, and the Particularists, Anti-Federals. The Federals had for leaders the brainiest and strongest men of the day, notably, Alexander Hamilton, James Madison and John Jay. The Anti-Federals had also some strong men, among whom were

Patrick Henry, and Samuel Adams, and the fight in the States over ratification was exceedingly fierce. Had not George Washington ranged himself with the Federalists, the result would have been uncertain; as it was, Congress was officially informed July 2d, 1788, that the needed nine States had ratified the Constitution, whereupon the first Wednesday in March, 1789, was fixed as the time "for commencing proceedings under the Constitution."

The people spontaneously nominated George Washington, for President, and John Adams for Vice-President, without any conventions. Washington selected his Cabinet from the leading minds of both parties, with the view undoubtedly of harmonizing all factions and obliterating party spirit. For a time this seemed to be the result, but soon party rancor became apparent, for even James Madison, who had been the leader of the Federalists, ranged himself under the Anti-Federalists' banner. During the third session of Congress, Vermont and Kentucky were admitted to the Union. Rhode Island and North Carolina, which had rejected the Constitution at first, reconsidered their action, the former in May, 1790, and the latter in November, 1789.

The election for members of the Second Congress, resulted in a Federal majority, and this Congress passed the first methodical apportionment bill, fixing representation at 33,000 for each Congressional district.

By 1793, party lines had become well drawn, the names being now the Federalists and the Republicans. George Washington was again the spontaneous choice of the people for President, and unanimously elected. John Adams received the support of the Federalists, and George Clinton, of New York, the support of the Republicans, for Vice-President. Adams was elected. In December, 1793, Jefferson left Washington's Cabinet, and retired to Monticello, where he busied himself in writing political essays and organizing the Republican party, of which he was the acknowledged head. Never before, nor hardly ever since, was political vituperation directed at exalted personages as in the closing days of Washington's administration, he being accused of shameful political crimes, and of winking at, if not being benefited by, frauds upon the public funds.

Accustomed as we are to all sorts of political abuse of prominent men, we can scarcely conceive it possible that the Father of his Country should have been so treated.

In 1796, the sentiment of the people crystallized upon the acknowledged leaders for President and Vice-President. Washington's farewell address had been issued in August, in which he announced his determination to serve no longer as President, or in any public capacity. The Federalists placed John Adams and Thomas Pinckney in nomination, while the Republicans named Thomas Jefferson and Aaron Burr. Both parties were plainly arrayed, and both confident; but so evenly were the parties divided the Electoral College chose John Adams, Federalist, President, and Thomas Jefferson, Republican, Vice-President. No political platform was adopted by either party. During this administration the celebrated Alien and Sedition law was passed, which authorized the President "to order all such aliens as he shall judge dangerous to the peace and safety of the United States, or shall have reasonable grounds to suspect are concerned in any treasonable or secret machinations against the Government thereof, to depart out of the territory of the United States within such time as shall be expressed in such order." These resolutions and the laws, passed in pursuance of this policy, gave a dangerous current "to political thought and action." Undoubtedly they were the immediate cause of the Kentucky and Virginia resolutions of 1798. Jefferson was the father of the former and Madison of the latter.

In 1800, John Adams was again nominated for President, and C. C. Pinckney for Vice-President. A "Congressional Convention," held in Philadelphia, nominated as the Republican candidates, for President and Vice-President, Thomas Jefferson and Aaron Burr. The Electors chosen voted 73 for Jefferson, 73 for Burr, and 65 for John Adams and 64 for Pinckney. Burr and Jefferson having the same number of votes, it was not legally decided which should be President or Vice-President, and the election had to go to the House of Representatives. The result was a protracted contest, which evoked the worst passions and even threatened civil war. It was the first practical test of the electoral system as then provided for in the Constitution. At that time each elector was required to vote for two persons, the one receiving the highest number of votes to be President, and the next highest Vice-President. This election showed conclusively that the man nominated for Vice-President might become the President, and the nominee for President the Vice-President; in other words, that the people's choice might not be ratified. On the thirty-sixth ballot in the House, Jefferson was chosen President, and Burr, Vice-President. An amendment to the Constitution was fully ratified by September 25th, 1804, requiring the Electors to ballot separately for President and Vice-President.

In the campaign of 1800, the first national party platform was adopted by the Republicans, and Jefferson and Burr were the first "Congressional Caucus" nominees. Epitomized, the platform of the Republican party was as follows: An inviolable preservation of the Federal Constitution, according to the true sense in which it was adopted by the States. Opposition to monarchizing its features by the forms of its administration, with a view to conciliate a transition, first to a President and Senate for life; secondly, to an hereditary tenure of those offices, and thus to worm out the elective principle. Preservation to the States of the powers not yielded by them to the Union. A rigorously frugal administration and all possible saving of public revenue, to be applied to payment of the public debt; resistance to all measures looking to a multiplication of offices and salaries, and a protest against the augmentation of the public debt on the principle of its being a public blessing. Reliance for internal defense solely upon the militia; no army or navy large enough to overawe public sentiment, or grind us with public burdens. Free commerce with all nations; political connections with none, and little or no diplomatic establishment. Opposition to linking ourselves by new treaties with the quarrels of Europe. Freedom of religion; freedom of speech and of the press; liberal naturalization laws; encouragement of the arts and sciences, to the end that the American people may become independent of all foreign monopolies, institutions and influences. The Federalists had no platform. During Jefferson's administration the first removal for political cause was made, and offices were first given as a reward for party fealty.

In 1804, the candidates of both parties were nominated by Congressional caucuses. Jefferson and Clinton were the Republican nominees, and Charles

C. Pinckney and Rufus King, were the nominees of the Federalists. Neither party adopted a platform of principles. In 1805, the Republicans dropped that name and took that of Democrats. In 1808, the usual Congressional caucus was held, nominating Madison and George Clinton, for the offices, respectively, of President and Vice-President. The Federalists supported C. C. Pinckney for President. Madison and Clinton were elected. In May, 1812, Madison was nominated by a Congressional caucus for reëlection to the Presidency, and John Langdon was nominated for Vice-President, but, declining on account of age, Elbridge Gerry, of Massachusetts, took his place.

In September, 1812, a

CONVENTION

of the opposition to Madison, representing in its delegates eleven States, was held in the City of New York, and nominated De Witt Clinton for President, and Jared Ingersoll for Vice-President. This was the first national political convention representing the people directly, and the Federalists must have the credit of establishing the precedent. Madison and Gerry were elected. Neither party presented a political platform. During this administration war was declared with Great Britain.

January 4th, 1815, the celebrated Hartford Convention passed a series of resolutions denunciatory of the forcible conscription, draft or imprisonment of citizens or the militia. It was a peace party in time of war; and it also proposed several amendments to the Constitution of the United States, the gist of which was as follows:

I. Representatives and direct taxes to be apportioned among the States, according to the respective number of *free* persons and those bound to service for a term of years; and excluding Indians and all other persons.

II. No new State to be admitted to the Union without the concurrence of two-thirds of both Houses of Congress.

III. No embargo on ships or vessels of citizens in the ports of the United States for a longer period than sixty days.

IV. Congress not to have power to interdict trade with foreign nations without concurrence of two-thirds of the members of both Houses.

V. Congress not to make nor declare war, nor authorize hostilities against any foreign nation, unless the United States be actually invaded, without concurrence of two-thirds of the members of both Houses.

VI. No person afterward naturalized to be eligible to Congress, or hold any civil office under the United States.

VII. Same person not to be eligible for reëlection to the Presidency; nor two citizens of same State, eligible for two terms in succession.

This was a Federalist platform. During this administration, Congress passed the first bill to promote internal improvements, but the President vetoed it. The first bill for the establishment of a national bank also passed, and was signed by Madison.

The Democrats, in 1816, nominated, through a Congressional caucus, James Monroe for President and Daniel D. Tompkins for Vice-President. The Federalists named Rufus King, of New York, and divided their vote for Vice-President. As usual, no political platforms. Monroe and Tompkins were elected. During this administration, the Monroe doctrine was enunciated, which has since become the unwritten law of the land.

The second election of Monroe occurred in 1820, and was practically without opposition, only one electoral vote being cast against him. Mr. Tompkins, candidate for Vice-President, was a little less esteemed, it would seem, since there were fourteen electoral votes cast against him. Neither party made any nominations or disseminated a platform. It was a case of spontaneity of expression, not likely to occur in our day or generation. During this administration, Missouri was admitted to the Union, and the Missouri Compromise passed. The sale of Government lands by the credit system was also changed to sales for cash and the price reduced.

In 1824, four candidates were before the people for President, namely: General Andrew Jackson, John Quincy Adams, William H. Crawford and Henry Clay. No one received a majority of the electoral votes, and for the second time in our history the House of Representatives was called upon to decide the struggle. The result was the selecting of John Quincy Adams for President and John C. Calhoun for Vice-President. The result made hard feelings and excited jealousies that were not allayed for many years. General Jackson had been the choice of the people, and his friends started the story, and professed to believe it, that there had been a corrupt bargain between Clay and Adams. The nominees had all been nominated by caucuses of Congressmen, and about all the good the bitter contest brought to the country was the destruction of that mode of nominating the Chief Magistrate of the Nation.

The election of 1824 really furnished a basis for the Whig party, for Mr. Clay, who had been a Democrat, was driven over to the National Republican (soon to be Whig) party.

In 1828, the National Republicans supported John Quincy Adams and Richard Rush, while the Democracy supported Andrew Jackson and John C. Calhoun. General Jackson received 178 Electoral votes, to 83 for Mr. Adams.

A convention was held in Philadelphia, in September, 1830, which adopted the following Anti-Masonic resolution : *Resolved*, That it is recommended to the people of the United States, opposed to secret societies, to meet in convention on Monday, the 26th day of September, 1831, at the city of Baltimore, by delegates equal to their representatives in both Houses of Congress, to make nominations of suitable candidates for the offices of President and Vice-President, to be supported at the next election, and for the transaction of such other business as the cause of Anti-Masonry may require.

In the month of December, 1831, the National Republican party held its Convention in Baltimore, and nominated Henry Clay for President, and John Sergeant for Vice-President. They issued a platform or address to the people, taking stand upon the questions of the tariff, internal improvements, removal of the Cherokee Indians, and in favor of the renewal of the United States Bank Charter. The Democrats put in nomination, General Jackson for reëlection as President, and John C. Calhoun as Vice-President, both of whom were elected by the popular vote and the Electoral College.

At a ratification meeting held in Washington (Whig party), May 11th, 1832, three resolutions were adopted as a platform for the party : 1st. Adequate protection to American industry ; 2d. Uniform system of internal improvements ; and 3d. That the " indiscriminate removal of public officers for a mere difference of political opinion is a gross abuse of power, and that the doctrine boldly preached in the United States Senate that 'to the victors belong the spoils of the vanquished,' is detrimental to the interests, corrupting to the morals and dangerous to the liberties of the country."

During this administration the public deposits were removed from the United States Bank, Roger B. Taney was made Chief Justice of the Supreme Court, and South Carolina, on the 24th of November, 1832, passed an ordinance to nullify certain acts of the Congress of the United States.

The Democracy held their Convention in 1836 at Baltimore, and nominated Martin Van Buren, for President.

The platform was constructed at New York, in January, 1836, and was known as the Locofoco Platform.

It declared that all men being created free and equal, each person has same rights as to person and property; that no man is under any greater duty than that of contributing to the necessities of society.

Unqualified hostility to bank notes and paper money as a circulating medium, because gold and silver is the only safe and constitutional currency. Hostility to all monopolies created by legislation; "hostility to the dangerous and unconstitutional creation of vested rights or prerogatives by legislation, because they are usurpations of the people's sovereign rights."

No legislature or other authority can, by charter or otherwise, exempt any man from trial by jury or give exemption from the jurisdiction of the laws. Acts of one legislature can be altered or repealed by a subsequent one.

The Whigs nominated William Henry Harrison and Francis Granger. There were scattering votes for Daniel Webster, Mr. Mangum and Hugh L. White, but Mr. Van Buren received 170 Electoral votes and Mr. Harrison 73.

The Whig resolutions were adopted at Albany, N. Y., February 3d, 1836, and in brief were: All citizens were invited to oppose Martin Van Buren, because he was the nominee of the Democrats in consequence of executive intrigue. That we support William Henry Harrison, not merely because of the value of his services as commander of our armies, but because we admire his talents and repose trust in his patriotism and principles.

In 1839, during the Twenty-sixth Congress, the practice of Members of Congress *pairing off* was first introduced. John Quincy Adams offered a resolution against the practice; it was placed on the calendar and not reached, hence not voted upon. The practice is now common.

In the campaign of 1840, Mr. Van Buren was again the Democratic nominee for President and Richard M. Johnson for Vice-President. Their Convention was held at Baltimore, and a platform adopted May 5th, 1840. The Convention made no nomination for Vice-President, several States having nominated different persons; but before the election Mr. Johnson was adopted. The Whigs held their Convention at Philadelphia, and nominated William Henry Harrison for President and John Tyler for Vice-President. The Whigs were victorious, the Electoral votes, 234, of nineteen States being given for them, and 60 Electoral votes from nine States were given to the Democratic nominees. General Harrison died April 4th, just one month after his inauguration, and John Tyler succeeded him as President. The Democrats gave to the country in this campaign a very elaborate platform, adopted at Baltimore, May 5th, 1840, and which we condense as follows:

That the Federal Government is one of limited powers, and that grants of power ought to be strictly construed by all the departments and agents of the Government.

That the Constitution does not confer upon the General Government the power to carry on a general system of internal improvements. The General Government has no right to assume the debts of the several States, or foster one branch of industry to the detriment of another; there must be equality of rights and privileges.

Rigid economy in National expenditures, and no more revenue raised than is required for that purpose. Congress has no power to charter a United States bank; no power to interfere with or control domestic institutions of the States. Denounced the Abolitionists. Money of the Government to be kept from banking institutions. No abridgment of present privilege of aliens becoming citizens.

This Convention made no choice for a candidate for Vice-President.

The first National platform of the Abolition party favored the abolition of slavery in the District of Columbia and the Territories; the Interstate slave trade and general opposition to slavery to the full extent of Constitutional power. During this administration the Democracy began to split on the free-soil issue, and discontented Whigs and Democrats united in forming a Liberty party, which, August 30th, 1843, in convention assembled at Buffalo, N. Y., promulgated a platform of twenty-one resolutions, the essential features of which were: That human brotherhood is a cardinal principle of true Democracy, as well as pure Christianity. Then followed a long exposition of what they deemed general, moral and Christian principles, winding up with the declaration, "That the laws of God are paramount to any laws of man." It was more a code of ethics than a declaration of political principles.

The next Presidential Nominating Convention was held at Baltimore, in May, 1844. This Convention had a majority of delegates favorable to the renomination of Mr. Van Buren, but a Chairman of the Convention opposed to his candidacy was selected, who, aided by a rule adopted by the Convention that a *two-thirds* vote should be necessary to nominate, the opposition headed by Calhoun's friends, were able to defeat him, and a dark horse in the person of James K. Polk, of Tennessee, carried off the prize. George M. Dallas, of Pennsylvania, was nominated for Vice-President. The Whig Convention at Baltimore, May 1st, 1844, adopted Henry Clay as its candidate for President and Theodore Frelinghuysen, of New Jersey, for Vice-President. The Abolitionists nominated James G. Birney, of Michigan, for President.

The Whig platform had one resolution which gave as their doctrine a tariff for revenue, discriminating with special reference to the protection of the domestic labor of the country, distribution of proceeds of the sales of public lands, a single term for the Presidency, and an efficient and economical administration. The Democratic platform reaffirmed the first nine resolutions of the platform of 1840; opposition to distribution of proceeds of sales of public lands among the States; against robbing the President of the qualified veto power, and affirming our title to the whole territory of Oregon, asking for its reoccupation, and the re-annexation of Texas, at the earliest practicable moment.

Polk and Dallas managed to be elected in consequence of the personal popularity of Silas Wright, who ran on the Democratic ticket for Governor of New York. The war with Mexico followed, Texas was annexed and anti-slavery agitation visibly increased in consequence of what was known as the Wilmot Proviso, namely: "That no part of the territory to be acquired (from Mexico) should be open to the introduction of slavery."

Preparatory to the Presidential election of 1848, the Democrats held their National Convention at Baltimore, May 21st, and nominated Levi Cass, of Michigan, for President, and General William O. Butler, of Kentucky, for Vice-President. The Whig Convention met at Philadelphia June 8th, 1848, and nominated General Zachary Taylor, of Louisiana, for President, and Millard Fillmore, of New York, for Vice-President. The disaffected Democracy, under the name of Free-Soil Democrats, met at Utica, N. Y., and nominated Martin Van Buren, of New York, for President, and Charles Francis Adams, of Massachusetts, for Vice-President. The Abolitionists nominated Gerritt Smith, of New York, for President. Each party put forth an elaborate platform of principles, and after an exciting canvass, General Taylor was elected. He died in about sixteen months from his inauguration, or on the 8th day of July, 1850.

The Democratic platform was adopted May 22d, and reaffirmed resolutions 1 to 4, and 7, 8 and 9, of the platform of 1840. They also reaffirmed their resolution of 1844, in relation to the distribution of proceeds of sale of the public lands and as to the veto power of the President; that the war with Mexico was provoked by that people, and while the party would rejoice over an honorable peace with Mexico, they demanded the ratification by the Mexican Government of the "treaty of peace," which had been prepared, and which provided for indemnity and security for the future; thanked the soldiers and sailors for their glorious achievements during the war; tendered congratulations to the French Republic; eulogized the administration of Polk, and congratulated the country on the establishment of a Constitutional Treasury, and the impulse given toward *free trade* by the repeal of the tariff of 1842 and substitution of that of 1846.

At a ratification meeting of the Whigs, held in Philadelphia, June 9th, instead of a regular platform they endorsed the nomination of General Zachary Taylor, for President, and eulogized him as a great soldier and a consistent, truthful man; that he would have voted in 1844,[*] if he could, for the Whig nominee, and was consistent in his support of the Whig party, and because he guaranteed to "make Washington's administration" a model for his, if elected. There was no distinct utterance of political principles in the resolutions. A popular soldier had been nominated, and he had simply pledged himself to carry out the principles of the party.

The Free Soil party also put out a long platform, aimed against slavery in particular, and denunciatory of the nominations of the Whig and Democratic parties, affirming that no opponent of slavery extension could consistently support the nominees. In their last resolution they said; "We inscribe on our banner, Free Soil, Free Speech, Free Labor and Free Men."

In 1852, it was becoming evident that unless the Whig party could be successful it would be dissolved, and a new party formed, more or less on

---

[*] There were doubts among the Whigs, as to whether General Taylor belonged to the party hence this declaration.

the slavery and sectional issues. The Free Soil Convention nominated John P. Hale, of New Hampshire, for President, at Pittsburg, August 11th, 1852. The Democrats nominated Franklin Pierce for President, at Baltimore, June 1st, 1852, and the Whigs, General Winfield Scott, at Baltimore, June 16th, 1852.

The Democracy, which clung to the two-thirds rule, nominated a dark horse, and the Whigs, a popular soldier. Each party, as had now become the custom, enunciated a platform of principles. The Democracy carried the day, and the Whig party ceased to exist as a national organization.

The Democratic platform was adopted June 1st, and re-affirmed the 1st to 7th resolutions of the platform of 1848. They declared for rigid economy in expenditures; that no more revenue should be raised than was necessary for that and the gradual extinction of the public debt; that Congress had no power to charter a National Bank; that the moneys of the Government should be kept separate from banking institutions; that the oppressed of every nation ought to be allowed to come here to become citizens and the owners of land. They also affirmed for non-interference, by Congress, with the domestic institutions of the States; resistance to anti-slavery agitation, in Congress or out of it; abided by the Kentucky and Virginia resolutions of 1792 and 1798; that the war with Mexico was just and necessary; rejoiced at the restoration of friendly relations with Mexico, and that in view of the condition of popular institutions in the Old World, a duty devolved upon the Democratic party to uphold and maintain the rights of every State, and thereby the union of States, and advance constitutional liberty by resisting all monopolies and exclusive legislation for the benefit of the few.

The Whig party adopted their platform June 16th. They declared that the Government of the United States is of limited character, and confined to the exercise of powers expressly granted by the Constitution; that reserved rights of States should be held secure and the general Government sustained in the exercise of its constitutional powers. That the Government should be conducted on the principles of strictest economy; and revenue sufficient for the expenses thereof, in time of peace, ought to be derived mainly from a duty on imports and not from direct taxes; and in laying such duties, sound policy requires a just discrimination, and when practicable by specific duties, whereby suitable encouragement may be offered to American industry, equal to all classes and to all portions of the country.

Congress has power to improve navigable waterways and harbors. Acquiesced in the series of laws of the Thirty-second Congress, including the "Fugitive Slave Law," as a settlement in principle and substance of dangerous and exciting questions. August 11th, 1852, "The Free Soil Party," in convention at Pittsburg, Pa., put forth a very long platform that affirmed, among other things, "That slavery is a sin against God, and a crime against man, which no human enactment or usage can make right; and that Christianity, humanity and patriotism alike demand its abolition." Denounced the "Fugitive Slave Law" and the compromise measures of 1850; the annexation of Texas, upon the terms upon which she was admitted to the Union; that all men have a natural right to a portion of the soil, and that the public lands of the United States belong to the people and should not be sold to individuals or corporations, but held as a sacred trust for the benefit of the people and should be granted in limited quantities, free of cost to landless settlers. These were distinctive principles, though it had others that were held in common by the Whig and Democratic parties.

About this time the Native American, or Know-Nothing, party arose; and the Kansas troubles were under full headway before Pierce's administration was over. The Dred Scott decision was also promulgated, and political excitement was at fever heat. The Free Soil Whigs and Democrats, and the disaffected of almost every shade of political opinion, formed a new party, named it the National Republican, the corner-stone of which was opposition to the extension of slavery. The American party met February 20th, 1856, at Philadelphia, and nominated for President Millard Fillmore, of New York, and for Vice-President, Andrew J. Donelson, of Tennessee. What was left of the Whig party met at Baltimore, September 17th, 1856, and endorsed the nominations of the American party. The first National Convention of the Republican party met at Philadelphia, June 18th, 1856, and nominated John C. Fremont for President, and William L. Dayton for Vice-President. The Democratic Convention met at Cincinnati, June 5th, 1856, and nominated James Buchanan for President, and John C. Breckinridge for Vice-President.

A most exciting canvass followed, resulting in the election of the Democratic ticket; but the vote cast for Fremont demonstrated that the Republican party was likely to succeed at the next trial. Then followed the excitement incident to the Kansas conflict, which became, on a small scale, actual war. Helper's Impending Crisis became a text-book; Douglas and Lincoln held their memorable debates, and John Brown made his insane raid on Harper's Ferry.

"The Know-Nothing," or "American party," met in Convention at Philadelphia, February 21st, 1856, their particular political object being embraced in the words "*Americans must rule America*, and to this end *native* born citizens should be selected for all State, Federal and municipal offices, or government employment in preference to all others. *Nevertheless*, persons born of American parents residing temporarily abroad, should be entitled to all the rights of native born citizens;" and that "no person should be selected for political station (whether of native or foreign birth) who recognizes any allegiance or obligation of any description to any foreign prince, potentate or power, or who refuses to recognize the Federal and State Constitutions (each within its sphere) as paramount to all other laws, or rule of political action."

It was, of course, tacitly understood that the last paragraph was aimed at Roman Catholic citizens. The party gained some local ascendancy but failed to become of national importance.

The Democratic National Platform was adopted June 6th, and in words was the longest that had ever been put forth in this country. However, the first ten resolutions were nearly the same as those of 1852. They took issue, of course, with the new "American party," declaring that it had met in secret conclave and agreed upon an adverse political test, and that "no party can justly be deemed to be national, constitutional or in accordance with American principles, which bases its exclusive organization upon religious opinions and accidental birth-place." It re-affirmed the doctrine of non-interference with the domestic institutions of the States; abided by the "Fugitive Slave Law;" said the territories, including Kansas and Nebraska, when they had sufficient population and made a constitution according to forms of law, should be admitted without, or with slavery, just as their constitution should provide; declared in favor of a preponderating influence in ways of communication across the Isthmus of Panama, and for our ascendency in the Gulf of Mexico.

The Republican National Platform was adopted June 17th, and its cardinal points were: opposition to the repeal of the Missouri compromise, of 1820; to the extension of slavery into free territory; in favor of admitting Kansas as a free State, and returning to the principles of Jefferson and Washington; denied "the authority of Congress, of a territorial legislature, of any individual, or association of individuals, to give legal existence to slavery in any territory of the United States, while the present constitution shall be maintained;" that Congress had sovereign right and power over the territories, and it was its duty to exclude from the territories those twin relics of barbarism, polygamy and slavery; arraigned the Democratic administration for various high crimes and misdemeanors, by allowing murder, rapine, suppression of free speech, test oaths of an extraordinary nature as a condition to the right of suffrage, denial of right of trial by jury, abridgment of the right of the people to keep and bear arms, and a number of other offenses aimed at the destruction of liberty. It also condemned the "Ostend circular," for its plea that "might makes right," and as being unworthy of American diplomacy.*

This platform also demanded the building of a railroad to the Pacific ocean.

The Whigs met at Baltimore, and, September 18th, resolved to support Millard Fillmore for President, the then nominee of the American party. They did so, without endorsing "the peculiar doctrines of that party."

Sectional excitement was running high in 1860; Senators in Congress were threatening the secession of their States, and there was throughout the country great unrest.

Amid profound excitement, the Democratic party convened its next National Convention at Charleston, S. C., on the 23d of April, 1860. The Convention did not get to balloting until Tuesday evening, May 1st—the eighth day of the session. They balloted until May 3d, when, finding it impossible to nominate, the Convention was adjourned to Baltimore, June 18th, 1860. This Convention debated until June 22d, and when on that day it was moved to go into a ballot, Virginia withdrew; North Carolina, Tennessee, Kentucky, Maryland, California, Oregon, and Arkansas followed. Georgia, Alabama, Mississippi, South Carolina, Texas, Louisiana, Arkansas, and Florida had been excluded from the Committee on Credentials in consequence of a resolution which had been introduced, and which was carried, referring "the credentials of all persons claiming seats in this Convention made vacant by the secession of delegates at Charleston to the Committee on Credentials." The Convention was now reduced to a minority of delegates from all the States. As a ballot was called for, when Massachusetts was reached, General B. F. Butler arose and refused to remain in a convention which represented a minority of States, or, what was personal to him-

---

* The "Ostend circular" was put forth by three American ministers to Europe, in favor of the buying, or, if that was not possible, the taking of Cuba by the United States.

self, in a convention where the African slave trade, which was piracy, was openly advocated. He then retired, followed by five others. The balloting proceeding, Stephen A. Douglas was nominated, with Senator Fitzpatrick, as candidates, respectively, for President and Vice-President. Mr. Fitzpatrick refused the honor, and the Executive Committee substituted Herschel V. Johnson. The same day, June 23d, another Convention assembled at Baltimore, styling itself the "National Democratic Convention," and nominated John C. Breckinridge for President, and Joseph Lane, of Oregon, for Vice-President. The Republican Convention assembled at Chicago, May 16th, 1860, and nominated Abraham Lincoln, of Illinois, for President, and Hannibal Hamlin, of Maine, for Vice-President. A "Constitutional Union" Convention met at Baltimore, May 9th, 1860, and nominated John Bell, of Tennessee, for President, and Edward Everett, of Massachusetts, for Vice-President.

Each party presented an elaborate platform, and made strenuous efforts to elect their candidates, it being apparent to thinking men that in the event of the success of the Republican party, the Gulf States and South Carolina at least would secede. Mr. Lincoln was elected, and all the Southern States did secede, excepting Maryland, Kentucky, and Missouri. The civil war followed, with what result all know. South Carolina seceded December 20th, 1860; Georgia, November 19th, 1860; Mississippi, January 9th, 1861; Florida, January 10th, 1861; Louisiana, January 25th, 1861; Alabama, January 11th, 1861; Arkansas rejected secession February 18th, 1861, seceded May 6th, 1861; Texas, February 1st, 1861; North Carolina, May 21st, 1861; Virginia, April 17th, 1861; secession vote of the people announced June 25th, 1861; Kentucky convened a rump conference at Russelville, October 29th, which passed a Declaration of Independence and a Secession Ordinance, November 20th, 1861; there was nothing regular or legal in this gathering. Tennessee was declared by Governor Isham G. Harris out of the Union, June 24th, 1861. In Missouri and Maryland, disaffected parties declared the States out of the Union, but in both it failed to have the sanction of the lawful authorities.

The remnant of the Whigs, who had not joined the new party or affiliated with the Democracy, and conservatives from the Democratic, American party, etc., under the name of the "Constitutional Union" party, put forth their principles, as follows:

"WHEREAS, Experience has demonstrated that platforms adopted by the partisan conventions of the country have had the effect to mislead and deceive the people, and at the same time to widen the political divisions of the country by the creation and encouragement of geographical and sectional parties; therefore,

"*Resolved*, That it is both the part of patriotism and of duty to *recognize* no political principles other than THE CONSTITUTION OF THE COUNTRY, THE UNION OF THE STATES, AND THE ENFORCEMENT OF THE LAWS. * * * * As representatives of the Constitutional Union men of the country, * * * * we hereby pledge ourselves to maintain, protect and defend, separately and unitedly, these great principles of public liberty and national safety against all enemies at home and abroad, believing that thereby peace may once more be restored to the country, and the rights of the people and of the States reëstablished."

Eight days after the Constitutional Union Convention, the Republican party put forth their platform. It declared that the declaration of the rights of man, as set forth in the Declaration of Independence, must be maintained; declared for the maintenance of the Union, and denounced all schemes of disunion. Maintained the right of each State to control its domestic institutions, and denounced the administration for trying to force the Lecompton Constitution upon Kansas. Declared that the new dogma that the Constitution, of its own force, carried slavery into any and all of the territories of the Union * * * * is revolutionary in its tendency and subversive of the peace and harmony of the country. That the normal condition of all the territory of the United States, is that of freedom; denounced the reopening of the African slave trade, and the vetoes of the Federal Governors of Kansas and Nebraska, of the acts of the Legislatures prohibiting slavery; that Kansas should be admitted at once as a free State; that while providing revenue for the support of the Government, by a duty upon imports, the duties should be so re-adjusted as to protect and encourage the industrial development of the country. In favor of the "Homestead law," against change in naturalization laws, for river and harbor improvements and a railroad to the Pacific Coast.

The Democratic party split in two, issued two platforms, that of the Douglas wing, declaring it reaffirmed the platform of 1856, and pledged the party to abide the decision of the United States Supreme Court upon all Constitutional questions; that the United States must protect all citizens at home and abroad; for speedy communication between the Atlantic and Pacific States; the acquisition of Cuba on terms honorable to this country and just to Spain; and that all acts of State Legislatures that defeat the faithful execution of the "Fugitive Slave law," are revolutionary.

The Breckinridge platform affirmed that all citizens have equal rights in all territories, and equal protection for all property they may take there. That it is the duty of the Federal Government, in all its departments, to defend the rights of persons and property in the territories. That any territory seeking admission as a State, with adequate population and a Constitution framed in accordance with law, should be admitted as a State, whether free or slave. This one plank was substantially the only difference between the two platforms.

In 1864, the Republicans re-nominated, June 7th, Abraham Lincoln for President, and Andrew Johnson, of Tennessee, for Vice-President. The Democrats held their Convention at Chicago, August 29th, and nominated General George B. McClellan for President, and George H. Pendleton for Vice-President. Lincoln was elected, and assassinated April 14th, 1865.

The Republican platform of 1864, adopted June 7th, upheld the Government in the war; declared slavery to be the cause of the conflict, and commended the "Emancipation Proclamation," and that there should be no peace except by unconditional surrender of the rebel armies. It thanked the soldiers and sailors of the army and navy; commended the use of the late slaves as Union soldiers; fostered foreign immigration, and the speedy construction of the Pacific Railroad; pledged the National faith to the redemption of the National debt, and that the Government would never regard with indifference the attempt of an European Government to overthrow by force or supplant by fraud, the institutions of any Republican Government on the Western Continent.

The Democratic National Convention, met at Chicago, August 29th, 1864. It declared that in the future, as in the past, we will adhere with unswerving fidelity to the Union and the Constitution; that four years of war had failed to restore the Union, and that there should be an immediate cessation of hostilities and a Convention of the States; that the recent interference of the military with the elections in Kentucky, Maryland, Missouri and Delaware, was a shameful violation of the Constitution; denounced the subversion of civil by the military law in States not in insurrection, and upbraided the administration for not exchanging prisoners; extended sympathy to the soldiers and sailors, and promised them care and protection in case the Democracy was restored to power.

In 1868, May 20th, the Republican National Convention met at Chicago, and nominated General Grant for President, and Schuyler Colfax for Vice-President, who were elected. The Democrats met at New York the 3d of July, 1868, and nominated Horatio Seymour for President, and General Francis P. Blair for Vice-President.

The Republican platform congratulated the country on the assured success of reconstruction measures, whereby equal civil and political rights were secured to all; denounced repudiation as a National crime; that it was due to the labor of the Nation that the debt should be equalized and reduced as rapidly as possible, but extented over a fair period at a low rate of interest; strictest economy in the carrying on of the Government; deplored the death of Abraham Lincoln and accession of Andrew Johnson to the Presidency; that the doctrine of Great Britain and other European powers, that because a man once a subject must always be one, should be resisted by the United States, at every hazard; under everlasting obligations to soldiers and sailors who saved the Union; sympathy with all oppressed people struggling for their rights, and fostered foreign emigration.

The Democratic platform, adopted July 4th, urged the immediate restoration to the Union of all the States, and to all their rights under the Constitution; general amnesty for all political offenses; payment of the public debt as soon as practicable, and one currency for all. It demanded economy in administration of the Government, a tariff for revenue upon foreign imports, and such taxation under the revenue laws as would afford incidental protection to manufacturers; reform of abuses in the Administration; equal rights and protection for naturalized and native-born citizens, at home or abroad; arraigned the Republican party for subversion of the Constitution and oligarchical methods. It sympathized with the workingmen of the country in their efforts to protect the rights and interests of the laboring classes, and tendered thanks to Chief Justice Chase for his justice, dignity and impartiality, while presiding over the court of impeachment of President Johnson.

May 1st, 1872, the "Liberal Republican" party met at Cincinnati, and nominated Horace Greely, of New York, for President, and B. Gratz Brown, of Missouri, for Vice-President. The regular Democratic Convention convened at Baltimore, June 9th, and endorsed the Liberal Republican candidates. A few straight-out Democrats met at Louisville, Ky., September 3d, and nominated Charles O'Conor, of New York, for President, and John Quincy Adams for Vice-President. The regular National Republican Convention met at Philadelphia, June 5th, and re-nominated General Grant for President, and nominated Henry Wilson, of Massachusetts, for Vice-President. Grant and Wilson were elected.

The Liberal Republican party adopted as their platform, the following: Equality of all men before the law; maintenance of the Union of the States, emancipation, enfranchisement and the 13th, 14th and 15th Amendments to the Constitution. Removal of all disabilities imposed on account of the Rebellion; local self-government and impartial suffrage; reform in civil service and one term for the Presidency. The 6th plank we give in full, as it marked a distinct departure in the settlement of the tariff question:

"We demand a system of Federal taxation which shall not unnecessarily interfere with the industry of the people, and which shall provide the means necessary to pay the expenses of the Government, economically administered, the pensions, the interest on the public debt, and a moderate reduction annually of the principal thereof; and recognizing that there are in our midst honest but irreconcilable differences of opinion with regard to the respective systems of protection and free trade, we remit the subject to the people in their Congressional Districts and the decision of Congress thereon, wholly free from Executive interference or dictation."

Public credit to be sacredly maintained; speedy return to specie payments; eulogized those who saved the Union; opposed further grants of lands to railroads or corporations; fair treatment of all nations, it being dishonorable to demand what is not right, or submit to what is wrong.

The Democratic party met in Convention at Baltimore, June 9th, and ratified the Liberal Republican platform and nominees.

The Republican platform, adopted June 5th, 1872, called attention to the achievements of the Republican party, in its eleven years of power; that despite reduction of taxation during General Grant's presidency, the public debt had been diminished $100,000,000 a year; that the amendments to the National Constitution must be sustained; for complete liberty and exact equality to all men, and protection to citizens everywhere; for civil service, and opposed to further grants of lands to railroads.

It demanded that the revenue over expenditures should be applied to the reduction of the public debt, and that revenue, except tax on tobacco and liquors, should be raised by duties on imports and so adjusted as to protect American labor, wages and manufactures; the abolishment of the franking privilege, legislation to be so shaped that both capital and labor, the creator of capital, shall be protected; denounced repudiation in every form; approved the extension of amnesty to those lately in rebellion, and that the Government should adopt such measures as would encourage and restore American commerce and ship-building. It also eulogized General Grant and Henry Wilson.

The Democratic (straight-out) platform was adopted at Louisville, Ky., September 3d, 1872.

In substance it was as follows: Recurrence to first principles and eternal vigilance against abuses, are the wisest provisions for liberty; and fidelity to our constitutional system is the only protection for either. Original basis of Union was consent of the States. Powers not delegated by the States to the General Government, are reserved to the States. All governmental powers, trust powers. Interests of labor and capital should not be permitted to conflict, but should be harmonized by judicious legislation. Principle should be preferred to power. That the party was betrayed at Baltimore.

In 1876, the Greenbackers held a Convention at Indianapolis, May 17th, and nominated Peter Cooper and Samuel F. Cary, for President and Vice-President. The National Republican Convention met at Cincinnati, June 14th, and nominated Rutherford B. Hayes for President, and William A. Wheeler for Vice-President. They were declared elected after a contest before the famous "Electoral Commission." The Democratic National Convention, met at St. Louis, June 28th, and nominated Samuel J. Tilden for President, and Thomas A. Hendricks for Vice-President.

The Independent (Greenback) platform adopted May 17th, 1876, demanded the immediate and unconditional repeal of the specie resumption act of January, 1875; a circulating medium to be issued by the Government, "convertible, on demand, into United States obligations bearing a rate of interest not exceeding one cent a day on each one hundred dollars (3.65 per cent.) and exchangeable for United States notes at par; to be legal tender for all obligations, except such as it is expressly provided shall be paid in coin." Declared it the paramount duty of the Government, in all its legislation, to keep in view the full development of all legitimate business, agricultural, mining, manufacturing and commercial. Protested against any more sales of gold bonds by which the people would be made for a long time "hewers of wood and drawers of water" for foreigners. Against sale of bonds to purchase silver for the enrichment of owners of silver mines.

The Republican platform, adopted June 14th, 1876, declared the United States is a Nation and not a league; that by the combined workings of the National and State governments, under their respective Constitutions, the rights of every citizen are secured, and the common welfare promoted; that the party was sacredly pledged to the permanent pacification of the South and the protection of all citizens in their rights. It promised the resumption of specie payments, and said Senators and Representatives should not dictate appointments to office; that no public funds or property should be devoted to any schools or institution under sectarian control; that duties on imports should be adjusted to promote the interests of American labor; opposed the further donation of public lands to corporations or monopolies, and that the National domain should be devoted to free homes for the people. Treaties with foreign nations to be modified, so that the same protection should be accorded adopted citizens as those native born; that Congress should investigate the effect of the immigration of Mongolians, upon the moral and material interests of the country; that that relic of barbarism, polygamy, be extirpated, and that all pledges made to the soldiers and sailors be fulfilled.

The Democratic National platform, adopted June 27th, 1876, reaffirmed their devotion to the Union and the Constitution; demanded reform as necessary to establish a sound currency, restore the public credit and maintain the National honor. Denounced the non-redemption of the legal tender notes and demanded repeal of redemption clause of 1875. Denounced the tariff in force as a master-piece of folly; that it has impoverished many industries to enrich a few. Declared that over 200,000,000 acres of public lands had been given to corporations, and out of thrice that amount, not over one-sixth to actual settlers.

In 1880, the National Republican Convention met at Chicago, June 5th, and nominated James A. Garfield, of Ohio, for President, and Chester A. Arthur for Vice-President. They were elected. The National Democratic Convention convened at Cincinnati, June 22d, and nominated General Winfield S. Hancock for President, and William H. English, of Indiana, for Vice-President. President Garfield was stricken down by an assassin, Charles J. Guiteau, July 2d, 1881, and died September 19th, 1881. Chester A. Arthur was sworn in as President, September 20th, 1881.

The Republican platform congratulated the country upon reconstruction; that the paper currency of the Nation had been raised from 38 per cent. to par with gold, and our credit so established; that 4 per cent. bonds sold at par, where previously 6 per cents. had sold at 86; railroad mileage had increased from 31,000, in 1860, to 82,000, in 1879; foreign trade from $700,000,000 to $1,150,000,000, and our exports which were $20,000,000 less, are now $264,000,000 more than our imports.

That the National debt had been reduced $888,000,000, while the pensions paid annually was over $30,000,000, and the interest on the National debt reduced from $151,000,000 to $89,000,000. Duties upon imports should be so levied as to favor American labor; Chinese immigration restrained, and denounced the Democratic party for trying to pack the United States House of Representatives.

The Democratic National platform opposed centralization and sumptuary laws; declared for separation of Church and State; the fostering of the public schools, home rule and honest money consistiting of gold, silver and paper convertible into coin on demand; maintenance of the public credit; a tariff for revenue only; subordination of the military to the civil power and a thorough reform of the civil service. It also denounced the fraud of 1876, whereby Hayes was seated as President; declared for free ships; no more Chinese immigration; public money and public credit for public purposes only, and the public land to be held for actual settlers.

Both the Democratic and Republican parties, in 1884, held their National Conventions in Chicago, the latter, June 3d-6th, and the former, July 10th. The Republican party went to the country with a declaration of its political opinions, as follows: Freedom and equality of all men; a united Nation; the rights of all citizens to be protected everywhere; the elevation of labor and an honest currency. That the first duty of a good government is to protect the rights and promote the interests of its own people; that duties upon imports be made not for revenue only, but they shall be so levied as to secure the American laborer against the low wages of Europe, and give the laboring man his full share in the National prosperity. Pledged the party to correct the inequalities of the tariff, reduce the surplus not by the indiscriminate process of horizonal reduction, but by such methods as will relieve the taxpayers without injuring the laborer, or the great productive interests of the country; the fostering of sheep husbandry and for bi-metalism by international agreement; regulation of commerce with foreign nations and between the States; a National bureau of labor; the enforcement of the eight hour law; a judicious system of general education; settlement of National difference by international arbitration; against Chinese immigration; completion of reform in the civil service, and public lands to go to actual settlers in small holdings. Suitable pensions for all disabled soldiers and sailors and their widows and orphans; no entanglement by alliances with foreign nations; restoration of the navy; officers in the Territories to be *bona-fide* citizens thereof, and the suppression of polygamy among the Mormons and the divorce of the political from the ecclesiastical power of the Mormon church.

James G. Blaine was nominated for President upon the fourth ballot, and John A. Logan for Vice-President upon the first ballot.

The political views of the Democrats, as expressed in their patform, were: That the fundamental principles of Democracy will always remain as the best security of the people and the continuance of free government; that personal rights must be preserved, for the equality of all citizens before the law; the reserved rights of the States to be maintained and the supremacy of the Federal Government within the limits of the Constitution; frequent changes of administration, that public officers long in service may not become arbitrary rulers; the Republican party as far as principles are concerned is a reminiscence. It then arraigned the Republican party for corruption, an effort to control State elections by Federal troops; subjected labor to the competition of convict and imported contract labor; for piling up a surplus of over $100,000,000, collected from a suffering people; that unnecessary taxation is unjust taxation, and that all taxation must be limited to the requirements of economical government. Only such import duties as will give manufacturers the difference between wages here and abroad; public lands for actual settlers; liberal support of the public schools; against importation of labor and for laws whereby labor organizations may be incorporated.

Grover Cleveland was nominated for President, and Thomas A. Hendricks for Vice-President, and were elected.

In 1888, the Democratic National Convention met at St. Louis, June 5th, and the Republican Convention assembled at Chicago, June 19th. The Democrats re-nominated Grover Cleveland for President, and Allen G. Thurman for Vice-President. The Republicans nominated Benjamin Harrison for President, and for Vice-President, Levi P. Morton, who were elected.

The Democratic platform endorsed the views of President Cleveland's message on tariff reduction, declared for honest reform in the civil service as it had been inaugurated by the Administration; that the rights of the people must be carefully guarded; that more money for pensions had been paid out under Cleveland than in any other four years; that it was Democratic policy to enforce frugality in public expenses and abolish unnecestaxation; revision of the tax laws with due allowance for the difference between the wages of American and foreign labor; sympathy with Home rule in Ireland, and for the speedy passage of the Mills (tariff) bill. In essentials it was the platform of 1884.

The Republican platform, in its political provisions, declared sympathy for Home Rule in Ireland; denounced the Mills bill, and avowed the protective system must be maintained; that wool must not be put on the free list, and that there should be reduction in the tax upon tobacco, and upon spirits used in the arts and for mechanical purposes; and for such revision of the tariff as shall lessen imports of such articles as we can produce. It declared against foreign contract labor; opposition to trusts; the public lands to go to actual settlers who are citizens, not aliens; that Territories should become

States whenever their population and material resources, public intelligence and morality is such as to insure stable governments; in favor of both gold and silver as money, and denounced the Democratic Administration for its efforts to demonetize silver. Fostered free schools; wanted rehabilitation of the American Marine; against a free ship bill as an injustice to American labor; the construction of a navy, coast defenses and modern ordnance. In other particulars the platform was a repetition of 1880 and 1884.

In 1892, the Republican National Convention met in Minneapolis, Minn., June 7th, and reported their platform on the 10th. Benjamin Harrison was renominated for President, and Whitelaw Reid, of New York, for Vice-President

The Democratic National Convention convened at Chicago, June 21st, and on the 22d adopted their platform. Grover Cleveland was for the third time re-nominated for President, and Adlai E. Stevenson for Vice-President. They were elected, and are now serving.

The People's party (Populist), which had carried some States and elected a few Representatives to Congress, and some Senators, met in National Convention at Omaha, Neb., July 2d, and adopted their platform July 4th. James B. Weaver, of Iowa, was nominated for President, and James G. Field, of Virginia, for Vice-President.

We give liberal quotations from their platform as to their attitude upon the money question, transportation, the public lands, and limitation of term of President:

"The national power to create money is appropriated to enrich bondholders; a vast public debt, payable in legal tender currency, has been funded into gold-bearing bonds, thereby adding millions to the burdens of the people. Silver, which has been accepted as coin since the dawn of history, has been demonetized to add to the purchasing power of gold by decreasing the value of all forms of property as well as human labor, and the supply of currency is purposely abridged to fatten usurers, bankrupt enterprise and enslave industry.

"A vast conspiracy against mankind has been organized on two continents, and it is rapidly taking possession of the world. If not met and overthrown at once, it forebodes terrible social convulsions, the destruction of civilization, or the establishment of an absolute despotism. We have witnessed, for more than a quarter of a century, the struggles of the two great political parties for power and plunder, while grievous wrongs have been inflicted upon the suffering people. We charge that the controlling influences dominating both these parties have permitted the existing dreadful conditions to develop without serious effort to prevent or restrain them. Neither do they now promise us any substantial reform. They have agreed together to ignore, in the coming campaign, every issue but one. They propose to drown the outcries of a plundered people with the uproar of a sham battle over the tariff, so that capitalists, corporations, national banks, rings, trusts, watered stock, the demonetization of silver, and the oppressions of the usurers may all be lost sight of. They propose to sacrifice our homes, lives and children on the altar of Mammon; to destroy the multitude in order to secure corruption funds from the millionaires.

"Transportation being a means of exchange and a public necessity, the Government should own and operate the railroads in the interest of the people. The telegraph and telephone, like the post-office system, being a necessity for the transmission of news, should be owned and operated by the Government in the interests of the people.

"The land, including all the natural sources of wealth, is the heritage of the people and should not be monopolized for speculative purposes, and alien ownership of land should be prohibited. All land now held by railroads and other corporations in excess of their actual needs, and all lands now owned by aliens, should be reclaimed by the Government and held for actual settlers only.

"Wealth belongs to him who creates it, and every dollar taken from industry without an equivalent is robbery. 'If any will not work, neither shall he eat.' The interests of rural and civic labor are the same; their enemies are identical.

"We believe that the time has come when the railroad corporations will either own the people or the people must own the railroads; and should the Government enter upon the work of owning and managing all railroads, we should favor an amendment to the Constitution by which all persons engaged in the Government service shall be placed under a civil service regulation of the most rigid character, so as to prevent the increase of the power of the National Administration by the use of such additional Government employés."

SUPPLEMENTARY RESOLUTION.

That we commend to the favorable consideration of the people and to the reform press the legislative system known as the initiative and referendum

That we favor a constitutional provision limiting the office of President and Vice-President to one term, and providing for the election of Senators of the United States by a direct vote of the people.

That we oppose any subsidy or National aid to any private corporation for any purpose.

The Democratic platform was denuncitory of "trusts" and "monopolies;" of the Elections bill; for a vigorous foreign policy; condemned oppression by the Russian Government of its Jewish and Lutheran citizens; against unrestricted immigration; in favor of just and liberal pensions; the Nicaragua canal; aid to the World's Fair; for public schools, and denounced Republican protection as a fraud and a robbery of the people, and for a tariff for revenue only.

The Republican party in its platform, demanded a free ballot, a fair count, so that every citizen should enjoy the sovereign right of suffrage. Denounced Southern outrages for political reasons; favored extension of our foreign commerce; restoration of our mercantile marine and a larger navy; against criminal, pauper or contract immigration; legislation to protect life or limb of employés engaged in carrying on inter-state commerce; liberty of thought and conscience and against union of Church and State.

It also denounced trusts and combinations of capital to arbitrarily control trade; cession of arid lands to the States subject to Homestead laws, and sympathy with all wise and legitimate laws intended to lessen intemperance. In other particulars, the platform was quite like that of the former campaign.

Readers of this book know as well as the writer, that platforms are not closely followed in all instances. In one thing they are mostly in unison, *viz.*, arraignment of the other party or parties.

The two absorbing subjects for 1896, are bi-metalism and the tariff. Upon the latter, the elections of 1894 completely reversed the decision of 1892.

ATTITUDE OF PARTIES UPON THE SILVER AND TARIFF QUESTIONS.

THE selection of delegates to National Conventions of the political parties of this country, and the formulation of distinctive party platforms, dates back only some seventy years. As late as 1832 the platform of the Democratic party was three resolutions, adopted at a mass meeting held in Washington May 11th of that year, to ratify the renomination of General Jackson.

Since then the practice of formulating elaborate platforms has grown, until they have come to contain not only a reference to all the issues before the country, the line of policy which the party pledges itself to pursue, but denunciation of the acts of the competing party and a reference to its sins of "omission and commission" whenever and wherever intrusted with power. The person or persons nominated are pledged to stand upon that platform; it is the law of the party, and is supposed to be obeyed; hence the only authoritative utterance of a party is its platform; the action of any single individual, or group of individuals, in the party, however exalted their position, does not bind the party as a whole.

In a work of this character only the leading parties can be considered, and at the present time they are three in number, namely, the Democratic, Republican and Populist. From the tendency of political talk now, it is altogether probable that the Populist party will, after the National Convention in July of this year (1896), be renamed the American party, and in speaking of it we shall call it by that name.

Upon the question of "silver and the tariff" the Democratic party, by its National platform, adopted June 22d, 1892, said:

TARIFF.—"We denounce Republican protection as a fraud, a robbery of the great majority of the American people for the benefit of the few. We declare it to be a fundamental principle of the Democratic party that the Federal Government has no constitutional power to impose and collect tariff duties, except for the purpose of revenue only, and we demand that the collection of such taxes shall be limited to the necessities of the Government when honestly and economically administered. We denounce the McKinley tariff law, enacted by the Fifty-first Congress, as the culminating atrocity of class legislation; we indorse the efforts made by the Democrats of the present Congress to modify its most oppressive feature in the direction of free raw materials and cheaper manufactured goods that enter into general consumption and we promise its repeal as one of the beneficent results that will follow the action of the people in intrusting power to the Democratic party."

Upon the question of silver it said: "We denounce the Republican legislation, known as the Sherman Act of 1890, as a cowardly makeshift, fraught with possibilities of danger in the future, which should make all of its supporters, as well as its author, anxious for its speedy repeal. We hold to the use of both gold and silver as the standard money of the country, and to the coinage of both gold and silver, without discriminating against either metal, or charge for mintage, but the dollar unit of coinage of both metals must be of equal intrinsic and exchangeable value, or be adjusted through international agreement, or by such safeguards of legislation as shall insure the maintenance of the parity of the two metals and the equal power of every dollar at all times in the markets, and in payments of debts; and we demand that all paper currency shall be kept at par with and redeemable in such coin."

The Republican National Convention of 1892 formulated their platform at Minneapolis, Minn., June 7th.

Upon the subject of the tariff they declared: "We reaffirm the American doctrine of protection. We call attention to its growth abroad. We maintain that the prosperous condition of our country is largely due to the wise revenue legislation of the Republican Congress. We believe that all articles which cannot be produced in the United States, except luxuries, should be admitted free of duty, and that on all imports coming into competition with the products of American labor there should be levied duties equal to the difference between wages abroad and at home. We assert that the prices of manufactured articles of general consumption have been reduced under the operations of the tariff act of 1890. We denounce the efforts of the Democratic majority of the House of Representatives to destroy our tariff laws piecemeal, as is manifested by their attacks upon wool, lead and lead ores, the chief products of a number of States, and we ask the people for their judgment thereon."

For reciprocity to increase our export trade.

For bi-metalism, "with such restrictions and under such provisions," as will keep silver on a parity with gold.

SILVER.—"The American people, from tradition and interest, favor bi-metalism, and the Republican party demands the use of both gold and silver as standard money, with such restrictions and under such provisions, to be determined by legislation, as will secure the maintenance of the parity of values of the two metals, so that the purchasing and debt-paying power of the dollar, whether of silver, gold or paper, shall be at all times equal. The interests of the producers of the country, its farmers and its workingmen, demand that every dollar, paper or coin, issued by the Government shall be as good as any other. We commend the wise and patriotic steps already taken by our Government to secure an international conference to adopt such measures as will insure a parity of value between gold and silver for use as money throughout the world."

The People's, popularly known as the Populist party, in National Convention at Omaha, Nebraska, July 2d, 1892, enunciated as the leading plank in their platform the following:

MONEY.—We demand a National currency, safe, sound and flexible, issued by the General Government only, a full legal tender for all debts public and private, and that without the use of banking corporations; a just, equitable and efficient means of distribution direct to the people, at a tax not to exceed 2 per cent. per annum, to be provided as set forth in the Sub-Treasury plan of the Farmers' Alliance, or a better system; also by payments in discharge of its obligations for public improvements.

(a) We demand free and unlimited coinage of silver and gold at the present legal ratio of 16 to 1.

(b) We demand that the amount of circulating medium be speedily increased to not less than $50 per capita.

(c) We demand a graduated income tax.

(d) We believe that the money of the country should be kept as much as possible in the hands of the people, and hence we demand that all State and National revenues shall be limited to the necessary expenses of the Government, economically and honestly administered.

(e) We demand that Postal Savings Banks be established by the Government for the safe deposit of the earnings of the people and to facilitate exchange.

At this writing, April 5th, 1896, it appears altogether probable that if the regular Democratic and Republican Conventions declare for the gold standard, the Populists and the disaffected (free silver) Republicans and Democrats will, at a National Convention to be held in July, 1896, nominate candidates upon a short crisp platform, something like that of the American League, which is as follows:

I. We demand legislation that will check and prevent the aggression of concentrated capital; that will provide means to discover dishonest over-capitalization of corporations, and enforce penalties against such over-capitalization.

II. We demand the maintenance of a true Protective system, a system that will:

(a) Protect American labor against underpaid and degraded European and Asiatic labor, and secure to American citizens the American markets.

(b) Extend American foreign commerce by adequate subsidies to American shipping.

(c) Remove all protective duties from imported articles which domestic "trusts" and combinations, created to control domestic production and repress domestic competition, have monopolized, destroying thus at home the benefit which protection along the frontier is intended to secure.

(d) Demonstrate that protection is a National question, not a class question, and that protective duties are not imposed for the benefit of any class, but for the public advantage of (1) diversified industries, (2) the industrial independence of the Nation, (3) the maintenance of comfort and intelligence among the people, and (4) the promotion of domestic commerce through extension and improvement of the means of communication.

III. We demand legislation that will establish on a permanent basis the unrestricted use of both gold and silver as money of the United States; that will admit to the mints of the United States for coinage, silver bullion from mines of the United States of America upon payment by the owner of a seigniorage absorbing three-fourths of the difference between the market (London) price and its value when coined; and that will admit foreign silver only for coinage purposes, at a seigniorage absorbing all of the difference between the market (London) price and its value when coined.

IV. We demand the extension of our external trade relations with countries having different soil, climate and products from those of the United States, especially when they use both gold and silver as money, unrestricted in amount and upon an agreed ratio, thereby establishing an International Trade League.

V. We demand legislation that will prohibit sale of public lands to aliens, and the ownership of lands by aliens.

VI. We demand legislation that will prohibit immigration of subjects or citizens of foreign countries, unless such immigrants intend to become citizens of the United States, and unless they can demonstrate that they have not been of the criminal or pauper classes in the countries from which they emigrated.

The ultra-silverites will, of course, contend for free coinage at the ratio of 16 to 1; but as compromises are usually made in conventions, it is not impossible a middle course will be pursued.

The Ohio Republican State Convention, recently held, had the following as the financial plank in their platform:

"We contend for honest money; for a currency of gold, silver and paper with which to measure our exchanges that shall be as sound as the Government and as untarnished as its honor; and to that end we favor bimetalism and demand the use of both gold and silver as standard money, either in accordance with a ratio to be fixed by an international agreement, if that can be obtained, or under such restrictions and such provisions to be determined by legislation as will secure the maintenance of the parities of value of the two metals, so that the purchasing and debt-paying power of the dollar, whether of silver, gold or paper, shall be at all times equal."

The New York State Republican Convention avoided all ambiguity by declaring as follows:

"The agitation of the free coinage of silver at the ratio of 16 to 1 seriously disturbs all industrial interests and calls for a clear statement of the Republican party's attitude upon this question, to the end that the trade of this country at home and abroad may again be placed upon a sound and stable foundation.

"We recognize in the movement for the free coinage of silver an attempt to degrade the long-established standard of our monetary system, and hence a blow to the public and private credit, at once costly to the National Government and harmful to our domestic and foreign commerce.

"Until there is a prospect of international agreement as to silver coinage, and while gold remains the standard of the United States and of the civilized world, the Republican party of New York declares itself in favor of the firm and honorable maintenance of that standard."

The Southern States, so far in their conventions, have declared for bimetalism, and generally for free coinage at the ratio of 16 to 1, without any qualifications.

There has been growing in this country a sentiment among the people that where the country has been appealed to on an issue, and the voters have elected a House of Representatives favorable to one or the other side of that issue, that the President ought not to interpose his veto to thwart the will of the people; and looking at it from the standpoint that the will of the people, as expressed at the polls, is and should be the law of the land, the President should not exercise this veto power. Hon. Chauncey F. Black, in an open letter, has just given his ideas upon the subject as follows:

"The Democratic party of the country must not be disrupted on the silver question. There is no constitutional principle involved in it. It is a matter of mere economy and expediency, about which Democrats may differ, with perfect freedom. Should we be weak and foolish enough to fight among ourselves and divide on this minor question of silver coinage, we would be simply throwing open the gates to let in the goths and vandals of monopoly and corruption to sack the country.

"Why not let us agree, gold standard and free silver Democrats—all of us who have stood together for generations in defense of the Constitution strictly construed—to abide the judgment of the majority in National Convention? Let us declare, and let us manfully keep the pledge, that, there being no constitutional question at issue, the candidate of the Democratic party for President will, if elected, sign any bill, covering the use of silver as money, which shall have passed Congress with a majority of the Democratic votes in its favor."

HISTORY OF SILVER AS MONEY.

MONEY has been defined as "any currency employed in buying and selling." Early in the history of mankind, as far back as there has been individual ownership of anything, a necessity has existed for something whereby one man could purchase that which he wanted and another had got. Undoubtedly, barter was the primitive way of men's dealing with each other; but as population increased and man began to form distinct communities, and advances in civilization increased his necessities, bartering would not do; there must be a *something* which would be lasting, easily transported and not too easily obtained. It is the general opinion that gold was the first metal discovered. It is a metal more generally diffused throughout the world than any other; it has in olden times been most easily obtained from mother earth, as the first mining was washing it from the sand and gravel; and it was generally pure, ductile and easily formed into any desirable shape. It is probable that this was the first metal upon which was bestowed a distinct value, and passed among men as worth a stated sum.

Copper was probably second, then silver. As we understand the word coin there was none for many centuries; and after gold and silver became of large value, a variety of substances was used as subsidiary coins and passed as current money among the people. Copper or bronze coins have for many centuries been the common vehicle for small payments, and to-day China only coins copper for general use among her citizens. Their common coin, called Cash or Tsien, is a small copper disc with a square hole in the centre, through which the owner puts a string. The value of the Cash is about $\frac{1}{10}$ of a cent. The Chinese know full well the value of gold and silver, but it passes only by weight and fineness.

The Hebrew Talent was equivalent to 3,000 Shekels, and worth, say, from $1,600 to $1,960. The gold Shekel contained 130 grains, the silver Shekel 224 grains and the copper 450 grains. That would make the Shekel in gold worth, say $5.00; silver, 60 cents, and copper, $1\frac{1}{2}$ cents—based upon our ratio of 1 gold, 16 silver. Silver was not in use, it appears, before the deluge, while brass and iron are spoken of.

"Money has always consisted of certain tangible pieces of some material, marked by public authority; its palpable characteristic has always been its mark of authority; its essential characteristic the possession of value, defined by law; its function the legal power to pay debts and mechanical power to facilitate the exchange of commodities" (*Del Mar*). That is undoubtedly true, since the world has had stable governments; but it is just as true that gold was used in the arts for ornaments long before it was used as money, and must have had value. Gold was probably first used as money in the Orient, before the time of authentic history. Bronze coins of Sung B. C. 2257, were *good for gold*.

Gold and silver multiple moneys have been known in India for many centuries; the common money was copper bronze, the gold and silver money (bars or pieces) over valued probably, and never used except to make up large sums.

The first monetary system of silver, positively based upon that metal, was that of the Greek States and Colonies; and like gold was simply used as multiples, bronze coins being the general money. Rome, during the Estruscan era, had gold, silver and copper coins. B. C. 269, the Romans coined a vast number of silver pieces. Del Mar says, "that from the fall of the Roman Commonwealth to the French Revolution, coins, made largely from old accumulations of metal, were substantially the only moneys of Europe. This stock of coins slowly but continually diminished until the tenth century, then slowly increased until the nineteenth century. First part of the fourteenth and last part of the eighteenth centuries almost the identical prices prevailed, in England, for corn, domestic animals and their products."

We think Mr. Del Mar is right, if instead of the French Revolution he had said, until the sixteenth century, for it is an undeniable fact that within one hundred years of the discovery of America the trade of Europe began to rapidly increase, as well as the comforts of the people, which was consequent upon the large amount of gold and silver (largely silver) obtained in the Western hemisphere. The more plentiful the currency of a nation, the greater and quicker the expansion of her business, the increase of her visible wealth in homes, lands and internal improvements. Pouring into the lap of Europe, during the sixteenth, seventeenth and eighteenth centuries, a constant stream of silver and gold, from North and South America, shot her ahead ten centuries—if we compare the development of those three centuries with the ten previous ones.

The relative value of gold and silver during the centuries that they have been used as money is hard to determine, and even since they have been coined and stamped, it is not easy to find out the value of silver as compared to gold, and partially for the reason that there was not a line of writing upon the Archaic moneys of India, Egypt or Greece. It has been no uncommon thing for rulers to arbitrarily change the value, and without any apparent reason. We do know for a certainty that the ratio has been 10 to 1, and has varied from that to 16 to 1, our present legal, though not the commercial, ratio. In view of all these facts, it may be said that previous to the dicovery of America, silver coins that passed from hand to hand were very scarce; and that copper was the common money of the people. Shall we or shall we not, therefore, infer that the strides forward in the pathway of human progress, during the past three centuries, have been due to an abundance of coin made from the white metal?

GOLD AND SILVER PRODUCED IN THE UNITED STATES.

The following estimate of the gold and silver produced in the United States, since the discovery of gold in California, is compiled from the official reports of the Director of the United States Mint:

Year.	Gold.	Silver.	Total.	Year.	Gold.	Silver.	Total.
1849	$40,000,000	$50,000	$40,050,000	1872	$36,000,000	$28,750,000	$64,750,000
1850	50,000,000	50,000	50,050,000	1873	36,000,000	35,750,000	71,750,000
1851	55,000,000	50,000	55,050,000	1874	33,490,902	37,324,594	70,815,496
1852	60,000,000	50,000	60,050,000	1875	33,467,856	31,727,560	65,195,416
1853	65,000,000	50,000	65,050,000	1876	39,929,166	38,783,016	78,712,182
1854	60,000,000	50,000	60,050,000	1877	46,897,390	39,793,573	86,690,963
1855	55,000,000	50,000	55,050,000	1878	51,206,360	45,281,385	96,487,745
1856	55,000,000	50,000	55,050,000	1879	38,899,858	40,812,132	79,711,990
1857	55,000,000	50,000	55,050,000	1880	36,000,000	38,150,000	74,450,000
1858	50,000,000	500,000	50,500,000	1881	34,700,000	43,000,000	77,700,000
1859	50,000,000	100,000	50,100,000	1882	32,500,000	46,800,000	79,300,000
1860	46,000,000	150,000	46,150,000	1883	30,000,000	46,200,000	76,200,000
1861	43,000,000	2,000,000	45,000,000	1884	30,800,000	48,800,000	79,600,000
1862	39,200,000	4,500,000	43,700,000	1885	31,800,000	51,600,000	83,400,000
1863	40,000,000	8,500,000	48,500,000	1886	35,000,000	51,000,000	86,000,000
1864	46,100,000	11,000,000	57,100,000	1887	33,000,000	53,357,000	86,357,000
1865	53,225,000	11,250,000	64,475,000	1888	33,175,000	59,195,000	92,370,000
1866	53,500,000	10,000,000	63,500,000	1889	32,800,000	64,646,000	97,446,000
1867	51,725,000	13,500,000	65,225,000	1890	32,845,000	70,464,000	103,309,000
1868	48,000,000	12,000,000	60,000,000	1891	33,175,000	75,416,565	108,591,565
1869	49,500,000	12,000,000	61,500,000	1892	33,000,000	82,101,010	115,101,010
1870	50,000,000	16,000,000	66,000,000	1893	35,955,000	77,575,757	113,530,757
1871	43,500,000	23,000,000	66,500,000				

Total Gold, $1,939,300,000. Silver, $1,154,817,575. Grand Total, $3,094,117,575.

COINAGE OF THE SILVER DOLLAR.

1794-95	$204,791	1849	$62,600	1873	$296,600
1796	72,920	1850	47,500	1874	
1797	7,776	1851	1,300	1875	
1798	327,536	1852	1,100	1876	
1799	423,515	1853	46,110	1877	
1800	220,920	1854	33,140	1878	22,495,550
1801	54,454	1855	26,000	1879	27,560,100
1802	41,650	1856	63,500	1880	27,397,355
1803	66,064	1857	94,000	1881	27,927,975
1804	19,570	1858		1882	27,574,100
1805	321	1859	636,500	1883	28,470,039
1836	1,000	1860	733,930	1884	28,136,875
1837		1861	78,500	1885	28,697,767
1838		1862	12,090	1886	31,423,886
1839	300	1863	27,660	1887	35,611,710
1840	61,005	1864	31,170	1888	31,990,883
1841	173,000	1865	47,000	1889	34,651,811
1842	184,618	1866	49,625	1890	38,043,004
1843	165,100	1867	60,325	1891	23,562,735
1844	20,000	1868	182,700	1892	6,333,245
1845	24,500	1869	424,300	1893	1,455,792
1846	169,600	1870	415,462	1894*	2,443,631
1847	140,750	1871	1,117,136		
1848	15,000	1872	1,118,600	Total	$429,807,646

*November 1, 1894. None coined since.

APPROXIMATE AMOUNT OF MONEY IN THE WORLD.

Gold, $4,261,830,000; silver, $4,361,902,200. In round numbers, the silver production of the world is, per annum, $200,000,000; and the gold production, $180,000,000.

Amount of money in the United States is estimated at $2,420,434,781. In circulation, $1,660,808,708. Population is, say, 68,397,000. Money per capita, $35.39. In circulation per capita, $24.28.

The silver dollar contains $371\frac{25}{1000}$ grains pure silver, or with alloy, $408\frac{375}{1000}$ grains.

MONETARY SYSTEMS AND APPROXIMATE STOCKS OF MONEY IN THE AGGREGATE AND PER CAPITA IN THE PRINCIPAL COUNTRIES OF THE WORLD.

(Up to November 1st, 1894, for the United States; to January 1st, 1894, as to all other countries.)

Countries.	Monetary System.	Ratio between Gold and Full Legal-tender Silver.	Ratio between Gold and Limited-tender Silver.	Population.	Stock of Gold.	Stock of Silver. Full-tender.	Stock of Silver. Limited-tender.	Uncovered Paper.	Per Capita. Gold.	Per Capita. Silver.	Per Capita. Paper.	Per Capita. Total.
United States	Gold and silver	1 to 15.98	1 to 14.95	68,900,000	$626,600,000	$549,700,000	$75,600,000	$175,700,000	$9.09	$9.08	$6.90	$25.07
United Kingdom	Gold		1 to 14.28	38,800,000	a550,000,000		b112,000,000	b113,400,000	14.18	2.88	2.92	19.98
France	Gold and silver	1 to 15½	1 to 14.38	38,300,000	a825,000,000	g434,300,000	g57,300,000	b88,500,000	21.54	12.85	2.31	36.70
Germany	Gold		1 to 13.957	49,400,000	a625,000,000	a105,000,000	a110,000,000	b88,000,000	12.65	4.35	1.78	18.78
Belgium	Gold and silver	1 to 15½	1 to 14.38	6,200,000	a55,000,000	a48,000,000	a6,900,000	b51,200,000	8.87	8.85	8.26	25.98
Italy	Gold and silver	1 to 15½	1 to 14.38	30,500,000	b96,000,000	a40,000,000	c20,000,000	b167,600,000	3.15	0.98	5.50	9.63
Switzerland	Gold and silver	1 to 15½	1 to 14.38	2,900,000	a15,000,000	a10,000,000	a5,000,000	c16,600,000	5.17	5.17	5.72	16.06
Greece	Gold and silver	1 to 15½	1 to 14.38	2,200,000	a500,000	d1,000,000	d2,000,000	b42,000,000	0.23	1.36	19.09	20.68
Spain	Gold and silver	1 to 14½	1 to 14.38	17,500,000	a40,000,000	a126,000,000	a10,000,000	b107,100,000	2.29	9.18	6.12	17.59
Portugal	Gold		1 to 14.08	4,700,000	b38,900,000		a21,800,000	b55,500,000	8.27	5.28	11.81	25.36
Roumania	Gold and silver			5,800,000	a15,000,000	a3,500,000	a5,000,000	b13,300,000	2.59	1.46	2.29	6.34
Servia	Gold and silver			2,200,000	b3,000,000	b1,900,000		c3,800,000	1.36	0.86	1.73	3.95
Austria-Hungary	Gold		1 to 13.69	43,200,000	a130,000,000	e81,000,000	e10,000,000	e 46,300,000	3.00	2.81	3.38	9.19
Netherlands	Gold and silver	1 to 15⅝	1 to 15	4,700,000	b27,600,000	b53,400,000	b3,100,000	b35,900,000	5.87	12.02	7.64	25.53
Scandinavian Un..												
Norway	Gold		1 to 14.88	2,000,000	b7,300,000		b1,900,000	b3,900,000	3.65	0.95	1.95	6.55
Sweden	Gold		1 to 14.88	4,800,000	b6,500,000		b1,800,000	b4,700,000	1.35	1.00	0.98	3.33
Denmark	Gold		1 to 14.88	2,200,000	b14,200,000		b5,400,000	b5,404,000	6.46	2.45	2.45	11.36
Russia & Finland	Silver	1 to 15½	1 to 12.90	124,000,000	a455,000,000		a18,000,000	b530,000,000	3.67	0.38	4.27	8.32
Turkey	Gold and silver	1 to 15⅞	1 to 15⅛	39,200,000	a50,000,000	a30,000,000	c10,000,000		1.27	1.02		2.29
Australia	Gold		1 to 14.28	4,700,000	a105,000,000		a7,000,000		22.34	1.49		23.83
Egypt	Gold		1 to 15.68	6,800,000	a120,000,000		a15,000,000		17.65	2.20		19.85
Mexico	Silver	1 to 16½		12,100,000	a5,000,000	a50,000,000		a2,000,000	0.41	4.13	0.17	4.71
Cent. Am. States	Silver	1 to 15½		3,300,000	b500,000	b8,000,000		b4,000,000	0.15	2.42	1.21	3.78
So. Am. States	Silver	1 to 15½		36,000,000	a40,000,000	a30,000,000		a550,000,000	1.11	0.83	15.28	17.22
Japan	Gold and silver	1 to 16.18		41,100,000	b80,000,000	b72,000,000	b16,300,000		1.95	2.14		4.09
India	Gold and silver	1 to 15		296,000,000		i950,000,000		h37,000,000		3.21	0.12	3.33
China	Silver			360,000,000		a750,000,000				2.08		2.08
Straits Settlements	Gold and silver			3,800,000		a115,000,000				3.26		3.26
Canada	Gold		1 to 14.28	4,800,000	a14,000,000		a5,000,000	d29,000,000	2.92	1.04	6.04	10.00
Cuba	Gold and silver	1 to 15½		1,600,000	a18,000,000	a1,500,000			11.25	0.94		12.19
Hayti	Gold and silver	1 to 15½		1,000,000	b2,000,000	b2,100,000	b800,000		2.00	2.90		4.90
Bulgaria	Gold and silver	1 to 15½	1 to 14.38	4,300,000	e800,000	e3,400,000	e3,400,000		0.18	1.58		1.76
Total					$3,965,900,000	$3,135,800,000	$619,900,000	$2,570,900,000				

a Estimate, Bureau of the Mint. b Information furnished through United States Representatives. c Haupt. d Credit Lyonnais. e L'Economist Europeen. f Sir Charles Fremantle. g A. De Foville. h Indian Currency Committee report. i F. C. Harrison.

Values of Foreign Coins in United States Money.

(Proclaimed by the Secretary of the Treasury, October 1st, 1894.)

Country.	Stand'rd	Monetary Unit.	Value in U.S. Gold Dollar.	Coins.
Argent. R.	Gld&Sil	Peso	$0.96.5	Gold: argentine ($4.82.4) and ½ argentine. Silver: peso and divisions.
Austria-H.	Gold	Crown	.20.3	Gold: former system—4 florins ($1.92.9), 8 florins ($3.85.8), ducat ($2.28.7), and 4 ducats ($9.15.8). Silver: 1 and 2 florins. Gold: present system—20 crowns ($4.05.2) and 10 crowns ($2.02.6).
Belgium	Gld&Sil	Franc	.19.3	Gold: 10 and 20 francs. Silver: 5 francs.
Bolivia	Silver	Boliviano	.46.4	Silver: boliviano and divisions.
Brazil	Gold	Milreis	.54.6	Gold: 5, 10 and 20 milreis. Silver: ½, 1 and 2 milreis.
Canada	Gold	Dollar	1.00	
Cent. Am.	Silver	Peso	.46.4	Silver: peso and divisions.
Chili	Gld&Sil	Peso	.91.2	Gold: escudo ($1.82.4), doubloon ($4.56.1), and condor ($9.12.3). Silver: peso and divisions.
China	Silver	Tael { Shanghai	.68.5	
		{ Haikwan	.76.3	
		{ Tientsin	.72.7	
Colombia	Silver	Peso	.46.4	Gold: condor ($9.64.7) and double-condor. Silver: peso.
Cuba	Gld&Sil	Peso	.92.6	Gold: doubloon ($5.01.7). Silver: peso.
Denmark	Gold	Crown	.26.8	Gold: 10 and 20 crowns.
Ecuador	Silver	Sucre	.46.4	Gold: condor ($9.64.7) and double-condor. Silver: Sucre and divisions.
Egypt	Gold	Pound (100 piasters)	4.94.3	Gold: pound (100 piasters), 5, 10, 20 and 50 piasters. Silver: 1, 2, 5, 10 and 20 piasters.
Finland	Gold	Mark	.19.3	Gold: 20 marks ($3.85.9), 10 marks ($1.91.4)
France	Gld&Sil	Franc	.19.3	Gold: 5, 10, 20, 50 and 100 francs. Silver 5 francs.
Germany	Gold	Mark	.23.8	Gold: 5, 10 and 20 marks.
Gt. Britain	Gold	Pound sterling	4.86.6½	Gold: sovereign (pound sterling) and ½ sovereign.
Greece	Gld&Sil	Drachma	.19.3	Gold: 5, 10, 20, 50 and 100 drachmas. Silver: 5 drachmas.
Hayti	Gld&Sil	Gourde	.96.5	Silver: gourde.
India	Silver	Rupee	.22	Gold: mohur ($7.10.5). Silver: rupee and divisions.
Italy	Gld&Sil	Lira	.19.3	Gold: 5, 10, 20, 50 and 100 lire. Silver: 5 lire.
Japan	G. & S.*	Yen { Gold.	.99.7	Gold: 1, 2, 5, 10 and 20 yen.
		{ Silver	.50	Silver: yen.
Liberia	Gold	Dollar	1.00	
Mexico	Silver	Dollar	.70.4	Gold: dollar ($0.98.3), 2½, 5, 10 and 20 dollars. Silver: dollar (or peso) and divis's.
Neth'lands	Gld&Sil	Florin	.40.2	Gold: 10 florins. Silver: ½, 1 and 2½ florins.
N'found'd.	Gold	Dollar	1.01.4	Gold: 2 dollars ($2.02.7).
Norway	Gold	Crown	.26.8	Gold: 10 and 20 crowns.
Peru	Silver	Sol	.46.4	Silver: sol and divisions.
Portugal	Gold	Milreis	1.08	Gold: 1, 2, 5 and 10 milreis.
Russia	Silver	Rouble { Gold.	.77.2	Gold: imperial ($7.71.8) and ½ imperial † ($3.86).
		{ Silver	.37.1	Silver: ¼, ½ and 1 rouble.
Spain	Gld&Sil	Peseta	.19.3	Gold: 25 pesetas. Silver: 5 pesetas.
Sweden	Gold	Crown	.26.8	Gold: 10 and 20 crowns.
Switz'land	Gld&Sil	Franc	.19.3	Gold: 5, 10, 20, 50 and 100 fr's. Silver: 5 fr's.
Tripoli	Silver	Mahbub of 20 piasters	.91.8	
Turkey	Gold	Piaster	.04.4	Gold: 25, 50, 100, 250 and 500 piasters.
Venezuela	Gld&Sil	Bolivar	.19.3	Gold: 5, 10, 20, 50 and 100 bolivars. Silver: 5 bolivars.

* Gold the nominal standard; silver practically the standard. † Coined since January 1st, 1886; old half-imperial $3.98.6. ‡ Silver the nominal standard; paper the actual currency, the depreciation of which is measured by the gold standard.

TABLE SHOWING THE VALUE OF FOREIGN COINS AND PAPER NOTES IN AMERICAN MONEY BASED UPON THE VALUES EXPRESSED IN THE ABOVE TABLE.

Number.	British £ Sterling.	German Mark.	French Franc Italian Lira.	Chinese Tael (Shanghai).	Dutch Florin.	Indian Rupee.	Russian Gold Rouble.	Austrian Crown
1	$1.86.65½	$0.23.8	$0.19.3	$0.68.5	$0.40.2	$0.22	$0.72.2	20.20.5
2	9.73.3	0.47.6	0.38.6	1.37	0.80.4	0.44	1.54.4	0.40.6
3	14.59.9½	0.71.4	0.57.9	2.05.5	1.20.6	0.66	2.31.6	0.60.9
4	19.46.6	0.95.2	0.77.2	2.74	1.60.8	0.88	3.08.8	0.81.2
5	24.33.2½	1.19	0.96.5	3.42.5	2.01	1.10	3.86	1.01.5
6	29.19.9	1.42.8	1.15.8	4.11	2.41.2	1.32	4.63.2	1.21.8
7	34.06.5½	1.66.6	1.35.1	4.79.5	2.81.4	1.54	5.40.4	1.42.1
8	38.93.2	1.90.4	1.54.4	5.48	3.21.6	1.76	6.17.6	1.62.4
9	43.79.8½	2.14.2	1.73.7	6.16.5	3.61.8	1.98	6.94.8	1.82.7
10	48.66.5	2.38	1.93	6.85	4.02	2.20	7.72	2.03
20	97.33	4.76	3.86	13.70	8.04	4.40	15.44	4.06
30	145.99.5	7.14	5.79	20.55	12.06	6.60	23.16	6.09
40	194.66	9.52	7.72	27.40	16.08	8.80	30.88	8.12
50	243.32.5	11.90	9.65	34.25	20.10	11.00	38.40	10.15
100	486.65	23.80	19.30	68.50	40.20	22.00	77.20	20.31

ELECTORAL VOTES FROM 1789 TO 1892.

1789.—Previous to 1804, each elector voted for two candidates for President. The one who received the largest number of votes was declared President and the one who received the next largest number of votes was declared Vice-President. The electoral votes for the first President of the United States were: George Washington, 69; John Adams, of Massachusetts, 34; John Jay, of New York, 9; R. H. Harrison, of Maryland, 6; John Rutledge, of South Carolina, 6; John Hancock, of Massachusetts, 4; George Clinton, of New York, 3; Samuel Huntingdon, of Connecticut, 2; John Milton, of Georgia, 2; James Armstrong, of Georgia, Benjamin Lincoln, of Massachusetts, and Edward Telfair, of Georgia, 1 vote each. Vacancies (votes not cast), 4. Washington was chosen President and Adams Vice-President.

1792.—George Washington, Federalist, received 132 votes; John Adams, Federalist, 77; George Clinton, of New York, Republican, 50; Thomas Jefferson, of Virginia, Republican, 4; Aaron Burr, of New York, Republican, 1 vote. Vacancies, 3. Washington was chosen President and Adams Vice-President.

1796.—John Adams, Federalist, 71; Thomas Jefferson, Republican, 68; Thomas Pickney, of South Carolina, Federalist, 59; Aaron Burr, of New York, Republican, 30; Samuel Adams, of Massachusetts, Republican 15; Oliver Ellsworth, of Connecticut, Independent, 11; George Clinton, of New York, Republican, 7; John Jay, of New York, Federalist, 5; James Iredell, of North Carolina, Federalist, 3; George Washington, of Virginia, ohn Henry, of Maryland, and S. Johnson, of North Carolina, all Federalists, 2 votes each; Charles Cotesworth Pickney, of South Carolina, Federalist, 1 vote. Adams was chosen President and Jefferson Vice-President.

1800.—Thomas Jefferson, Republican, 73; Aaron Burr, Republican, 73; John Adams, Federalist, 65; Charles C. Pickney, Federalist, 64; John Jay, Federalist, 1 vote. There being a tie vote for Jefferson and Burr, the choice devolved upon the House of Representatives. Jefferson received the votes of ten States, which, being the largest vote cast for a candidate, elected him President. Burr received the votes of four States, which, being the next largest vote, elected him Vice-President. There were two blank votes.

1804.—The Constitution of the United States having been amended, the electors at this election voted for a President and a Vice-President. The result was as follows: For President, Thomas Jefferson, Republican, 162; Charles C. Pinckney, Federalist, 14. For Vice-President, George Clinton, Republican, 162; Rufus King, of New York, Federalist, 14. Jefferson was chosen President and Clinton Vice-President.

1808.—For President, James Madison, of Virginia, Republican, 122; Charles C. Pinckney, of South Carolina, Federalist, 47; George Clinton, of New York, Republican, 6. For Vice-President, George Clinton, Republican, 113; Rufus King, of New York, Federalist, 47; John Langdon, of New Hampshire, 9; James Madison, 3; James Monroe, 3. Vacancy, 1. Madison was chosen President and Clinton Vice-President.

1812.—For President, James Madison, Republican, 128; DeWitt Clinton, of New York, Federalist, 89. For Vice-President, Elbridge Gerry, of Massachusetts, Republican, 131; Jared Ingersoll, of Pennsylvania, Federalist, 86. Vacancy, 1. Madison was chosen President and Gerry Vice-President.

1816.—For President, James Monroe, of Virginia, Republican, 183; Rufus King, of New York, Federalist, 34. For Vice-President, Daniel D. Tompkins, of New York, Republican, 183; John Eager Howard, of Maryland, Federalist, 22; James Ross, of Pennsylvania, 5; John Marshall, of Virginia, 4; Robert G. Harper, of Maryland, 3. Vacancies, 4. Monroe was chosen President and Tompkins Vice-President.

1820.—For President, James Monroe, of Virginia, Republican, 231 John Q. Adams, of Massachusetts, Republican, 1. For Vice-President, Daniel D. Tompkins, Republican, 218; Richard Stockton, of New Jersey, 8; Daniel Rodney, of Delaware, 4; Robert G. Harper, of Maryland, and Richard Rush, of Pennsylvania, 1 vote each. Vacancies, 3. Monroe was chosen President and Tompkins Vice-President.

1824.—For President, Andrew Jackson, of Tennessee, Republican, 99; John Q. Adams, of Massachusetts, Republican, 84; Henry Clay, of Kentucky, Republican, 37; William H. Crawford, of Georgia, Republican, 41. For Vice-President, John C. Calhoun, of South Carolina, Republican, 182; Nathan Sanford, of New York, Republican, 30; Nathaniel Macon, of North Carolina, Republican, 24; Andrew Jackson, of Tennessee, Republican, 13; Martin Van Buren, of New York, Republican, 9; Henry Clay, of Kentucky, Republican, 2. No candidate having a majority of the electoral vote, the House of Representatives elected Adams as President. Calhoun was chosen Vice-President.

1828.—For President, Andrew Jackson, of Tennessee, Democrat, 178; John Q. Adams, of Massachusetts, National Republican, 83. For Vice-President, John C. Calhoun, of South Carolina, Democrat, 171; Richard Rush, of Pennsylvania, National Republican, 83; William Smith, of South Carolina, Democrat, 7. Jackson was chosen President and Calhoun Vice-President.

1832.—For President, Andrew Jackson, of Tennessee, Democrat, 219; Henry Clay, of Kentucky, National Republican, 49; John Floyd, of Georgia, Independent, 11; William Wirt, of Maryland, Anti-Masonic, 7. For Vice-President, Martin Van Buren, of New York, Democrat, 189; John Sergeant, of Pennsylvania, National Republican, 49; Henry Lee, of Massachusetts, Independent, 11; Amos Ellmaker, of Pennsylvania, Anti-Masonic, 7; William

Wilkins, of Pennsylvania, Democrat, 30. Jackson was chosen President and Van Buren Vice-President.

1836.—For President, Martin Van Buren, of New York, Democrat, 170; W. H. Harrison, of Ohio, Whig, 73; Hugh L. White, of Tennessee, Whig, 26; Daniel Webster, of Massachusetts, Whig, 14; Willie P. Mangum, of North Carolina, Whig, 11. For Vice-President, R. M. Johnson, of Kentucky, Democrat, 147; Francis Granger, of New York, Whig, 77; John Tyler, of Virginia, Whig, 47; William Smith, of Alabama, Democrat, 23. Van Buren was chosen President, and there being no choice for Vice-President, the Senate elected Johnson.

1840.—For President, W. H. Harrison, of Ohio, Whig, 234; Martin Van Buren, of New York, Democrat, 60. For Vice-President, John Tyler, of Virginia, Whig, 234; R. M. Johnson, of Kentucky, Democrat, 48; L. W. Tazewell, of Virginia, Democrat, 11; James K. Polk, of Tennessee, Democrat, 1. Harrison was chosen President and Tyler Vice-President.

1844.—For President, James K. Polk, of Tennessee, Democrat, 170; Henry Clay, of Kentucky, Whig, 105. For Vice-President, George M. Dallas, of Pennsylvania, Democrat, 170; F. Frelinghuysen, of New Jersey, Whig, 105. Polk was chosen President and Dallas Vice-President.

1848.—For President, Zachary Taylor, of Louisiana, Whig, 163; Lewis Cass, of Michigan, Democrat, 127. For Vice-President, Millard Fillmore, of New York, Whig, 163; William O. Butler, of Kentucky, Democrat, 127. Taylor was chosen President and Fillmore Vice-President.

1852.—For President, Franklin Pierce, of New Hampshire, Democrat, 254; Winfield Scott, of New Jersey, Whig, 42. For Vice-President, William R. King, of Alabama, Democrat, 254; William A. Graham, of North Carolina, Whig, 42. Pierce was chosen President and King Vice-President.

1856.—For President, James Buchanan, of Pennsylvania, Democrat, 174; John C. Fremont, of California, Republican, 114; Millard Fillmore, of New York, American, 8. For Vice-President, J. C. Breckenridge, of Kentucky Democrat, 174; William L. Dayton, of New Jersey, Republican, 114; A J. Donelson, of Tennessee, American, 8. Buchanan was chosen President and Breckenridge Vice-President.

1860.—For President, Abraham Lincoln, of Illinois, Republican, 180; Stephen A. Douglas, of Illinois, Democrat, 12; J. C. Breckenridge, of Kentucky, Democrat, 72; John Bell, of Tennessee, Union, 39. For Vice-President, Hannibal Hamlin, of Maine, Republican, 180; H. V. Johnson, of Georgia, Democrat, 12; Joseph Lane, of Oregon, Democrat, 72; Edward Everett, of Massachusetts, Union, 39. Lincoln was chosen President and Hamlin Vice-President.

1864.— For President, Abraham Lincoln, of Illinois, Republican, 212; George B. McClellan, of New Jersey, Democrat, 21. For Vice-President, Andrew Johnson, of Tennessee, Republican, 212; George H. Pendleton, of Ohio, Democrat, 21. Lincoln was chosen President and Johnson Vice-President.

1868.—For President, Ulysses S. Grant, of Illinois, Republican, 214; Horatio Seymour, of New York, Democrat, 80. For Vice-President, Schuyler Colfax, of Indiana, Republican, 214; F. P. Blair, Jr., of Missouri, Democrat, 80. Grant was chosen President and Colfax Vice-President.

1872.—For President, Ulysses S. Grant, of Illinois, Republican, 286;

Horace Greeley, of New York, Democrat and Liberal Republican, died, and the Democratic electors scattered their vote; Thomas A. Hendricks, of Indiana, Democrat, 42; B. Gratz Brown, of Missouri, Democrat, 18; Charles J. Jenkins, of Georgia, Democrat, 2; David Davis, of Illinois, Independent, 1. For Vice-President, Henry Wilson, of Massachusetts, Republican, 286; B. Gratz Brown, of Missouri, Democrat and Liberal Republican, 47; George W. Julian, of Indiana, Liberal, 5; A. H. Colquitt, of Georgia, Democrat, 5; John M. Palmer, of Illinois, Democrat, 3; T. E. Bramlett, of Kentucky, Democrat, 3; W. S. Groesbeck, of Ohio, Democrat, 1; Willis B. Machen, of Kentucky, Democrat, 1; N. P. Banks, of Massachusetts, Liberal, 1. Grant was chosen President and Wilson Vice-President.

1876.—For President, Samuel J. Tilden, of New York, Democrat, 184; Rutherford B. Hayes, of Ohio, Republican, 185. For Vice-President, Thomas A. Hendricks, of Indiana, Democrat, 184; William A. Wheeler, of New York, Republican, 185. Hayes was chosen President and Wheeler Vice-President.

1880.—For President, James A. Garfield, of Ohio, Republican, 214; Winfield S. Hancock, of Pennsylvania, Democrat, 155. For Vice-President, Chester A. Arthur, of New York, Republican, 214; William H. English, of Indiana, Democrat, 155. Garfield was chosen President and Arthur Vice-President.

1884.—For President, Grover Cleveland, of New York, Democrat, 219; James G. Blaine, of Maine, Republican, 182. For Vice-President, Thomas A. Hendricks, of Indiana, Democrat, 219; John A. Logan, of Illinois, Republican, 182. Cleveland was chosen President and Hendricks Vice-President.

1888.—For President, Benjamin Harrison, of Indiana, Republican, 233; Grover Cleveland, of New York, Democrat, 168. For Vice-President, Levi P. Morton, of New York, Republican, 233; Allen G. Thurman, of Ohio, Democrat, 168. Harrison was chosen President and Morton Vice-President.

1892.—For President, Grover Cleveland, Democrat, 277; Benjamin Harrison, Republican, 145; James B. Weaver, of Iowa, People's Party, 22. For Vice-President, Adlai E. Stevenson, of Illinois, Democrat, 277; Whitelaw Reid, of New York, Republican, 145; James G. Field, of Virginia, People's Party, 22. Cleveland was chosen President and Stevenson Vice-President.

POPULAR VOTE FOR PRESIDENTIAL CANDIDATES FROM 1824 to 1892.

NOTE.—Properly speaking, there is no popular vote for President and Vice-President; the people vote for electors, who meet in each State and vote for the candidates. The record of any popular vote for electors prior to 1824 is so imperfect that a compilation would be useless. In most of the States for more than a quarter of a century following the establishment of the Government, the State Legislatures "appointed" the Presidential electors, and the people voted only indirectly for them, their choice being expressed by their votes for members of the Legislature.

1824.—J. Q. Adams had 105,321 to 155,872 for Jackson, 44,282 for Crawford, and 46,587 for Clay. Jackson over Adams, 50,551. Adams less than combined vote of others, 140,869. Of the whole vote Adams had 29.92 per cent., Jackson 44.27, Clay 13.23, Crawford 13.23. Adams elected by House of Representatives.

1828.—Jackson had 647,231 to 509,097 for J. Q. Adams. Jackson's majority, 138,134. Of the whole vote Jackson had 55.97 per cent., Adams 44.03.

1832.—Jackson had 687,502 to 530,189 for Clay, and 33,108 for Boyd and Wirt combined. Jackson's majority, 124,205. Of the whole vote Jackson had 54.96 per cent., Clay 42.39, and the others combined 2.65.

1836.—Van Buren had 761,549 to 736,656, the combined vote for Harrison, White, Webster and Mangum. Van Buren's majority, 24,893. Of the whole vote Van Buren had 50.83 per cent., and the others combined 49.17.

1840.—Harrison had 1,275,017 to 1,128,702 for Van Buren, and 7,059 for Birney. Harrison's majority, 139,256. Of the whole vote Harrison had 52.89 per cent., Van Buren, 46.82, and Birney .29.

1844.—Polk had 1,337,243 to 1,299,068 for Clay and 62,300 for Birney. Polk over Clay, 38,175. Polk less than others combined, 24,125. Of the whole vote Polk had 49.55 per cent., Clay 48.14, and Birney 2.21.

1848.—Taylor had 1,360,101 to 1,220,544 for Cass, and 291,263 for Van Buren. Taylor over Cass 139,577. Taylor less than others combined, 151,706. Of the whole vote Taylor had 47.36 per cent., Cass 42.50, and Van Buren 10.14.

1852.—Pierce had 1,601,474 to 1,386,578 for Scott, and 156,149 for Hale. Pierce over all, 58,747. Of the whole vote Pierce had 50.90 per cent., Scott 44.10, and Hale 4.97.

1856.—Buchanan had 1,838,169 to 1,341,264 for Fremont, and 874,534 for Fillmore. Buchanan over Fremont, 496,905. Buchanan less than combined vote of others, 377,629. Of the whole vote Buchanan had 45.34 per cent., Fremont 33.09, and Fillmore 21.57.

1860.—Lincoln had 1,866,352 to 1,375,157 for Douglas, 845,763 for Breckenridge, and 589,581 for Bell. Lincoln over Breckenridge, 491,195. Lincoln less than Douglas and Breckenridge combined, 354,568. Lincoln less than combined vote of all others, 944,149. Of the whole vote Lincoln had 39.91 per cent., Douglas 29.40, Breckenridge 18.08, and Bell, 12.61.

1864.—Lincoln had 2,216,067 to 1,808,725 for McClellan (eleven States not voting, viz.: Alabama, Arkansas, Florida, Georgia, Louisiana, Mississippi, North Carolina, South Carolina, Tennessee, Texas and Virginia). Lincoln's majority, 408,342. Of the whole vote Lincoln had 55.06 per cent. and McClellan 44.94.

1868.—Grant had 3,015,071 to 2,709,613 for Seymour (three States not voting, viz.: Mississippi, Texas and Virginia). Grant's majority, 305,458. Of the whole vote Grant had 52.67 per cent. and Seymour 47.33.

1872.—Grant had 3,597,070 to 2,834,079 for Greeley, 29,408 for O'Conor, and 5,608 for Black. Grant's majority, 729,975. Of the whole vote Grant had 55.63 per cent., Greeley 43.83, O'Conor .15, Black .09.

1876.—Hayes had 4,033,950 to 4,284,885 for Tilden, 81,740 for Cooper, 9,522 for Smith, and 2,636 scattering. Tilden's majority over Hayes, 250,935. Tilden's majority of the entire vote cast, 157,037. Hayes less than the combined vote of others, 344,833. Of the whole vote cast Hayes had 47.95 per cent., Tilden 50.94, Cooper .97, Smith .11, scattering .03.

1880.—Garfield had 4,449,053 to 4,442,035 for Hancock, 307,306 for Weaver, and 12,576 scattering. Garfield over Hancock, 7,018. Garfield less than the combined vote for the others, 313,864. Of the popular vote Garfield had 48.26 per cent., Hancock 48.25, Weaver 3.33, scattering .13.

1884.—Cleveland had 4,874,986 to 4,851,981 for Blaine, 150,369 for St. John, 173,370 for Butler. Cleveland had over Blaine 23,006. Cleveland had 48.48 per cent., Blaine 48.22, St. John 1.49, Butler 1.74.

1888.—Harrison had 5,441,902 to 5,538,560 for Cleveland, 249,937 for Fisk, 147,521 for Streeter, 3,073 for Cowdrey, 1,591 for Curtis, and 9,845 scattering. Harrison had 96,658 less than Cleveland. Of the whole vote Harrison had 47.83 per cent., Cleveland 48.63, Fisk 2.21, and Streeter 1.30.

1892.—Cleveland had 5,556,562 to 5,162,874 for Harrison, 264,066 for Bidwell, 1,055,424 for Weaver, and 22,613 for Wing. Of the whole vote Cleveland had 45.73 per cent., Harrison 42.49, Bidwell, 2.17, and Weaver 8.67.

Adams, Federalist; Polk, Buchanan and Cleveland, Democrats; Taylor, Whig; Lincoln, Hayes, Garfield and Harrison, Republicans, did not, when elected, receive a majority of the popular vote. The highest percentage of popular vote received by any President was 55.97 for Jackson, Democrat, in 1828, and the lowest, 39.91 for Lincoln, Republican, in 1860.

ELECTORAL VOTE, 1872-92.

States.	1892			1888		1884		1880		1876		1872	
	Rep	Peo	Dem	Rep	Dem	Rep	Dem	Rep	Dem	Rep	Dem	Rep	Dem
Alabama			11		10		10		10		10	10	
Arkansas			8		7		7		6		6	*	*
California	1		8	8	8			1	5	6		6	
Colorado		4		3	3		3			3			
Connecticut			6	6		6	6				6	6	
Delaware			3		3		3		3		3	3	
Florida			4	4			4	4		4			4
Georgia			13		12		12		11		11		
Idaho	3												
Illinois			24	22	22			21		21		21	
Indiana			15		15		15	15			15	15	
Iowa	13				13	13		11		11		11	
Kansas		10		9	9			5		5		5	
Kentucky			13	13			13		12		12		8
Louisiana			8	8			8	8		8		*	*
Maine	6			6	6			7		7		7	
Maryland			8	8			8		8		8		8
Massachusetts	15			14	14			13		13		13	
Michigan	9		5	13	13			11		11		11	
Minnesota	9			7	7			5		5		5	
Mississippi			9		9			9		8		8	
Missouri			17		16		16		15		15		6
Montana	3												
Nebraska	8			5	5			3		3		3	
Nevada		3		3	3				3	3		3	
New Hampshire	4			4	4			5		5		5	
New Jersey			10	9			9		9		9	9	
New York			36	36			36	35		35		35	
North Carolina			11	11			11		10		10	10	
North Dakota	1	1	1										
Ohio	22			23	23			22		22		22	
Oregon	3	1		3	3			3		3		3	
Pennsylvania	32			30	30			29		29		29	
Rhode Island	4			4	4			4		4		4	
South Carolina			9	9			9		7		7	7	
South Dakota	4												
Tennessee			12	12			12		12		12		12
Texas			15	13			13		8		8		8
Vermont	4			4	4			5		5		5	
Virginia			12	12			12		11		11	11	
Washington	4												
West Virginia			6	6			6		5		5	5	
Wisconsin			12	11	11			10		10		10	
Wyoming	3												
Total	145	22	277	168	233	182	219	214	155	185	184	286	42

* Rejected.

CANDIDATES FOR PRESIDENT AND VICE-PRESIDENT FROM 1789 TO 1892.

AGGREGATE POPULAR VOTE AND ELECTORAL VOTE FOR CANDIDATES FOR PRESIDENT AND VICE-PRESIDENT AT EACH ELECTION.

ELECTORAL VOTES.

1789.—Previous to 1804, each elector voted for two candidates for President. The one who received the largest number of votes was declared President, and the one who received the next largest number of votes was declared Vice-President. The electoral votes for the first President of the United States were: George Washington, 69; John Adams, of Massachusetts, 34; John Jay, of New York, 9; R. H. Harrison, of Maryland, 6; John Rutledge, of South Carolina, 6; John Hancock, of Massachusetts, 4; George Clinton, of New York, 3; Samuel Huntingdon, of Connecticut, 2; John Milton, of Georgia, 2; James Armstrong, of Georgia, Benjamin Lincoln, of Massachusetts, and Edward Telfair, of Georgia, 1 vote each. Vacancies (votes *not* cast), 4. George Washington was chosen President and John Adams Vice-President.

1792.—George Washington, Federalist, received 132 votes; John Adams, Federalist, 77; George Clinton, of New York, Republican (*a*), 50; Thomas Jefferson, of Virginia, Republican, 4; Aaron Burr, of New York, Republican, 1 vote. Vacancies, 3. George Washington was chosen President and John Adams Vice-President.

1796.—John Adams, Federalist, 71; Thomas Jefferson, Republican, 68; Thomas Pinckney, of South Carolina, Federalist, 59; Aaron Burr, of New York, Republican, 30; Samuel Adams, of Massachusetts, Republican, 15; Oliver Ellsworth, of Connecticut, Independent, 11; George Clinton, of New York, Republican, 7; John Jay, of New York, Federalist, 5; James Iredell, of North Carolina, Federalist, 3; George Washington, of Virginia, John Henry, of Maryland, and S. Johnson, of North Carolina, all Federalists, 2 votes each; Charles Cotesworth Pinckney of South Carolina, Federalist, 1 vote. John Adams was chosen President and Thomas Jefferson Vice-President.

1800.—Thomas Jefferson, Republican, 73; Aaron Burr, Republican, 73; John Adams, Federalist, 65; Charles C. Pinckney, Federalist, 64; John Jay, Federalist, 1 vote. There being a tie vote for Jefferson and Burr, the choice devolved upon the House of Representatives. Jefferson received the votes of ten States, which, being the largest vote cast for a candidate, elected him President. Burr received the votes of four States, which, being the next largest vote, elected him Vice-President. There were two blank votes.

1804.—The Constitution of the United States having been amended, the electors at this election voted for a President and a Vice-President, instead of for two candidates for President. The result was as follows: For President, Thomas Jefferson, Republican, 162; Charles C. Pinckney, Federalist, 14. For Vice-President, George Clinton, Republican, 162; Rufus King, of New York, Federalist, 14. Jefferson was chosen President and Clinton Vice-President.

1808.—For President, James Madison, of Virginia, Republican, 122; Charles C. Pinckney, of South Carolina, Federalist, 47; George Clinton, of

New York, Republican, 6. For Vice-President, George Clinton, Republican, 113; Rufus King, of New York, Federalist, 47; John Langdon, of New Hampshire, 9; James Madison, 3; James Monroe, 3. Vacancy, 1. Madison was chosen President and Clinton Vice-President.

1812.—For President, James Madison, Republican, 128; De Witt Clinton, of New York, Federalist, 89. For Vice-President, Elbridge Gerry, of Massachusetts, Republican, 131; Jared Ingersoll, of Pennsylvania, Federalist, 86. Vacancy, 1. Madison was chosen President and Gerry Vice-President.

1816.—For President, James Monroe, of Virginia, Republican, 183; Rufus King, of New York, Federalist, 34. For Vice-President, Daniel D. Tompkins, of New York, Republican, 183; John Eager Howard, of Maryland, Federalist, 22; James Ross, of Pennsylvania, 5; John Marshall, of Virginia, 4; Robert G. Harper, of Maryland, 3. Vacancies, 4. Monroe was chosen President and Tompkins Vice-President.

1820.—For President, James Monroe, of Virginia, Republican, 231; John Q. Adams, of Massachusetts, Republican, 1. For Vice-President, Daniel D. Tompkins, Republican, 218; Richard Stockton, of New Jersey, 8; Daniel Rodney, of Delaware, 4; Robert G. Harper, of Maryland, and Richard Rush, of Pennsylvania, 1 vote each. Vacancies, 3. James Monroe was chosen President and Daniel D. Tompkins Vice-President.

ELECTORAL AND POPULAR VOTES.

Year of Election	Candidates for President	States	Political Party	Popular Vote	Plurality	Electoral Vote	Candidates for Vice-President	States	Political Party	Electoral Vote
1824	Andrew Jackson	Tenn.	Rep.	155,872	50,551 (b)	99	John C. Calhoun*	S. C.	Rep.	182
	John Q. Adams*	Mass.	Rep.	105,321		84	Nathan Sanford	N. Y.	Rep.	30
	Henry Clay	Ky.	Rep.	46,587		37	Nathaniel Macon	N. C.	Rep.	24
	Wm. H. Crawford*	Ga.	Rep.	44,282		41	Andrew Jackson	Tenn.	Rep.	13
							M. Van Buren	N. Y.	Rep.	9
							Henry Clay	Ky.	Rep.	2
1828	Andrew Jackson*	Tenn.	Dem.	647,231	138,134	178	John C. Calhoun*	S. C.	Dem.	171
	John Q. Adams	Mass.	Nat. R.	509,097		83	Richard Rush	Pa.	Nat. R.	83
							William Smith	S. C.	Dem.	7
1832	Andrew Jackson*	Tenn.	Dem.	687,502	157,313	219	M. Van Buren	N. Y.	Dem.	189
	Henry Clay	Ky.	Nat. R.	530,189		49	John Sergeant	Pa.	Nat. R.	49
	John Floyd	Ga.	Ind.	} 33,108		11	Henry Lee	Mass.	Ind.	11
	William Wirt (c)	Md.	An. M.			7	Amos Ellmaker (c)	Pa.	Anti M.	7
							Wm. Wilkins	Pa.		30
1836	Martin Van Buren*	N. Y.	Dem.	761,549	24,893	172	R. M. Johnson (d)*	Ky.	Dem	147
	W. H. Harrison	O.	Whig			73	Francis Granger	N. Y.	Whig	77
	Hugh L. White	Tenn.	Whig	} 736,656		26	John Tyler	Va.	Whig	47
	Daniel Webster	Mass.	Whig			14	William Smith	Ala.	Dem.	23
	Willie P. Mangum	N. C.	Whig			11				
1840	W. H. Harrison*	O.	Whig	1,275,017	146,315	234	John Tyler*	Va.	Whig	234
	Martin Van Buren	N. Y.	Dem.	1,128,702		60	R. M. Johnson	Ky.	Dem.	48
	James G. Birney	N. Y.	Lib.	7,059			L. W. Tazewell	Va.	Dem.	11
							James K. Polk	Tenn.	Dem.	1
1844	James K. Polk*	Tenn.	Dem.	1,337,243	38,175	170	George M. Dallas*	Pa.	Dem.	170
	Henry Clay	Ky.	Whig	1,299,068		105	T. Frelinghuysen	N. J	Whig	105
	James G. Birney	N. Y.	Lib.	62,300			Thomas Morris	O.	Lib.	
1848	Zachary Taylor*	La.	Whig	1,360,101	139,557	163	Millard Fillmore*	N. Y.	Whig	163
	Lewis Cass	Mich.	Dem.	1,220,544		127	William O. Butler	Ky.	Dem	127
	Martin Van Buren	N. Y.	F. Soil.	291,263			Charles F. Adams	Mass.	F. Soil.	
1852	Franklin Pierce*	N. H.	Dem.	1,601,474	220,896	254	William R. King*	Ala.	Dem.	254
	Winfield Scott	N. J	Whig	1,380,576		43	William A. Graham	N. C.	Whig	42
	John P. Hale	N. H.	F.D.(i)	156,149			George W. Julian	Ind	F. D.	

CANDIDATES FOR PRESIDENT AND VICE-PRESIDENT—Continued.

Year of Election	Candidates for President.	States.	Political Party.	Popular Vote.	Plurality.	Electoral Vote.	Candidates for Vice-President.	States.	Political Party.	Electoral Votes.
1856	James Buchanan*	Pa.	Dem	1,838,169	496,905	174	J. C. Breckinridge*	Ky.	Dem	174
	John C. Fremont	Cal.	Rep	1,341,264		114	William L. Dayton	N. J.	Rep	114
	Millard Fillmore	N. Y.	Amer.	874,538		8	A. J. Donelson	Tenn.	Amer	8
1860	Abraham Lincoln*	Ill.	Rep	1,866,352	491,195	180	Hannibal Hamlin*	Me.	Rep	180
	Stephen A. Douglas	Ill.	Dem	1,375,157		12	H. V. Johnson	Ga.	Dem	12
	J. C. Breckinridge	Ky.	Dem	845,763		72	Joseph Lane	Ore	Dem	72
	John Bell	Tenn.	Union	589,581		39	Edward Everett	Mass.	Union	39
1864	Abraham Lincoln*	Ill.	Rep	2,216,067	407,342	(e)212	Andrew Johnson*	Tenn.	Rep	212
	George B. McClellan	N. J.	Dem	1,808,725		21	George H. Pendleton	O	Dem	21
1868	Ulysses S. Grant*	Ill.	Rep	3,015,071	305,456	(f)214	Schuyler Colfax*	Ind	Rep	214
	Horatio Seymour	N. Y.	Dem	2,709,615		80	F. P. Blair, Jr.	Mo.	Dem	80
1872	Ulysses S. Grant*	Ill.	Rep	3,597,070	762,991	286	Henry Wilson*	Mass.	Rep	286
	Horace Greeley	N. Y.	D. & L.	2,834,079		(g)	B. Gratz-Brown	Mo	D. L.	47
	Charles O'Conor	N. Y.	Dem	29,408			John Q. Adams	Mass.	Dem	
	James Black	Pa.	Temp	5,608			John Russell	Mich.	Temp	
	Thomas A. Hendricks	Ind	Dem			42	George W. Julian	Ind	Lib	5
	B. Gratz-Brown	Mo.	Dem			18	A. H. Colquitt	Ga.	Dem	5
	Charles J. Jenkins	Ga.	Dem			2	John M. Palmer	Ill.	Dem	3
	David Davis	Ill.	Ind			1	T. E. Bramlette	Ky.	Dem	3
							W. S. Groesbeck	O	Dem	1
							Willis B. Machen	Ky.	Dem	1
							N. P. Banks	Mass.	Lib	1
1876	Samuel J. Tilden	N. Y.	Dem	4,284,885	250,935	184	T. A. Hendricks	Ind	Dem	184
	Rutherford B. Hayes*	O	Rep	4,033,950		(h)185	William A. Wheeler*	N. Y.	Rep	185
	Peter Cooper	N. Y.	Gre'nb.	81,740			Samuel F. Cary	O	Gre'nb.	
	Green Clay Smith	Ky.	Pro	9,522			Gideon T. Stewart	O	Pro	
	James B. Walker	Ill.	Amer.	2,636			D. Kirkpatrick	N. Y.	Amer.	
1880	James A. Garfield*	O	Rep	4,449,053	7,018	214	Chester A. Arthur*	N. Y.	Rep	214
	W. S. Hancock	Pa.	Dem	4,442,035		155	William H. English	Ind	Dem	155
	James B. Weaver	Iowa	Gre'nb.	307,306			B. J. Chambers	Tex	Gre'nb.	
	Neal Dow	Me.	Pro	10,305			H. A. Thompson	O	Pro	
	John W. Phelps	Vt.	Amer.	707			S. C. Pomeroy	Kan	Amer.	
1884	Grover Cleveland*	N. Y.	Dem	4,911,017	62,683	219	T. A. Hendricks*	Ind	Dem	219
	James G. Blaine	Me.	Rep	4,848,331		182	John A. Logan	Ill.	Rep	233
	John P. St. John	Kans.	Pro	151,809			William Daniel	Md.	Pro	
	Benjamin F. Butler	Mass	Peop.	133,825			A. M. West	Miss.	Peop.	
	P. D. Wigginton	Cal.	Amer.						Amer.	
1888	Grover Cleveland	N. Y.	Dem	5,538,233	98,017	168	Allen G. Thurman	O	Dem	168
	Benjamin Harrison*	Ind	Rep	5,440,216		233	Levi P. Morton*	N. Y.	Rep	182
	Clinton B. Fisk	N. J.	Pro	249,307			John A. Brooks	Mo.	Pro	
	Alson J. Streeter	Ill.	U'd. L.	148,105			C. E. Cunningham	Ark.	U'd L.	
	R. H. Cowdry	Ill.	U'd. L.	2,808			W. H. T. Wakefield	Kans	U'd L.	
	James L. Curtis	N. Y.	Amer.	1,591			James R. Greer	Tenn.	Amer.	
1892	Grover Cleveland*	N. Y.	Dem	5,556,918	380,810	277	Adlai E. Stevenson*	Ill.	Dem	277
	Benjamin Harrison	Ind.	Rep	5,176,108		145	Whitelaw Reid	N. Y.	Rep	145
	James B. Weaver	Iowa.	Peop.	1,041,028		22	James G. Field	Va.	Peop.	22
	John Bidwell	Cal.	Pro	264,133			James B. Cranfill	Tex	Pro	
	Simon Wing	Mass.	Soc. L.	21,164			Charles H. Matchett	N. Y.	Soc. L.	

* The candidates starred were elected. (a) The first Republican party is claimed by the present Democratic party as its progenitor. (b) No candidates having a majority of the electoral vote, the House of Representatives elected Adams. (c) Candidates of the Anti-Masonic Party. (d) There being no choice, the Senate elected Johnson. (e) Eleven Southern States, being within the belligerent territory, did not vote. (f) Three Southern States disfranchised. (g) Horace Greeley died after election, and Democratic electors scattered their votes. (h) There being a dispute over the electoral votes of Florida, Louisiana, Oregon and South Carolina, they were referred by Congress to an electoral commission composed of eight Republicans and seven Democrats, which, by a strict party vote, awarded 185 electoral votes to Hayes and 184 to Tilden. (i) Free Democrat.

ELECTORAL COLLEGE BY STATES.

ELECTORAL COLLEGE in 1892 was the same as it is in 1896, except that Utah, having just been admitted as a State, is entitled to three votes, making the number of votes in 1896, 447, against 444 in 1892.

Therefore 224 votes must be cast for some one candidate, or the election will go to the House of Representatives, where each State is entitled to only one vote, making the vote of twenty-three States for some candidate necessary for his election.

The following is the electoral vote by States: Alabama, 11; Arkansas, 8; California, 9; Colorado, 4; Connecticut, 6; Delaware, 3; Florida, 4; Georgia, 13; Idaho, 3; Illinois, 24; Indiana, 15; Iowa, 13; Kansas, 10; Kentucky, 13; Louisiana, 8; Maine, 6; Maryland, 8; Massachusetts, 15; Michigan, 14; Minnesota, 9; Mississippi, 9; Missouri, 17; Montana, 3; Nebraska, 8; Nevada, 3; New Hampshire, 4; New Jersey, 10; New York, 36; North Carolina, 11; North Dakota, 3; Ohio, 23; Oregon, 4; Pennsylvania, 32; Rhode Island, 4; South Carolina, 9; South Dakota, 4; Tennessee, 12; Texas, 15; Utah, 3; Vermont, 4; Virginia, 12; Washington, 4; West Virginia, 6; Wisconsin, 12, and Wyoming, 3.

HOW THE PRESIDENT OF THE UNITED STATES IS CHOSEN.

Technically speaking, the President is not elected by the people, and the people do not vote directly for any Presidential candidate. They cast their ballots for electors, and these electors choose a President and Vice-President. In each State the number of electors is equal to the number of Senators and Representatives which the State has in Congress. Each party has an electoral ticket with the names of its electors printed on it.

The electoral ticket which receives the greatest number of popular ballots in the State would be chosen by the people, and the electors named on it will be entitled to give their votes for the candidate whom they represent.

The electors who are chosen will meet in each State on the second Monday in January, and cast their votes for a President and Vice-President. As a matter of law, they can then vote for whom they please. As a matter of usage and public trust, they are expected to vote for the candidate whom they are pledged to support.

The following law, given in full, passed February 3d, 1887, governs the counting of the electoral vote:

An act to fix the day for the meeting of the electorals of President and Vice-President, and to provide for and regulate the counting of the votes for President and Vice-President, and the decision of questions arising thereon.

BE IT ENACTED BY THE SENATE AND HOUSE OF REPRESENTATIVES OF THE UNITED STATES OF AMERICA IN CONGRESS ASSEMBLED, That the electors of each State shall meet and give their votes on the second Monday in January next following their appointment at such place in each State as the Legislature of such State shall direct.

SEC. 2. That if any State shall have provided, by laws enacted prior to the day fixed for the appointment of the electors, for its final determination of any controversy or contest concerning the appointment of all or any of the electors of such State, by judicial or other methods or procedures, and such determination shall have been made at least six days before the time fixed for the meeting of the electors, such determination made pursuant to such law so existing on said day, and made at least six days prior to the said time of meeting of the electors, shall be conclusive, and shall govern in the counting of the electoral votes as provided in the Constitution, and as hereinafter regulated, so far as the ascertainment of the electors appointed by such State is concerned.

SEC. 3. That it shall be the duty of the Executive of each State, as soon as practicable after the conclusion of the appointment of electors in such State, by the final ascertainment under and in pursuance of the laws of such State providing for such ascertainment, to communicate, under the seal of the State, to the Secretary of State of the United States, a certificate of such ascertainment of the electors appointed, setting forth the names of such electors and the canvass or other ascertainment under the laws of such State of the number of votes given or cast for each person for whose appointment any and all votes have been given or cast; and it shall also thereupon be the duty of the Executive of each State to deliver to the electors of such State, on or before the day on which they are required by the preceding section to meet, the same certificate, in triplicate, under the seal of the State; and such certificate shall be inclosed and transmitted by the electors at the same time and in the same manner as is provided by law for transmitting by such electors to the seat of government the lists of all persons voted for as President and of all persons voted for as Vice-President; and section one hundred and thirty-six of the Revised Statutes is hereby repealed; and if there shall have been any final determination in a State of a controversy or contest as provided for in section two of this act, it shall be the duty of the Executive of such State, as soon as practicable after such determination, to communicate, under the seal of the State, to the Secretary of State of the United States a certificate of such determination, in form and manner as the same shall have been made; and the Secretary of State of the United States, as soon as practicable after the receipt at the State Department of each of the certificates hereinbefore directed to be transmitted to the Secretary of State, shall publish, in such public newspaper as he shall designate, such certificates in full; and at the first meeting of Congress thereafter he shall transmit to the two Houses of Congress copies in full of each and every such certificate so received theretofore at the State Department.

SEC. 4. That Congress shall be in session on the second Wednesday in February succeeding every meeting of the electors. The Senate and House of Representatives shall meet in the Hall on the House of Representatives, at the hour of one o'clock in the afternoon on that day, and the President of the Senate shall be their presiding officer. Two tellers shall be previously appointed on the part of the Senate and two on the part of the House of Representatives, to whom shall be handed, as they are opened by the President of the Senate, all the certificates and papers purporting to be certificates of the electoral votes, which certificates and papers shall be opened, presented and acted upon in the alphabetical order of the States, beginning with the letter A; and said tellers, having then read the same in the presence and hearing of the two Houses, shall make a list of the votes as they shall appear from the said certificates, and the votes having been ascertained and counted in the manner and according to the rules in this Act provided, the result of the same shall be delivered to the President of the Senate, who shall thereupon announce the state of the vote, which announcement shall be deemed a sufficient declaration of the persons, if any, elected President and Vice-President of the United States, and, together with a list of the votes, be entered on the Journals of the two Houses. Upon such reading of any such certificate or paper, the President of the Senate shall call for objections, if any. Every objection shall be made in writing, and shall state clearly and concisely, and without argument, the ground thereof, and shall be signed by at least one Senator and one member of the House of Representatives before the same shall be received. When all objections, so made to any vote or paper from a State shall have been received and read, the Senate shall thereupon withdraw, and such objections shall be submitted to the Senate for its decision; and the Speaker of the House of Representatives shall in like manner submit such objections to the House of Representatives for its decision, and no electoral vote or votes from any State which shall have been regularly given by electors whose appointment has been lawfully certified to according to Section 3 of this Act, from which but one return has been received, shall be rejected, but the two Houses concurrently may reject the vote or votes when they agree that such vote or votes have not been so regularly given by electors whose appointment has been so certified. If more than one return, or paper purporting to be a return from a State, shall have been received by the President of the Senate, those votes, and those only, shall be counted which shall have been regularly given by the electors who are shown by the determination mentioned in Section 2 of this Act to have been appointed, if the determination in said Section provided for shall have been made, or by such successors or substitutes, in case of a vacancy in the Board of Electors so ascertained, as have been appointed to fill such vacancy in the mode provided by the laws of the State ; but in case there shall arise the question which of two or more of such State authorities determining what electors have been appointed as mentioned in Section 2 of this Act, is the lawful tribunal of such State, the votes regularly given of those electors, and those only, of such State, shall be counted whose title as electors the two Houses, acting separately, shall concurrently decide is supported by the decision of such State so authorized by its laws; and in such case of more than one return or paper purporting to be a return from a State, if there shall have been no such determination of the question in the State aforesaid, then those votes, and those only, shall be counted which the two Houses shall concurrently decide were cast by lawful electors appointed in accordance with the laws of the State, unless the two Houses, acting separately, shall concurrently decide such votes not to be the lawful votes of the legally appointed electors of such State. But if the two Houses shall disagree in respect of the counting of such votes, then, and in that case, the votes of the electors whose appointment shall have been certified by the Executive of the State, under the seal thereof, shall be counted. When the two Houses have voted, they shall immediately again meet, and the presiding officer shall then announce the decision of the questions submitted. No votes or papers from any other State shall be acted upon until the objections previously made to the votes or papers from any State shall have been finally disposed of.

SEC. 5. That while the two Houses shall be in meeting as provided in this act the President of the Senate shall have power to preserve order; and no debate shall be allowed and no question shall be put by the presiding officer except to either House on a motion to withdraw.

SEC. 6. That when the two Houses separate to decide upon an objection that may have been made to the counting of any electoral vote or votes from any State, or other question arising in the matter, each Senator and Representative may speak to such objection or question five minutes, and not more than once; but after such debate shall have lasted two hours, it shall be the duty of the presiding officer of each House to put the main question without further debate.

SEC. 7. That at such joint meeting of the two Houses seats shall be provided as follows: For the President of the Senate, the Speaker's chair; for the Speaker, immediately upon his left; the Senators, in the body of the Hall, upon the right of the presiding officer; for the Representatives, in the body of the Hall not provided for the Senators; for the tellers, Secretary of the Senate and Clerk of the House of Representatives, at the Clerk's desk; for the other officers of the two Houses, in front of the Clerk's desk and upon each side of the Speaker's platform. Such joint meeting shall not be dissolved until the count of electoral votes shall be completed and the result declared; and no recess shall be taken unless a question shall have arisen in regard to counting any such votes, or otherwise under this act, in which case it shall be competent for either House, acting separately, in the manner hereinbefore provided, to direct a recess of such House not beyond the next calendar day, Sunday excepted, at the hour of ten o'clock in the forenoon. But if the counting of the electoral votes and the declaration of the result shall not have been completed before the fifth calendar day next after such first meeting of the two Houses, no further or other recess shall be taken by either House.

The representation in 1896 is 357, Utah having been admitted as a State in 1896, and is entitled to one Representative. Add the 50 Senators, and the whole electoral vote in 1896 is 447.

Governors of all States and Territories, Corrected to Date, with Term of Office, Salary and State Capitals.

State.	Governors.	Term.	Term Began.	Term Ends.	Salary.	Capital.
Alabama	William C. Oates	2 yrs.	Dec. 1, '94.	Dec. 1, '96.	$3,000	Montgomery.
Arkansas	James P. Clarke	2 "	Jan., '95.	Jan., '97.	3,000	Little Rock.
California	James H. Budd	4 "	" '95.	" '99.	6,000	Sacramento.
Colorado	A. W. McIntyre	2 "	" '95.	" '97.	5,000	Denver.
Connecticut	O. Vincent Collin	2 "	" 9, '95.	" 9, '97.	4,000	Hartford.
Delaware	Joshua H. Marvil	4 "	3d Tues. Jan., '95.	3d Tues. Jan., '99.	2,500	Dover.
Florida	Henry L. Mitchell	4 "	Jan. 3, '93.	Jan. 3, '97.	3,500	Tallahassee.
Georgia	Wm. Y. Atkinson	2 "	Nov. 1, '94.	Nov. 1, '96.	3,000	Atlanta.
Idaho	W. J. McConnell	2 "	Jan., '95.	Jan., '97.	3,000	Boise City.
Illinois	J. P. Altgeld	4 "	" 10, '93.	" 10, '97.	6,000	Springfield.
Indiana	Claude Matthews	4 "	" 9, '93.	" 9, '97.	5,000	Indianapolis.
Iowa	Francis M. Drake	2 "	" '94.	" '98.	3,000	Des Moines.
Kansas	E. N. Morrill	2 "	" '95.	" '97.	3,000	Topeka.
Kentucky	W. O. Bradley	4 "	Dec. 10, '95.	Dec. 10, '99.	5,000	Frankfort.
Louisiana*	Murphy J. Foster	4 "	May 21, '92.	May 21, '96.	4,000	Baton Rouge.
Maine	Henry B. Cleaves	2 "	Jan., '95.	Jan., '97.	2,000	Augusta.
Maryland	Lloyd Lowndes	4 "	1896.	1900.	4,500	Annapolis.
Massachusetts	F. T. Greenhalge‡	1 "	1st Wed. Jan., '96.	1st Wed. Jan., '97.	8,000	Boston.
Minnesota	D. M. Clough§	2 "	Jan. 1, '95.	Jan. 1, '97.	5,000	St. Paul.
Michigan	John G. Rich	2 "	" '95.	" '97.	4,000	Lansing.
Mississippi	Anselm J. McLaurin	4 "	" '96.	" 1900.	4,000	Jackson.
Missouri	William J. Stone	4 "	" '93.	" '97.	5,000	Jefferson City.
Montana	John E. Rickards	4 "	" 2, '93.	" 2, '97.	5,000	Helena.
Nebraska	S. A. Holcomb	2 "	" 3, '95.	" 3, '97.	2,500	Lincoln.
Nevada	J. E. Jones	4 "	" '95.	" '99.	5,000	Carson City.
New Hampshire	Charles A. Busiel	2 "	" '95.	" '97.	2,000	Concord.
New Jersey	John W. Griggs	3 "	" 20, '96.	" 20, '99.	10,000	Trenton.
New York	Levi P. Morton	2 "	" 1, '95.	Dec. 31, '96.	10,000	Albany.
North Carolina	Elias Carr	4 "	" 1, '93.	Jan. 1, '97.	3,000	Raleigh.
North Dakota	Roger Allin	2 "	" 1, '95.	" 1, '97.	3,000	Bismarck.
Ohio	Asa S. Bushnell	2 "	2d Mon. Jan., '96.	2d Mon. Jan., '98.	8,000	Columbus.
Oregon	W. P. Lord	4 "	Jan., '95.	Jan., '99.	1,500	Salem.
Pennsylvania	D. H. Hastings	4 "	3d Tues. Jan., '95.	3d Tues. Jan., '99.	10,000	Harrisburg.
Rhode Island	Charles W. Lippitt	1 "	May 26, '95.	May 26, '96.	3,000	Providence.
South Carolina	J. Gary Evans	2 "	Dec. 4, '94.	Dec. 4, '96.	3,500	Columbia.
South Dakota	C. H. Sheldon	2 "	Jan. 1, '95.	Jan. 1, '97.	2,500	Pierre.
Tennessee	Peter Turney¶	2 "	" 15, '95.	" 15, '97.	4,000	Nashville.
Texas	Chas. A. Culberson	2 "	" '95.	" '97.	4,000	Austin.
Utah†	Caleb W. West					
Vermont	U. A. Woodbury	2 "	Oct. 6, '94.	Oct. 6, '96.	1,500	Montpelier.
Virginia	Charles T. O'Ferrall	4 "	Jan. 1, '94.	Dec. 31, '97.	5,000	Richmond.
Washington	J. H. McGraw	4 "	" 11, '93.	Jan. 11, '97.	4,000	Olympia.
West Virginia	Wm. H. McCorkle	4 "	Mar. 4, '93.	Mar. 4, '97.	2,700	Charleston.
Wisconsin	Wm. H. Upham	2 "	Jan. 8, '95.	Jan. 8, '97.	5,000	Madison.
Wyoming	W. A. Richards	4 "	" '95.	" '99.	2,500	Cheyenne.

Territories.

Alaska	James Sheakley	4 "	Apr. 19, '92.	Aug. 28, '96.	3,000	Sitka.
Arizona	Louis C. Hughes	4 "	1893.	1897.	2,600	Phoenix.
Indian		4 "	1895.	1899.	2,000	Tahlequah.
New Mexico	Wm. T. Thornton	4 "	Jan. 1, '95.	Jan. 1, '99.	2,000	Santa Fe.
Oklahoma	W. C. Renfrew	4 "	May 11, '93.	May 10, '97.	2,600	Guthrie.

* Elected to serve from May, 1896, to May, 1900.
† Admitted as a state 1896.
‡ Died 1896. Roger Wolcott Acting Governor.
§ Succeeded Governor Knute Nelson, who was elected United States Senator.
¶ On the face of the returns H. Clay Evans was elected, but Legislature declared Turney elected on account of irregularities in election.

BRIEF SKETCHES OF THE PRESIDENTS.

GEORGE WASHINGTON was born February 22d, 1732, near Bridges Creek, Westmoreland county, Va. His parents were Augustine and Mary (Ball) Washington. He was a surveyor in early life and afterward a planter. Married, 1759, Mrs. Martha (Dandridge) Custis. No children. Died at Mount Vernon, Va., December 14th, 1799.

John Adams was born October 19th, 1735, at Quincy, Norfolk county, Mass. His parents were John and Susanna (Boylston) Adams. He was a teacher in early life and afterward a lawyer. Graduated Harvard, 1755. Married, 1764, Abigail Smith. Three sons and two daughters. Died at Quincy, Mass., July 4th, 1826.

Thomas Jefferson was born April 13th, 1743, at Shadwell, Albemarle county, Va. His parents were Peter and Jane (Randolph) Jefferson. He was a lawyer. Graduated William and Mary College, 1762. Married, 1772, Mrs. Martha (Wayles) Skelton. One son and five daughters. Died at Monticello, Va., July 4th, 1826.

James Madison was born March 16th, 1751, at Port Conway, King George county, Va. His parents were James and Nelly (Conway) Madison. He was a lawyer. Graduated Princeton, 1771. Married, 1794, Mrs. Dolly (Payne) Todd. No children. Died at Montpelier, Vt., June 28th, 1836.

James Monroe was born April 28th, 1758, at Head of Monroe's Creek, Westmoreland county, Va. His parents were Spence and Eliza (Jones) Monroe. He was a lawyer in early life, but abandoned that profession. Graduated William and Mary College, 1776. Married, 1786, Eliza Kortright. Two daughters. Died at New York city, July 4th, 1831, in almost extreme poverty.

John Quincy Adams was born July 11th, 1767, at Quincy, Norfolk county, Mass. His parents were John and Abigail (Smith) Adams. He was a lawyer. Graduated Harvard, 1787. Married, 1797, Louisa Catherine Johnson. Three sons and one daughter. Died at Washington, D. C., February 23d, 1848. His mortal illness came upon him in the House of Representatives, while a member of that body.

Andrew Jackson was born March 15th, 1767, near Cureton's Pond, Union county, N. C. His parents were Andrew and Elizabeth (Hutchinson) Jackson. He was a lawyer. Married, 1794, Mrs. Rachel (Donelson) Robards. No children. Died at Hermitage, Tenn., June 8th, 1845.

Martin Van Buren was born December 5th, 1782, at Kinderhook, Columbia county, N. Y. His parents were Abraham and Maria (Hoes) Van Buren. He was a lawyer. Married, 1807, Hannah Hoes. Four sons. Died at Lindenwold, N. Y., July 24th, 1862.

William Henry Harrison was born February 9th, 1773, at Berkeley, Charles City county, Va. His parents were Benjamin and Elizabeth (Bassett) Harrison. He was a soldier and farmer. Graduated Hampden-Sydney, 1790. Married, 1795, Anna Symmes. Six sons and four daughters. Died at Washington, D. C., April 4th, 1841.

John Tyler was born March 29th, 1790, at Greenway, Charles City county, Va. His parents were John and Mary (Armistead) Tyler. He was a lawyer. Graduated William and Mary College, 1807. Married, 1813, Letitia Christian and 1844 Julia Gardiner. Three sons and four daughters by first wife, five sons and two daughters by second wife. Died at Richmond, Va., January 17th, 1862.

James Knox Polk was born November 2d, 1795, near Pineville, Mecklenburg, county, N. C. His parents were Samuel and Jane (Knox) Polk. He was a lawyer. Graduated University of North Carolina, 1818. Married, 1824, Sarah Childress. No children. Died at Nashville, Tenn., June 15th, 1849.

Zachary Taylor was born November 24th, 1784, near Orange Court House, Va. His parents were Richard and Sarah (Strother) Taylor. He was a soldier. Married, 1810, Margaret Smith. One son and three daughters. Died at Washington, D. C., July 9th, 1850.

Millard Fillmore was born January 7th, 1800, at Summerhill, Cayuga county, N. Y. His parents were Nathaniel and Phebe (Millard) Fillmore. He was a tailor in early life and afterward a lawyer. Married, 1826, Abigail Powers and 1858 Mrs. Caroline (Carmichael) McIntosh. One son and one daughter by first wife. Died at Buffalo, N. Y., March 9th, 1874.

Franklin Pierce was born November 23d, 1804, at Hillsborough, Hillsborough county, N. H. His parents were Benjamin and Anna (Kendrick) Pierce. He was a lawyer. Graduated Bowdoin, 1824. Married, 1834, Jane Means Appleton. Three sons. Died at Concord, N. H., October 8th, 1869.

James Buchanan was born April 23d, 1791, at Core Gap, Franklin county, Pa. His parents were James and Elizabeth (Speer) Buchanan. He was a lawyer. Graduated Dickinson College, 1809. Unmarried. Died at Wheatland, Pa., June 1st, 1868.

Abraham Lincoln was born February 12th, 1809, near Hodgenville, Larue county, Ky. His parents were Thomas and Nancy (Hanks) Lincoln. He was a farm laborer in early life and afterward a lawyer. Married, 1842, Mary Todd. Four sons. Assassinated at Washington, D. C., April 15th, 1865.

Andrew Johnson was born December 29th, 1808, at Raleigh, Wake county, N. C. His parents were Jacob and Mary (McDonough) Johnson. He was a tailor in early life. Married, 1827, Eliza McCardle. Three sons and two daughters. Died at Carter's Depot, Tenn., July 31st, 1875.

Ulysses S. Grant was born April 27th, 1822, at Point Pleasant, Clermont county, Ohio. His parents were Jesse Root and Harriet (Simpson) Grant. He was a soldier. Graduated West Point, 1843. Married, 1848, Julia Dent. Three sons and one daughter. Died at Mt. McGregor, N. Y., July 23d, 1885.

Rutherford B. Hayes was born October 4th, 1822, at Delaware, Delaware county, Ohio. His parents were Rutherford and Sophia (Birchard) Hayes. He was a lawyer. Graduated Kenyon College, 1842. Married, 1852, Lucy Ware Webb. Seven sons and one daughter. Died at Fremont, Ohio, January 17th, 1893.

James A. Garfield was born November 19th, 1831, at Orange township, Cuyahoga county, Ohio. His parents were Abram and Eliza (Ballou) Garfield. He was a teacher in early life and afterward a lawyer. Graduated Williams College, 1856. Married, 1858, Lucretia Rudolph. Four sons and one daughter. Died at Long Branch, N. J., September 19th, 1881.

Chester A. Arthur was born October 5th, 1830, at Fairfield, Franklin county, Vt. His parents were William and Malvina (Stone) Arthur. He was a teacher in early life and afterward a lawyer. Graduated Union College, 1848. Married, 1859, Ellen Lewis Herndon. One son and one daughter. Died at New York city, November 18th, 1886.

Grover Cleveland (see sketch of life and portrait in this book. President 1885-89 and chosen again in 1892. Now serving).

Benjamin Harrison was born August 20th, 1833, at North Bend, Ohio. His father was John Scott Harrison, who was a member of Congress. His grandfather was General William Henry Harrison (Tippecanoe) and President of the United States. Benjamin Harrison was a General in the Army of the Rebellion, United States Senator from Indiana, and was chosen President over Grover Cleveland in 1888, and served from March 4th, 1889, to March 4th, 1893. His wife, Caroline L. Scott, died in the White House. After his term expired Mr. Harrison returned to Indianapolis and resumed the practice of the law. April 8th, 1896, he was again married to Mrs. Dimmick, of New York city.

VICE-PRESIDENTS OF THE UNITED STATES.

	Name.	Birthplace.	Year.	Paternal Ancestry.	Residence.	Qualified.	Politics.	Place of Death.	Year.	Age at Death.
1	John Adams	Quincy, Mass.	1735	English	Mass.	1789	Fed.	Quincy, Mass.	1826	91
2	Thomas Jefferson	Shadwell, Va.	1743	Welsh	Va.	1797	Rep.	Monticello, Va.	1826	83
3	Aaron Burr	Newark, N. J.	1756	English	N. Y.	1801	Rep.	Staten Island, N. Y.	1836	80
4	George Clinton	Ulster Co., N. Y.	1739	English	N. Y.	1805	Rep.	Washington, D. C.	1812	73
5	Elbridge Gerry	Marblehead, Mass.	1744	English	Mass.	1813	Rep.	Washington, D. C.	1814	70
6	Daniel D. Tompkins	Scarsdale, N. Y.	1774	English	N. Y.	1817	Rep.	Staten Island, N. Y.	1825	51
7	John C. Calhoun	Abbeville, S. C.	1782	Scotch-Irish	S. C.	1825	Rep.	Washington, D. C.	1850	68
8	Martin Van Buren	Kinderhook, N. Y.	1782	Dutch	N. Y.	1834	Dem.	Kinderhook, N. Y.	1862	80
9	Richard M. Johnson	Louisville, Ky.	1780	English	Ky.	1837	Dem.	Frankfort, Ky.	1850	70
10	John Tyler	Greenway, Va.	1790	English	Va.	1841	Dem.	Richmond, Va.	1862	72
11	George M. Dallas	Philadelphia, Pa.	1792	English	Pa.	1845	Dem.	Philadelphia, Pa.	1864	72
12	Millard Fillmore	Summer Hill, N. Y.	1800	English	N. Y.	1849	Whig	Buffalo, N. Y.	1874	74
13	William R. King	Sampson Co., N. C.	1786	English	Ala.	1853	Dem.	Dallas Co., Ala.	1853	67
14	John C. Breckinridge	Lexington, Ky.	1821	Scotch	Ky.	1857	Dem.	Lexington, Ky.	1875	54
15	Hannibal Hamlin	Paris, Me.	1809	English	Me.	1861	Rep.	Bangor, Me.	1891	81
16	Andrew Johnson	Raleigh, N. C.	1808	English	Tenn.	1865	Rep.	Carter Co., Tenn.	1875	67
17	Schuyler Colfax	New York City.	1823	English	Ind.	1869	Rep.	Mankato, Minn.	1885	62
18	Henry Wilson	Farmington, N. H.	1812	English	Mass.	1873	Rep.	Washington, D. C.	1875	63
19	William A. Wheeler	Malone, N. Y.	1819	English	N. Y.	1877	Rep.	Malone, N. Y.	1887	68
20	Chester A. Arthur	Fairfield, Vt.	1830	Scotch-Irish	N. Y.	1881	Rep.	New York City.	1886	56
21	Thos. A. Hendricks	Muskingum Co., O.	1819	Scotch-Irish	Ind.	1885	Dem.	Indianapolis, Ind.	1885	66
22	Levi P. Morton	Shoreham, Vt.	1824	Scotch	N. Y.	1889	Rep.			
23	Adlai E. Stevenson	Christian Co., Ky.	1835	Scotch-Irish	Ill.	1893	Dem.			

PRESIDENTS PRO TEMPORE OF THE UNITED STATES SENATE.

John Langdon, N. H., 1789-92; Richard H. Lee, Va., 1792; John Langdon, N. H., 1792 94; Ralph Izard, S. C., 1794-95; Henry Tazewell, Va., 1795-96; Samuel Livermore, N. H., 1796-97; William Bingham, Pa., 1797; William Bradford, R. I., 1797; Jacob Read, S. C., 1797-98; Theodore Sedgwick, Mass., 1798; John Laurence, N. Y., 1798-99; James Ross, Pa., 1799; Samuel Livermore, N. H., 1799-1800; Uriah Tracy, Conn., 1800; John E. Howard, Md., 1800-01; James Hillhouse, Conn., 1801; Abraham Baldwin, Ga., 1801-02; Stephen R. Bradley, Vt., 1802-03; John Brown, Ky., 1803-04; Jesse Franklin, N. C., 1804-05; Joseph Anderson, Tenn., 1805; Samuel

Smith, Md., 1805-08; Stephen R. Bradley, Vt., 1808-09; John Milledge, Ga., 1809; Andrew Gregg, Pa., 1809-10; John Gaillard, S. C., 1810-11; John Pope, Ky., 1811-12; William H. Crawford, Ga., 1812-13; Joseph B. Varnum, Mass., 1813-14; John Gaillard, S. C., 1814-18; James Barbour, Va., 1818-19; John Gaillard, S. C., 1820-26; Nathaniel Macon, N. C., 1826-28; Samuel Smith, Md., 1828-32; L. W. Tazewell, Va., 1832; Hugh L. White, Tenn., 1832-34; George Poindexter, Miss., 1834-35; John Tyler, Va., 1835-36; William R. King, Ala., 1836-41; Samuel L. Southard, N. J., 1841-42; W. P. Mangum, N. C., 1842-46; D. R. Atchison, Mo., 1846-49; William R. King, Ala., 1850-52; D. R. Atchison, Mo., 1852 54; Jesse D. Bright, Ind., 1854-57; James M. Mason, Va., 1857; Benjamin Fitzpatrick, Ala., 1857-61; Solomon Foot, Vt., 1861-64; Daniel Clark, N. H., 1864-65; Lafayette S. Foster, Conn., 1865-67; Benjamin F. Wade, O., 1867-69; Henry B. Anthony, R. I., 1869-73; M. H. Carpenter, Wis., 1873-75; Thomas W. Ferry, Mich., 1875-79; A. G. Thurman, O., 1879-81; Thomas F. Bayard, Del., 1881; David Davis, Ill., 1881-83; George F. Edmunds, Vt., 1883-85; John Sherman, O., 1885-87; John J. Ingalls, Kan., 1887-91; C. F. Manderson, Neb., 1891-93; Isham G. Harris, Tenn., 1893-94; William P. Frye, Me., 1896.

SPEAKERS OF THE UNITED STATES HOUSE OF REPRESENTATIVES.

F. A. Muhlenburg, Pa., 1781-91; Jonathan Trumbull, Conn., 1791-93; F. A Muhlenburg, Pa., 1793-95; Jonathan Dayton, N. J., 1795-99; Theodore Sedgwick, Mass., 1799-1801; Nathaniel Macon, N. C., 1801-07; Joseph B. Varnum, Mass., 1807-11; Henry Clay, Ky., 1811-14; Langdon Cheves, S. C., 1814-15; Henry Clay, Ky., 1815-20; John W. Taylor, N. Y., 1820-21; Philip B. Barbour, Va., 1821-23; Henry Clay, Ky., 1823 25; John W. Taylor, N. Y., 1825-27; Andrew Stevenson, Va., 1827-34; John Bell, Tenn., 1834-35; James K. Polk, Tenn., 1835-39; R. M. T. Hunter, Va., 1839-41; John White, Ky., 1841-43; John W. Jones, Va., 1843 45; John W. Davis, Ind., 1845-47; Robert C. Winthrop, Mass., 1847-49; Howell Cobb, Ga., 1849-51; Linn Boyd, Ky., 1851-55; Nathaniel P. Banks, Mass., 1856-57; James L. Orr, S. C., 1857-59; William Pennington, N. J., 1860-61; Galusha A. Grow, Pa., 1861-63; Schuyler Colfax, Ind., 1863-69; James G. Blaine, Me., 1869-75; Michael C. Kerr, Ind., 1875-76; Samuel J. Randall, Pa., 1876-81; John W. Keifer, O., 1881-83; John G. Carlisle, Ky., 1883-89; Thomas B. Reed, Me., 1889-91; Chas. F. Crisp, Ga., 1891-95; Thomas B. Reed, 1895-97.

PRESIDENTIAL CABINET OFFICERS.
With States to which Accredited and Years of Appointment.

SECRETARIES OF STATE.—Thomas Jefferson, Va., 1789; Edmund Randolph, Va., 1794; Timothy Pickering, Mass., 1795 and 1797; John Marshall, Va., 1800; James Madison, Va., 1801; Robert Smith, Md., 1809; James Monroe, Va., 1811; John Quincy Adams, Mass., 1817; Henry Clay, Ky., 1825; Martin Van Buren, N. Y., 1829; Edward Livingston, La., 1831; Louis McLane, Del., 1833; John Forsyth, Ga., 1834 and 1837; Daniel Webster,

Mass., 1841; Hugh S. Legaré, S. C., 1843; Abel P. Upshur, Va., 1843; John C. Calhoun, S. C., 1844; James Buchanan, Pa., 1845; John M. Clayton, Del., 1849; Daniel Webster, Mass., 1850; Edward Everett, Mass., 1852; William L. Marcy, N. Y., 1853; Lewis Cass, Mich., 1857; Jeremiah S. Black, Pa., 1860; William H. Seward, N. Y., 1861 and 1865; Elihu B. Washburn, Ill., 1869; Hamilton Fish, N. Y., 1869; William M. Evarts, N. Y., 1877; James G. Blaine, Me., 1881 and 1889; F. T. Frelinghuysen, N. J., 1881; Thomas F. Bayard, Del., 1885; John W. Foster, Ind., 1892; Walter Q. Gresham, Ill., 1893.

SECRETARIES OF THE TREASURY.—Alexander Hamilton, N. Y., 1789; Oliver Wolcott, Conn., 1795 and 1797; Samuel Dexter, Mass., 1801; Albert Gallatin, Pa., 1801 and 1809; Geo. W. Campbell, Tenn., 1814; Alexander J. Dallas, Pa., 1814; William H. Crawford, Ga., 1816 and 1817; Richard Rush, Pa., 1825; Samuel D. Ingham, Pa., 1829; Louis McLane, Del., 1831; William J. Duane, Pa., 1833; Roger B. Taney, Md., 1833; Levi Woodbury, N. H., 1834 and 1837; Thomas Ewing, O., 1841; Walter Forward, Pa., 1841; John C. Spencer, N. Y., 1843; George M. Bibb, Ky., 1844; Robert J. Walker, Miss., 1845; William M. Meredith, Pa., 1849; Thomas Corwin, O., 1850; James Guthrie, Ky., 1853; Howell Cobb, Ga., 1857; Philip F. Thomas, Md., 1860; John A. Dix, N. Y., 1861; Salmon P. Chase, O., 1861; William P. Fessenden, Me., 1864; Hugh McCulloch, Ind., 1865; George S. Boutwell, Mass., 1869; William A. Richardson, Mass., 1873; Benjamin H. Bristow, Ky., 1874; Lot M. Morrill, Me., 1876; John Sherman, O., 1877; William Windom, Minn., 1881 and 1889; Charles J. Folger, N. Y., 1881; Walter Q. Gresham, Ind., 1884; Hugh McCulloch, Ind., 1884; Daniel Manning, N. Y., 1885; Charles S. Fairchild, N. Y., 1887; Charles Foster, O., 1891; John G. Carlisle, Ky., 1893.

SECRETARIES OF WAR.—Henry Knox, Mass., 1789; Timothy Pickering, Mass., 1795; James McHenry, Md., 1796 and 1797; John Marshall, Va., 1800; Samuel Dexter, Mass., 1800; Roger Griswold, Conn., 1801; Henry Dearborn, Mass., 1801; William Eustis, Mass., 1809; John Armstrong, N. Y., 1813; James Monroe, Va., 1814; William H. Crawford, Ga., 1815; Isaac Shelby, Ky., 1817; George Graham, (*ad in.*), 1817; John C. Calhoun, S. C., 1817; James Barbour, Va., 1825; Peter B. Porter, N. Y., 1828; John H. Eaton, Tenn., 1829; Lewis Cass, O., 1831; Benjamin F. Butler, N. Y., 1837; Joel R. Poinsett, S. C., 1837; John Bell, Tenn., 1841; John McLean, O., 1841; John C. Spencer, N. Y., 1841; James M. Porter, Pa., 1843; William Wilkins, Pa., 1844; William L. Marcy, N. Y., 1845; George W. Crawford, Ga., 1849; Edward Bates, Mo., 1850; Charles M. Conrad, La., 1850; Jefferson Davis, Miss., 1853; John B. Floyd, Va., 1857; Joseph Holt, Ky., 1861; Simon Cameron, Pa., 1861; Edwin M. Stanton, O., 1862 and 1865; U. S. Grant (*ad in.*), Ill., 1867; Lorenzo Thomas (*ad in.*), 1868; John M. Schofield, N. Y., 1868; John A. Rawlins, Ill., 1869; William T. Sherman, O., 1869; William W. Belknap, Jr., 1869; Alphonso Taft, O., 1876; James Don Cameron, Pa., 1876; George W. McCrary, Ia., 1877; Alexander Ramsey, Minn., 1879; Robert T. Lincoln, Ill., 1881; William C. Endicott, Mass., 1885; Redfield Proctor, Vt., 1889; Stephen B. Elkins, W. Va., 1891; Daniel S. Lamont, N. Y., 1893.

SECRETARIES OF THE INTERIOR.—Thomas Ewing, O., 1849; James A. Pearce, Md., 1850; Thomas M. T. M'Kernon, Pa., 1850; Alexander H. H.

Stuart, Va., 1850; Robert McClelland, Mich., 1853; Jacob Thompson, Miss., 1857; Caleb B. Smith, Ind., 1861; John P. Usher, Ind., 1863 and 1865; James Harlan, Ia., 1865; Orville H. Browning, Ill., 1866; Jacob D. Cox, O., 1869; Columbus Delano, O., 1870; Zachariah Chandler, Mich., 1875; Carl Schurz, Mo., 1877; Samuel J. Kirkwood, Ia., 1881; Henry M. Teller, Col., 1882; Lucius Q. C. Lamar, Miss., 1885; William F. Vilas, Wis., 1888; John W. Noble, Mo., 1889; Hoke Smith, Ga., 1893.

SECRETARIES OF THE NAVY.—George Cabot, Mass., 1798; Benjamin Stoddert, Md., 1798 and 1801; Robert Smith, Md., 1801; Jacob Crowninshield, Mass., 1805; Paul Hamilton, S. C., 1809; William Jones, Ia., 1813; B. W. Crowninshield, Mass., 1814 and 1817; Smith Thompson, N. Y., 1818; Samuel L. Southard, N. J., 1823 and 1825; John Branch, N. C., 1829; Levi Woodbury, N. H., 1831; Mahlon Dickerson, N. J., 1834 and 1837; James K. Paulding, N. Y., 1838; George E. Badger, N. C., 1841; Abel P. Upshur, Va., 1841; David Henshaw, Mass., 1843; Thomas W. Gilmer, Va., 1844; John Y. Mason, Va., 1844 and 1846; George Bancroft, Mass., 1845; William B. Preston, Va., 1849; William A. Graham, N. C., 1850; John P. Kennedy, Md., 1852; James C. Dobbin, N. C., 1853; Isaac Toucey, Conn., 1857; Gideon Welles, Conn., 1861 and 1865; Adolph E. Borie, Pa., 1869; George M. Robeson, N. J., 1869; Richard W. Thompson, Ind., 1877; Nathan Goff, Jr., W. Va., 1881; William H. Hunt, La., 1881; William E. Chandler, N. H., 1882; William C. Whitney, N. Y., 1885; Benjamin F. Tracy, N. Y., 1889; Hilary A. Herbert, Ala., 1893.

SECRETARIES OF AGRICULTURE—Norman J. Colman, Mo., 1889; Jeremiah M. Rusk, Wis., 1889; J. Sterling Morton, Neb., 1893.

POSTMASTERS-GENERAL.*—Samuel Osgood, Mass., 1789; Timothy Pickering, Mass., 1791; Joseph Habersham, Ga., 1795, 1797, and 1801; Gideon Granger, Conn., 1801 and 1809; Return J. Meigs, Jr., O., 1814 and 1817; John McLean, O., 1823 and 1825; William T. Barry, Ky., 1829; Amos Kendall, Ky., 1835 and 1837; John M. Niles, Conn., 1840; Francis Granger, N. Y., 1841; Charles A. Wickliffe, Ky., 1841; Cave Johnson, Tenn., 1845; Jacob Collamer, Vt., 1849; Nathan K. Hall, N. Y., 1850; Samuel D. Hubbard, Conn., 1852; James Campbell, Pa., 1853; Aaron V. Brown, Tenn., 1857; Joseph Holt, Ky., 1859; Horatio King, Me., 1861; Montgomery Blair, Md., 1861; William Dennison, O., 1864 and 1865; Alexander W. Randall, Wis., 1866; John A. J. Cresswell, Md., 1869; James W. Marshall, Va., 1874; Marshall Jewell, Conn., 1874; James N. Tyner, Ind., 1876; David McK. Key, Tenn., 1877; Horace Maynard, Tenn., 1880; Thomas L. James, N. Y., 1881; Timothy O. Howe, Wis., 1881; Walter Q. Gresham, Ind., 1883; Frank Hatton, Ia., 1884; William F. Vilas, Wis., 1885; Don M. Dickinson, Mich., 1888; John Wanamaker, Pa., 1889; Wilson S. Bissell, N. Y., 1893.

ATTORNEYS-GENERAL.—Edmund Randolph, Va., 1789; William Bradford, Pa., 1794; Charles Lee, Va., 1795 and 1797; Theophilus Parsons, Mass., 1801; Levi Lincoln, Mass., 1801; Robert Smith, Md., 1805; John Breckinridge, Ky., 1805; Cæsar A. Rodney, Del., 1807 and 1809; William Pinkney, Md., 1811; Richard Rush, Pa., 1814 and 1817; William Wirt, Va., 1817 and 1825; John M'P. Berrien, Ga., 1829; Roger B. Taney, Md., 1831; Benjamin F. Butler, N. Y., 1833 and 1837; Felix Grundy, Tenn., 1838; Henry D. Gilpin, Pa., 1840; John J. Crittenden, Ky., 1841; Hugh S. Legaré, S. C., 1841;

* Postmasters-General were not considered Cabinet officers until 1829.

John Nelson, Md., 1843; John Y. Mason, Va., 1845; Nathan Clifford, Me., 1846; Isaac Toucey, Conn., 1848; Reverdy Johnson, Md., 1849; John J. Crittenden, Ky., 1850; Caleb Cushing, Mass., 1853; Jeremiah S. Black, Pa., 1857; Edwin M. Stanton, O., 1860; Edward Bates, Mo., 1861; Titian J. Coffee (ad in.), Pa., 1863; James Speed, Ky., 1864 and 1865; Henry Stanbery, O., 1866; William M. Evarts, N. Y., 1868; Ebenezer R. Hoar, Mass., 1869; Amos T. Ackerman, Ga., 1870; George H. Williams, Ore., 1871; Edwards Pierrepont, N. Y., 1875; Alphonso Taft, O., 1876; Charles Devens, Mass., 1877; Wayne McVeagh, Pa., 1881; Benjamin H. Brewster, Pa., 1881; Augustus H. Garland, Ark., 1885; William H. H. Miller, Ind., 1889; Richard Olney, Mass., 1893.

JUSTICES OF THE UNITED STATES SUPREME COURT.

Name.	Term.	Born.	Died.	Name.	Term.	Born.	Died.
*John Jay, N. Y.	1789–1795	1745	1829	Peter V. Daniel, Va.	1841–1860	1785	1860
John Rutledge, S. C.	1789–1791	1739	1800	Samuel Nelson, N. Y.	1845–1872	1792	1873
William Cushing, Mass.	1789–1810	1733	1810	Levi Woodbury, N. H.	1845–1851	1789	1851
James Wilson, Pa.	1789–1798	1742	1798	Robert C. Grier, Pa.	1846–1870	1794	1870
John Blair, Va.	1789–1796	1732	1800	Benj. R. Curtis, Mass.	1851–1857	1809	1874
Robert H. Harrison, Md.	1789–1790	1745	1790	John A. Campbell, Ala.	1853–1861	1811	1889
James Iredell, N. C.	1790–1799	1751	1799	Nathan Clifford, Maine	1858–1881	1803	1881
Thomas Johnson, Md.	1791–1793	1732	1819	Noah H. Swayne, Ohio	1861–1881	1804	1884
William Paterson, N. J.	1793–1806	1745	1806	Samuel F. Miller, Iowa	1862–1890	1816	1890
*John Rutledge, S. C.	1795–1795	1739	1800	David Davis, Ill.	1862–1877	1815	1885
Samuel Chase, Md.	1796–1811	1741	1811	Stephen J. Field, Cal.	1863–	1816	
*Oliver Ellsworth, Conn.	1796–1800	1745	1807	*Salmon P. Chase, Ohio	1864–1873	1808	1873
Bush. Washington, Va.	1798–1829	1762	1829	William Strong, Pa.	1870–1880	1808	
Alfred Moore, N. C.	1799–1804	1755	1810	Joseph P. Bradley, N. J.	1870–1892	1813	1892
*John Marshall, Va.	1801–1835	1755	1835	Ward Hunt, N. Y.	1872–1882	1811	1889
William Johnson, S. C.	1804–1834	1771	1834	*Morrison R. Waite, O.	1874–1888	1816	1888
Broc. Livingston, N. Y.	1806–1823	1757	1823	John M. Harlan, Ky.	1877–	1833	
Thomas Todd, Ky.	1807–1826	1765	1826	William B. Woods, Ga.	1880–1887	1824	1887
Joseph Story, Mass.	1811–1845	1779	1845	Stanley Matthews, O.	1881–1889	1824	1889
Gabriel Duval, Md.	1811–1836	1752	1844	Horace Gray, Mass.	1881–	1828	
Smith Thompson, N. Y.	1823–1843	1767	1843	Samuel Blatchford, N.Y.	1882–1893	1820	1893
Robert Trimble, Ky.	1826–1828	1777	1828	Luc. Q. C. Lamar, Miss.	1888–1893	1825	1893
John McLean, Ohio	1829–1861	1785	1861	*Melville W. Fuller, Ill.	1888–	1833	
Henry Baldwin, Pa.	1830–1844	1779	1844	David J. Brewer, Kan.	1889–	1837	
James M. Wayne, Ga.	1835–1867	1790	1867	Henry B. Brown, Mich.	1890–	1836	
*Roger B. Taney, Md.	1836–1864	1777	1864	George Shiras, Jr., Pa.	1892–	1832	
Philip P. Barbour, Va.	1836–1841	1783	1841	How. E. Jackson, Tenn.	1893–	1832	
John Catron, Tenn.	1837–1865	1786	1865	Edw. D. White, La.	1894–	1845	
John McKinley, Ala.	1837–1852	1789	1852				

*Chief Justices.

SIGNERS OF THE DECLARATION OF INDEPENDENCE, IN CONGRESS ASSEMBLED, JULY 4th, 1776.

The following list of members of the Continental Congress, who signed the Declaration of Independence, is here given, for the purpose of showing the places and dates of their birth, and the times of their respective deaths, for convenient reference:

NAMES OF SIGNERS.	BORN AT	DELEGATED FROM	DIED.
Adams, John	Braintree, Mass., 19 Oct., 1735	Massachusetts	4 July, 1826.
Adams, Samuel	Boston, Mass., 27 Sept., 1722	Massachusetts	2 Oct., 1803.
Bartlett, Josiah	Amesbury, Mass., in Nov., 1729	New Hampshire	19 May, 1795.
Braxton, Carter	Newington, Va., 10 Sept., 1736	Virginia	10 Oct., 1797.
Carroll, Chas. of Carrollton	Annapolis, Md., 20 Sept., 1737	Maryland	11 Nov., 1832.
Chase, Samuel	Somerset Co., Md., 17 April, 1741	Maryland	19 June, 1811.
Clark, Abraham	Elizabethtown, N. J., 15 Feb., 1726	New Jersey	— Sept., 1794.
Clymer, George	Philadelphia, Pa., in 1739	Pennsylvania	23 Jan., 1813.
Ellery, William	Newport, R. I., 22 Dec., 1727	R. I. and Prov. Pl.	15 Feb., 1820.
Floyd, William	Suffolk Co., N. Y., 17 Dec., 1734	New York	4 Aug., 1821.
Franklin, Benjamin	Boston, Mass., 17 Jan., 1706	Pennsylvania	17 April, 1790.
Gerry, Elbridge	Marblehead, Mass., 1 July, 1744	Massachusetts	23 Nov., 1814.
Gwinnett, Button	England, in 1732	Georgia	27 May, 1777.
Hall, Lyman	Connecticut, in 1731	Georgia	— Feb., 1790.
Hancock, John	Braintree, Mass., in 1737	Massachusetts	8 Oct., 1793.
Harrison, Benjamin	Berkley, Va., ——	Virginia	— April, 1791.
Hart, John	Hopewell, N. J., in 1715	New Jersey	—— 1780.
Heyward, Thomas, Jr	St. Lukes, S. C., in 1746	South Carolina	— March, 1809.
Hewes, Joseph	Kingston, N. J., in 1730	North Carolina	10 Oct., 1779.
Hooper, William	Boston, Mass., 17 June, 1742	North Carolina	— Oct., 1790.
Hopkins, Stephen	Scituate, Mass., 7 March, 1707	R. I. and Prov. Pl.	13 July, 1785.
Huntington, Samuel	Windham, Conn., 3 July, 1732	Connecticut	5 Jan., 1796.
Hopkinson, Francis	Philadelphia, Pa., in 1737	New Jersey	9 May, 1790.
Jefferson, Thomas	Shadwell, Va., 13 April, 1743	Virginia	4 July, 1826.
Lee, Richard Henry	Stratford, Va., 20 Jan., 1732	Virginia	19 June, 1794.
Lee, Francis Lightfoot	Stratford, Va., 14 Oct., 1734	Virginia	— April, 1797.
Lewis, Francis F.	Landaff, Wales, in March, 1713	New York	30 Dec., 1803.
Livingston, Philip	Albany, N. Y., 15 Jan., 1716	New York	12 June, 1778.
Lynch, Thomas, Jr	St. George's, S. C., 5 Aug., 1749	South Carolina	Lost at sea, 1779.
McKean, Thomas	Chester Co., Pa., 19 March, 1734	Delaware	24 June, 1817.
Middleton, Arthur	Middleton Place, S. C., in 1743	South Carolina	1 Jan., 1787.
Morris, Lewis	Morrisania, N. Y., in 1726	New York	22 Jan., 1798.
Morris, Robert	Lancashire, Eng., Jan., 1733-4	Pennsylvania	8 May, 1806.
Morton, John	Ridley, Pa., in 1724	Pennsylvania	— April, 1777.
Nelson, Thomas, Jr	York, Va., 26 Dec., 1738	Virginia	4 Jan., 1789.
Paca, William	Wye-Hill, Md., 31 Oct., 1740	Maryland	——, 1799.
Paine, Robert Treat	Boston, Mass., in 1731	Massachusetts	11 May, 1804.
Penn, John	Caroline Co., Va., 17 May, 1741	North Carolina	26 Oct., 1829.
Read, George	Cecil Co., Md., in 1734	Delaware	——, 1798.
Rodney, Cæsar	Dover, Del., in 1730	Delaware	——, 1783.
Ross, George	New Castle, Del., in 1730	Pennsylvania	— July, 1779.
Rush, Benjamin, M. D.	Byberry, Pa., 24 Dec., 1745	Pennsylvania	19 April, 1813.
Rutledge, Edward	Charleston, S. C., in Nov., 1749	South Carolina	23 Jan., 1800.
Sherman, Roger	Newton, Mass., 19 April, 1721	Connecticut	23 July, 1793.
Smith, James	——, Ireland, ——	Pennsylvania	11 July, 1806.
Stockton, Richard	Princeton, N. J., 1 Oct., 1730	New Jersey	28 Feb., 1781.
Stone, Thomas	Charles Co., Md., in 1742	Maryland	5 Oct., 1787.
Taylor, George	——, Ireland, in 1716	Pennsylvania	23 Feb., 1781.
Thornton, Matthew	——, Ireland, in 1714	New Hampshire	24 June, 1803.
Walton, George	Frederick Co., Va., in 1740	Georgia	2 Feb., 1804.
Whipple, William	Kittery, Maine, in 1730	New Hampshire	28 Nov., 1785.
Williams, William	Lebanon, Conn., 8 April, 1731	Connecticut	2 Aug., 1811.
Wilson, James	Scotland, about 1742	Pennsylvania	28 Aug., 1798.
Witherspoon, John	Yester, Scotland, 5 Feb., 1722	New Jersey	15 Nov., 1794.
Wolcott, Oliver	Windsor, Conn., 26 Nov., 1726	Connecticut	1 Dec., 1797.
Wythe, George	Elizabeth City Co., Va., in 1726	Virginia	8 June, 1806.

PRESIDENTS OF THE CONTINENTAL CONGRESS AND OF THE CONGRESS OF THE CONFEDERATION, 1774-1788.

Peyton Randolph, Va., September 5th, 1774; Henry Middleton, S. C., October 22d, 1774; Peyton Randolph, Va., May 10th, 1775; John Hancock, Mass., May 24th, 1775; Henry Laurens, S. C., November 1st, 1777; John Jay, N. Y., December 10th, 1778; Samuel Huntington, Conn., September 28th, 1779; Thomas McKean, Del., July 10th, 1781; John Hanson, Md., November 5th, 1781; Elias Boudinot, N. J., November 4th, 1782; Thomas Mifflin, Pa., November 3d, 1783; Richard H. Lee, Va., November 30th, 1784; Nathaniel Gorham, Mass., June 6th, 1786; Arthur St. Clair, Pa., February 2d, 1787; Cyrus Griffin, Va., January 22d, 1788.

NATURALIZATION LAWS OF THE UNITED STATES.

The conditions under and the manner in which an alien may be admitted to become a citizen of the United States are prescribed by Sections 2, 165-74 of the Revised Statutes of the United States.

DECLARATION OF INTENTIONS.

The alien must declare upon oath before a Circuit or District Court of the United States, or a District or Supreme Court of the Territories, or a Court of Record of any of the States having common law jurisdiction and a seal and clerk, two years at least prior to his admission; that it is, *bona fide*, his intention to become a citizen of the United States, and to renounce forever all allegiance and fidelity to any foreign prince or State, and particularly to the one of which he may be at the time a citizen or subject.

OATH ON APPLICATION FOR ADMISSION.

He must at the time of his application to be admitted declare on oath, before some one of the courts above specified, "that he will support the Constitution of the United States, and that he absolutely and entirely renounces and abjures all allegiance and fidelity to every foreign prince, potentate, State, or sovereignty, and particularly, by name, to the prince, potentate, State, or sovereignty of which he was before a citizen or subject," which proceedings must be recorded by the clerk of the court.

CONDITIONS FOR CITIZENSHIP.

If it shall appear to the satisfaction of the court to which the alien has applied, that he has made a declaration to become a citizen two years before applying for final papers, and has resided continuously within the United States for at least five years, and within the State or Territory where such court is at the time held one year at least; and that during that time "he has behaved as a man of good moral character, attached to the principles of the Constitution of the United States, and well disposed to the good order and happiness of the same," he will be admitted to citizenship.

TITLES OF NOBILITY.

If the applicant has borne any hereditary title or order of nobility he must make an express renunciation of the same at the time of his application.

SOLDIERS.

Any alien of the age of twenty-one years and upward who has been in the armies of the United States, and has been honorably discharged therefrom, may become a citizen on his petition, without any previous declaration of intention, provided that he has resided in the United States at least one year previous to his application, and is of good moral character. (It is judicially decided that residence of one year in a particular State is not requisite).

MINORS.

Any alien under the age of twenty-one years who has resided in the United States three years next preceding his arrival at that age, and who has continued to reside therein to the time he may make application to be admitted a citizen thereof, may, after he arrives at the age of twenty-one years, and after he has resided five years within the United States, including the three years of his minority, be admitted a citizen; but he must make a declaration on oath, and prove to the satisfaction of the court, that for two years next preceding it has been his *bona fide* intention to become a citizen.

CHILDREN OF NATURALIZED CITIZENS.

The children of persons who have been duly naturalized, being under the age of twenty-one years at the time of the naturalization of their parents, shall, if dwelling in the United States, be considered as citizens thereof.

CITIZENS' CHILDREN WHO ARE BORN ABROAD.

The children of persons who now are or have been citizens of the United States are, though born out of the limits and jurisdiction of the United States, considered as citizens thereof.

CHINESE.

The naturalization of Chinamen is expressly prohibited by Section 14, Chapter 126, Laws of 1882.

PROTECTION ABROAD TO NATURALIZED CITIZENS.

Section 2000 of the Revised Statutes of the United States declares that "all naturalized citizens of the United States while in foreign countries are entitled to and shall receive from this Government the same protection of person and property which is accorded to native-born citizens."

THE RIGHT OF SUFFRAGE.

The right to vote comes from the State, and is a State gift. Naturalization is a Federal right and is a gift of the Union, not of any one State. In nearly one-half of the Union (aliens who have declared intentions) vote and have the right to vote equally with naturalized or native-born citizens. In the other half only actual citizens may vote. (See Table of Qualifications for voting in each State, on another page.) The Federal naturalization laws apply to the whole Union alike, and provide that no alien may be naturalized until after five years' residence. Even after five years' residence and due naturalization he is not entitled to vote unless the laws of the State confer the privilege upon him, and he may vote in several States six months after landing, if he has declared his intention, under United States law, to become a citizen.

CONSTITUTION

OF THE

UNITED STATES OF AMERICA.*

We, the people of the United States, in order to form a more perfect union, establish justice, insure domestic tranquillity, provide for the common defense, promote the general welfare, and secure the blessings of liberty to ourselves and our posterity, do ordain and establish this Constitution for the United States of America. [See 1 Wheat., 324; 4 Wheat., 405.]

ARTICLE I.
Of the Legislature.

SECTION 1. All legislative powers herein granted shall be vested in a Congress of the United States, which shall consist of a Senate and House of Representatives.

Of the House of Representatives.

SECT. II. 1. The House of Representatives shall be composed of members chosen every second year by the people of the several States; and the electors in each State shall have the qualifications requisite for electors of the most numerous branch of the state Legislature.

Qualifications of Members.

2. No person shall be a Representative who shall not have attained the age of twenty five years, and have been seven years a citizen of the United States, and who shall not, when elected, be an inhabitant of that state in which he shall have been elected.

Apportionment of Representatives and Direct Taxes—Census.

3. Representatives and direct taxes shall be apportioned among the several States, which may be included within this Union, according to the respective numbers, which shall be determined by adding to the whole number of free persons, including those bound to service for a number of years, and excluding Indians not taxed, three-fifths of all other persons. The actual enumeration shall be made within three years after the first meeting of the Congress of the United States, and within every subsequent term of ten years, in such manner as they shall by law direct. The number of Representatives shall not exceed one for every thirty thousand, but each State shall have at least one Representative; and until such enumeration shall be made, the State of New Hampshire shall be entitled to choose three, Massachusetts eight, Rhode Island and Providence Plantations one, Connecticut five, New York six, New Jersey four, Pennsylvania eight, Delaware one, Maryland six, Virginia ten, North Carolina five, South Carolina five, and Georgia three. [See 5 Wheat., 317.]

Vacancies.

4. When vacancies happen in the representation from any State, the executive authority thereof shall issue writs of election to fill such vacancies.

Of their Officers—Impeachment.

5. The House of Representatives shall choose their Speaker and other officers, and shall have the sole power of impeachment.

Of the Senate.

SECT. III. 1. The Senate of the United States shall be composed of two Senators from each state, chosen by the Legislature thereof, for six years, and each Senator shall have one vote. [See 6 Wheat., 299.]

Their Classes.

2. Immediately after they shall be assembled, in consequence of the first election, they shall be divided as equally as may be into three classes. The seats of the Senators of the first class shall be vacated at the expiration of the second year; of the second class, at the expiration of the fourth year; and of the third class, at the expiration of the sixth year, so that one-third may be chosen every second year. And if vacancies happen by resignation, or other-

---

* This Constitution went into operation on the first Wednesday in March, 1789. [5 Wheat., 420.]

wise, during the recess of the Legislature of any State, the executive thereof may make temporary appointments until the next meeting of the Legislature, which shall then fill such vacancies.

Qualifications of the Senators.

3. No person shall be a Senator who shall not have attained the age of thirty years, and been nine years a citizen of the United States, and who shall not, when elected, be an inhabitant of that State for which he shall be chosen.

Of the Vice-President.

4. The Vice-President of the United States shall be President of the Senate, but shall have no vote unless they be equally divided.

Of the Officers of the Senate.

5. The Senate shall choose their other officers, and also a President *pro tempore*, in the absence of the Vice-President, or when he shall exercise the office of President of the United States.

Of Impeachment.

6. The Senate shall have the sole power to try all impeachments. When sitting for that purpose they shall be on oath or affirmation. When the President of the United States is tried, the Chief Justice shall preside. And no person shall be convicted without the concurrence of two-thirds of the members present.

7. Judgment, in case of impeachment, shall not extend further than to removal from office, and disqualification to hold and enjoy any office of honor, trust or profit, under the United States; but the party convicted shall, nevertheless, be liable and subject to indictment, trial, judgment and punishment according to law.

Manner of Electing Members of Congress.

SECT. IV. 1. The times, places and manner of holding elections for Senators and Representatives shall be prescribed by each State, by the Legislature thereof; but the Congress may, at any time, by law, make or alter such regulations, except as to the place of choosing Senators.

Of the Meetings of Congress.

2. Congress shall assemble at least once in every year and such meetings shall be on the first Monday in December, unless they shall by law appoint a different day.

Powers of Each House.

SECT. V. 1. Each House shall be the judge of the elections, returns and qualifications of its own members; and a majority of each shall constitute a quorum to do business: but a smaller number may adjourn from day to day, and may be authorized to compel the attendance of the absent members, in such manner and under such penalties as each House may provide.

Expulsion.

2. Each House may determine the rules of its proceedings, punish its members for disorderly behavior, and with the concurrence of two-thirds, expel a member. [*See* 1 *Hall's Am. Law Journal,* 459.]

Journals and Yeas and Nays.

3. Each House shall keep a journal of its proceedings, and from time to time publish the same, excepting such parts as may in their judgment require secrecy; and the yeas and nays of members of either House, on any question, shall, at the desire of one-fifth of those present, be entered on the journal.

Of Adjournment.

4. Neither House, during the session of Congress, shall, without the consent of the other, adjourn for more than three days, nor to any other place than to that in which the two Houses shall be sitting.

Compensation, Privileges and Incapacities of Members.

SECT. VI. The Senators and Representatives shall receive a compensation for their services, to be ascertained by law, and paid out of the treasury of the United States. They shall, in all cases, except treason, felony and breach of the peace, be privileged from arrest during their attendance at the session of their respective Houses, and in going to and returning from the same; and for any speech or debate in the House they shall not be questioned in any other place.

Exclusion from Office.

2. No Senator or Representative shall, during the time for which he was elected, be appointed to any civil office under the authority of the United States, which shall have been created, or the emoluments whereof shall have been increased, during such time; and no person holding any office under the United States shall be a member of either House during his continuance in office.

Revenue Bills.

SECT. VII 1. All bills for raising revenue shall originate in the House of Representatives; but the Senate may propose or concur with amendments, as on other bills.

Manner of Passing Bills, Etc.

2. Every bill which shall have passed the House of Representatives and the Senate shall, before it becomes a law, be presented to the President of the United States; if he approve, he shall sign it; but if not, he shall return it, with his objections, to the House in which it shall have originated, who shall enter the objections at large on their journal, and proceed to reconsider it. If, after such reconsideration, two thirds of that House shall agree to pass the bill, it shall be sent, together with the objections, to the other House, by which it shall likewise be reconsidered, and if approved by two thirds of that House, it shall become a law. But in all cases the votes of both Houses shall be determined by yeas and nays, and the names of the persons voting for and against the bill shall be entered on the journal of each House respectively. If any bill shall not be returned by the President within ten days (Sundays excepted) after it shall have been presented to him, the same shall be a law, in like manner as if he had signed it, unless Congress, by their adjournment, prevent its return, in which case it shall not be a law.

Orders, Resolutions and Votes.

3. Every order, resolution or vote, to which the concurrence of the Senate and House of Representatives may be necessary (except on the question of adjournment) shall be presented to the President of the United States, and before the same shall take effect, shall be approved by him, or, being disapproved by him, shall be repassed by two thirds of the Senate and House of Representatives, according to the rules and limitations prescribed in the case of bills.

General Powers of Congress.

SECT. VIII. Congress shall have power:

1. To lay and collect taxes, duties, imposts and excises, to pay the debts and provide for the common defense and general welfare of the United States but all duties, imposts and excises shall be uniform throughout the United States [See 5 Wheaton, 317.]
2. To borrow money on the credit of the United States.
3. To regulate commerce with foreign nations, and among the several States, and with the Indian tribes. [See 9 Wheaton, 1-2; Hall's Am. L. Jour., 255, 272; Johns., 488.]
4. To establish a uniform rule of naturalization, and uniform laws on the subject of bankruptcies, throughout the United States. [See 4 Wheaton, 122, 193, 209; 2 Wheaton, 396; 20 Johns., 251.]
5. To coin money, regulate the value thereof, and of foreign coins, and fix the standard of weights and measures.
6. To provide for the punishment of counterfeiting the securities and current coin of the United States.
7. To establish post offices and post roads.
8. To promote the progress of science and useful arts by securing, for limited times, to authors and inventors, the exclusive right to their respective writings and discoveries. [See Wheaton's App., n 2, p. 13; 7 Wheaton, 356.]
9. To constitute tribunals inferior to the Supreme Court.
10. To define and punish piracies and felonies committed on the high seas, and offences against the law of nations. [5 Wheaton, 76, 153, 184; 3 Wheaton, 336.]
11. To declare war, grant letters of marque and reprisal, and make rules concerning captures on land and waters. [8 Cranch, 110, 154.]
12. To raise and support armies; but no appropriation of money to that use shall be for a longer period than two years.
13. To provide and maintain a navy. [See 1 Mason, 79, 81; 4 Binn., 487.]
14. To make rules for the government and regulation of the land and naval forces.
15. To provide for calling forth the militia to execute the laws of the Union, suppress insurrection and repel invasion. [See 5 Wheaton, 1; 19 Johns., 7.]

16. To provide for organizing, arming and disciplining the militia, and for governing such part of them as may be employed in the service of the United States, reserving to the States, respectively, the appointment of officers and the authority of training the militia according to the discipline prescribed by Congress. [4 S. & R., 169; 5 Wheaton, 1; 19 Johns., 2.]

17. To exercise exclusive legislation, in all cases whatsoever, over such district (not exceeding ten miles square) as may, by cession of particular States and the acceptance of Congress, become the seat of government of the United States; and to exercise like authority over all places purchased by the authority of the Legislature of the State in which the same shall be, for the erection of forts, magazines, arsenals, dock-yards and other needful buildings: and—[See 2 Mason, 60; 5 Wheaton, 317, 324; 6 Wheaton 440; Jour. of Juris., 47, 156; 17 Johns., 225.]

18. To make all laws which shall be necessary and proper for carrying into execution the foregoing powers, and all other powers vested by this Constitution in the government of the United States, or in any department or officer thereof. [4 Wheaton, 413; 6 Wheaton, 264.]

Limitations of the Powers of Congress.

SECT. IX. 1. The migration or importation of such persons as any of the States now existing shall think proper to admit shall not be prohibited by Congress, prior to the year one thousand eight hundred and eight; but a tax or duty may be imposed on such importation, not exceeding ten dollars for each person.

2. The privileges of the writ of *habeas corpus* shall not be suspended unless, when in case of rebellion or invasion, the public safety may require it.

3. No bill of attainder or *ex post facto* law shall be passed. [See 3 Dallas, 386, 396; 6 Binn., 271.]

4. No capitation or other direct tax shall be laid, unless in proportion to the census or enumeration hereinbefore directed to be taken. [See 5 Wheat., 317; 3 Dall., 171.]

5. No tax or duty shall be laid on articles exported from any State. No preference shall be given, by any regulation of commerce or revenue, to the ports of one State over those of another; nor shall vessels bound to or from one State be obliged to enter, clear, or pay duties in another.

6. No money shall be drawn from the treasury but in consequence of appropriations made by law; and a regular statement of any account of receipts and expenditures of all public money shall be published from time to time.

7. No title of nobility shall be granted by the United States; and no person holding any office of profit or trust under them shall, without the consent of Congress, accept of any present, emolument, office, or title of any kind whatever, from any king, prince or foreign State.

Limitations of the Powers of the Individual States.

SECT. X. 1. No State shall enter into any treaty, alliance, or confederation; grant letters of marque or reprisal; coin money; emit bills of credit; make anything but gold and silver coin a tender in payment of debts; pass any bill of attainder, *ex post facto* law, or law impairing the obligation of contracts; or grant any title of nobility. [See 8 Wheat., 84, 92, 256, n. 464; 5 Wheat., 420; 4 Wheat., 519, 1,209; 6 Wheat., 131; 16 Johns., 233; 13 Mass., 16; 1 Johns. Ch. R., 202; 2 Conn., 696.]

2. No State shall, without the consent of Congress, lay any imposts or duties on imports or exports, except what may be absolutely necessary for executing its inspection laws; and the net produce of all duties and imposts laid by any State on imports and exports, shall be for the use of the Treasury of the United States; and all such laws shall be subject to the revision and control of Congress. No State shall, without the consent of Congress, lay any duty on tonnage, keep troops or ships of war in time of peace, enter into any agreement or compact with another State, or with a foreign power, or engage in war, unless actually invaded, or in such imminent danger as will not admit of delay.

ARTICLE II.
OF THE PRESIDENT.
Of the Executive Power.

SECTION I. 1. The Executive power shall be vested in a President of the United States of America. He shall hold his office during the term of four years, and together with the Vice-President, chosen for the same term, be elected as follows:

Manner of Election.

2. Each State shall appoint, in such manner as the Legislature thereof may direct, a

number of electors equal to the whole number of Senators and Representatives to which the State may be entitled in Congress; but no Senator or Representative, or person holding an office of trust or profit under the United States, shall be appointed an elector.

Altered—See Amendments, Article XII.

3. The electors shall meet in their respective States, and vote by ballot, for two persons, of whom one, at least, shall not be an inhabitant of the same State with themselves. And they shall make a list of all the persons voted for, and of the number of votes for each; which list they shall sign and certify, and transmit, sealed, to the seat of government of the United States, directed to the President of the Senate. The President of the Senate shall, in the presence of the Senate and House of Representatives, open all the certificates, and the votes shall then be counted. The person having the greatest number of votes shall be the President, if such number be a majority of the whole number of electors appointed; and if there be more than one who have such majority, and have an equal number of votes, then the House of Representatives shall immediately choose by ballot, one of them for President; and if no person have a majority, then, from the five highest on the list, the said House shall in like manner choose the President. But in choosing the President, the votes shall be taken by States, the representation from each State having one vote; a quorum for this purpose shall consist of a member or members from two-thirds of the states, and a majority of all the states shall be necessary to a choice. In every case, after the choice of the President, the person having the greatest number of the votes of the electors, shall be the Vice-President. But if there should remain two or more who have equal votes, the Senate shall choose from them, by ballot, the Vice-President. (*This clause is altogether altered and supplied by the XIIth amendment.*)

4. Congress may determine the time of choosing the electors, and the day on which they shall give their votes, which day shall be the same throughout the United States.

Who May Be Elected President.

5. No person, except a natural born citizen, or a citizen of the United States at the time of the adoption of this Constitution, shall be eligible to the office of President; neither shall any person be eligible to that office who shall not have attained to the age of thirty-five years, and been fourteen years a resident within the United States. [*See also as to the Vice-President. See XII amendment, post.*]

In Case of Removal, etc., of the President, His Power Devolves Upon the Vice-President, etc.

6. In case of the removal of the President from office, or of his death, resignation or inability to discharge the powers and duties of the said office, the same shall devolve on the Vice-President; and Congress may, by law provide for the case of removal, death, resignation, or inability, both of the President and Vice-President, declaring what officer shall then act as President, and such officer shall act accordingly, until the disability be removed, or a President shall be elected.

President's Compensation.

7. The President shall, at stated times, receive for his services a compensation which shall neither be increased nor diminished during the period for which he shall have been elected; and he shall not receive, within that period, any other emolument from the United States or any of them.

8. Before he enter on the execution of his office, he shall take the following oath or affirmation.

His Oath.

"I do solemnly swear (or affirm) that I will faithfully execute the office of President of the United States, and will, to the best of my ability, preserve, protect and defend the Constitution of the United States."

Power and Duties of the President.

SECT. II. 1. The President shall be Commander-in-Chief of the Army and Navy of the United States, and of the militia of the several States, when called into the actual service of the United States; he may require the opinion, in writing, of the principal officer in each of the executive departments, upon any subject relating to the duties of their respective offices, and he shall have power to grant reprieves and pardons, for offences against the United States, except in cases of impeachment.

Of Making Treaties.

2. He shall have power, by and with the advice and consent of the Senate, to make treaties, provided two-thirds of the Senate present concur; and he shall nominate, and by and

with the advice and consent of the Senate, shall appoint Ambassadors, and other public Ministers, and Consuls, Judges of the Supreme Court, and all other officers of the United States, whose appointments are not herein otherwise provided for, and which shall be established by law. But Congress may, by law, vest the appointment of such inferior offices as they think proper, in the President alone, in the courts of law, or in the heads of departments.

Power of Appointment.

3. The President shall have power to fill up all vacancies that may happen during the recess of the Senate, by granting commissions which shall expire at the end of their next session.

Further Powers and Duties.

SECT. III. He shall, from time to time, give to Congress information of the state of the Union, and recommend to their consideration such measures as he shall judge necessary and expedient; he may, on extraordinary occasions, convene both Houses, or either of them; and in case of disagreement between them, with respect to the time of adjournment, he may adjourn them to such a time as he shall think proper; he shall receive ambassadors and other public ministers; he shall take care that the laws be faithfully executed, and shall commission all the officers of the United States. [See 1 Cranch, 137.]

Of Impeachment.

SECT. IV. The President, Vice-President, and all civil officers of the United States, shall be removed from office on impeachment for, and conviction of, treason, bribery, or other high crimes and misdemeanors.

ARTICLE III.
OF THE JUDICIARY.
Of the Judicial Power—Concerning the Judges.

SECTION I. The judicial power of the United States shall be vested in one Supreme Court, and in such inferior courts as Congress may, from time to time, ordain and establish. The judges, both of the Supreme and inferior courts, shall hold their offices during good behavior, and shall, at stated times, receive for their services a compensation, which shall not be diminished during their continuance in office. [See 7 Johns. Ch. R., 305.]

Extent of the Judicial Power—This Clause Altered Postea—See Amendments, Art. XI.

SECT. II. The judicial power shall extend to all cases in law and equity, arising under this Constitution, the laws of the United States, and treaties made, or which shall be made, under their authority; to all cases affecting ambassadors, or other public ministers and consuls; to all cases of admiralty and maritime jurisdiction; to controversies to which the United States shall be a party; to controversies between two or more States; between a State and citizens of another State; between citizens of different States; between citizens of the same State, claiming lands under grants of different States, and between a State, or the citizens thereof and foreign States, citizens or subjects. [See 2 Dall., 297; 6 Wheat., 264, 405; 2 Mason, 472; 9 Wheat., 819.]

Of Original and Appellate Jurisdiction of the Supreme Court.

2. In all cases affecting ambassadors, other public ministers and consuls, and those in which a State shall be a party, the Supreme Court shall have original jurisdiction. In all other cases before mentioned, the Supreme Court shall have appellate jurisdiction, both as to law and fact, with such exceptions, and under such regulations, as Congress shall make. [5 Sergt. & R., 545; 1 Binn., 138.]

Of Trials for Crimes.

3. The trial of all crimes, except in cases of impeachment, shall be by jury; and such trial shall be held in the state where the said crime shall have been committed; but when not committed within any state, the trial shall be at such place or places as Congress may, by law, have directed.

Of Treason.

SECT. III. 1. Treason against the United States shall consist only in levying war against them, or in adhering to their enemies, giving them aid and comfort. No person shall be convicted of treason, unless on the testimony of two witnesses to the same overt act, or on confession in open court. [4 Cranch App, Note B., 470, 136.]

2. Congress shall have power to declare the punishment of treason, but no attainder of treason shall work corruption of blood, or forfeiture, except during the life of the person attainted

ARTICLE IV.
OF STATE RECORDS.

SECT. I. Full faith and credit shall be given, in each state, to the public acts, records, and judicial proceedings of every other State. And Congress may, by general laws, prescribe the manner in which such acts, records and proceedings shall be proved, and the effect thereof. [See 7 Cranch, 481; 3 Wheat., 234; 1 Peters, 81, 354; 6 Wheat., 129.]

OF CITIZENSHIP.

SECT. II. 1. The citizens of each State shall be entitled to all privileges and immunities of citizens in the several States.* [See 4 Johns. Ch. R., 430.]

OF FUGITIVES FROM JUSTICE.

2. A person charged in any State for treason, felony, or other crime, who shall flee from justice and be found in another State, shall, on demand of the executive authority of the State from which he fled, be delivered up, to be removed to the State having jurisdiction of the crime. [See 4 Johns. Ch. R., 106.]

OF PERSONS HELD TO SERVICE.

3. No person held to service or labor in one State, under the laws thereof, escaping into another, shall, in consequence of any law or regulation therein, be discharged from such service or labor, but shall be delivered up, on the claim of the party to whom such service or labor may be due. [See 2 S. & R., 306; 3 S. & R., 4; 5 S. & R., 62.]

OF THE ADMISSION OF NEW STATES.

SECT. III. 1. New States may be admitted by Congress into this Union; but no new State shall be formed or erected within the jurisdiction of any other State, nor any State be formed by the junction of two or more States or parts of States, without the consent of the Legislatures of the states concerned, as well as of Congress.

OF TERRITORIES.

2. Congress shall have power to dispose of, and make all needful rules and regulations respecting the territory or other property belonging to the United States; and nothing in this Constitution shall be so construed as to prejudice any claims of the United States, or any particular State.

OF THE STATE FORMS OF GOVERNMENT.
Republican Form of Government Guarantied to the Several States.

SECT. IV. The United States shall guarantee to every State in this Union a republican form of government, and shall protect each of them against invasion; and on application of the Legislature, or of the executive (when the Legislature cannot be convened), against domestic violence.

ARTICLE V.
OF AMENDMENTS TO THE CONSTITUTION.

Congress, whenever two-thirds of both Houses shall deem it necessary, shall propose amendments to this Constitution, or on the application of the Legislatures of two-thirds of the several states, shall call a Convention for proposing amendments, which in either case shall be valid, to all intents and purposes, as part of this Constitution, when ratified by the Legislatures of three-fourths of the several States, or by Conventions in three-fourths thereof, as the one or the other mode of ratification may be proposed by Congress: *Provided*, That no amendment which may be made prior to the year eighteen hundred and eight, shall in any manner affect the first and fourth clauses in the ninth section of the first article; and that no State, without its consent, shall be deprived of its equal suffrage in the Senate.

ARTICLE VI.
OF PUBLIC DEBT.

SECTION I. All debts contracted, and engagements entered into, before the adoption of this Constitution, shall be as valid against the United States under this Constitution as under the confederation.

OF THE SUPREME LAW OF THE LAND.

SECT. II. This Constitution, and the laws of the United States which shall be made in pursuance thereof, and all treaties made, or which shall be made, under the authority of the United States, shall be the supreme law of the land; and the judges in every state shall be bound thereby, anything in the Constitution or laws of any state to the contrary notwithstanding.

---

* Free negroes and mulattoes are not citizens within the meaning of the Constitution. [1 Litt., 335.]

OF THE CONSTITUTIONAL OATH AND RELIGIOUS TEST.

SECT. III. The Senators and Representatives before mentioned, and the members of the several State Legislatures, and all executive and judicial officers, both of the United States and of the several States, shall be bound by oath or affirmation, to support this Constitution; but no religious test shall ever be required as a qualification to any office of public trust under the United States.

ARTICLE VII.
RATIFICATION OF THE CONSTITUTION.

The ratification of the Conventions of nine States shall be sufficient for the establishment of this Constitution, between the States so ratifying the same. [5 *Wheat.*, 422.]

DONE in the Convention, by the unanimous consent of the States present, the seventeenth day of September, in the year of our Lord one thousand seven hundred and eighty-seven, and of the Independence of the United States of America the twelfth.

IN WITNESS WHEREOF, we have hereunto subscribed our names.

GEO. WASHINGTON, *President,*
And Deputy from Virginia.

NEW HAMPSHIRE.
JOHN LANGDON,
NICHOLAS GILMAN.

MASSACHUSETTS.
NATHANIEL GORMAN,
RUFUS KING.

CONNECTICUT.
WILLIAM SAMUEL JOHNSON,
RODGER SHERMAN.

PENNSYLVANIA.
BENJAMIN FRANKLIN,
THOMAS MIFFLIN,
ROBERT MORRIS,
GEORGE CLYMER,
THOMAS FITZSIMONS,
JARED INGERSOLL,
JAMES WILSON,
GOUV. MORRIS.

VIRGINIA.
JOHN BLAIR,
JAMES MADISON, JUN.

MARYLAND.
DANIEL OF ST. THOMAS JENIFER,
JAMES MCHENRY,
DANIEL CARROLL.

NEW JERSEY.
WILLIAM LIVINGSTON,
DAVID BREARLY,
WILLIAM PATTERSON,
JONATHAN DAYTON.

NEW YORK.
ALEXANDER HAMILTON.

DELAWARE.
GEORGE READ,
GUNNING BEDFORD, JUN.,
JOHN DICKINSON,
RICHARD BASSETT,
JACOB BROOM.

SOUTH CAROLINA.
JOHN RUTLEDGE,
CHARLES COTESWORTH PINCKNEY,
CHARLES PINCKNEY,
PIERCE BUTLER.

NORTH CAROLINA.
WILLIAM BLOUNT,
RICHARD DOBBS SPAIGHT,
HUGH WILLIAMSON.

GEORGIA.
WILLIAM BALDWIN,
ABRAHAM FEW.

Attest: WILLIAM JACKSON, *Secretary.*

AMENDMENTS.

The following articles proposed by Congress, in addition to and amendments of the Constitution of the United States, having been ratified by the Legislatures of three-fourths of the States, are become a part of the Constitution.

ARTICLE I.
First Congress, First Session, March 5th, 1789.
Of the Right of Conscience, Freedom of the Press, etc.

Congress shall make no law respecting the establishment of religion, or prohibiting the free exercise thereof; or abridging the freedom of speech, or of the press; or the right of the people peaceably to assemble, and to petition the government for a redress of grievances. [See 3 Yeates, 520.]

ARTICLE II.
Of the Right to Bear Arms.

A well regulated militia being necessary to the security of a free State, the right of the people to keep and bear arms shall not be infringed.

ARTICLE III.
Of Quartering Troops.

No soldier shall, in time of peace, be quartered in any house without the consent of the owner; nor in time of war, but in a manner to be prescribed by law.

ARTICLE IV.
Of the Right to be Secure from Search, etc.

The right of the people to be secure in their persons, houses, papers and effects, against unreasonable searches and seizures, shall not be violated; and no warrant shall issue but upon probable cause, supported by oath or affirmation, and particularly describing the place to be searched, and the persons or things to be seized. [3 Cranch., 448, 453; 6 Binn., 316.]

ARTICLE V.
Of Indictments, Punishments, etc.

No person shall be held to answer for a capital, or otherwise infamous crime, unless on a presentment or indictment of a grand jury, except in cases arising in the land or naval forces, or in the militia, when in actual service in time of war or public danger; nor shall any person be subject, for the same offense, to be twice put in jeopardy of life or limb; nor shall be compelled in any criminal case to be a witness against himself; nor be deprived of life, liberty, or property, without due process of law, nor shall private property be taken for public use without just compensation. [18 Johns., 187, 201; 3 Yeates, 362; 6 Binn., 500; 2 Dall., 312; 4 Johns. Ch. R., 164; 1 S. & R., 382; 6 Cowen, 530; 8 Wend., 85; 7 Pet., 243.]

ARTICLE VI.
Of Trial in Criminal Cases and the Rights of a Defendant.

In all criminal prosecutions, the accused shall enjoy the right to a speedy and public trial, by an impartial jury of the State and district wherein the crime shall have been committed, which district shall have been previously ascertained by law, and to be informed of the nature and cause of the accusation; to be confronted with the witnesses against him; to have compulsory process for obtaining witnesses in his favor, and to have the assistance of counsel for his defense.

ARTICLE VII.
Of Trials in Civil Cases.

In suits at common law, where the value in controversy shall exceed twenty dollars, the right of trial by jury shall be preserved; and no fact tried by a jury shall be otherwise reexamined in any court of the United States, than according to the rules of the common law. [See 8 Wheat., 85, 674.]

ARTICLE VIII.
Of Bail and Fines.

Excessive bail shall not be required, nor excessive fines imposed, nor cruel and unusual punishments inflicted. [*See 20 Johns.*, 457; *3 Cowen*, 686.]

ARTICLE IX.
Of Rights Reserved.

The enumeration in the Constitution, of certain rights, shall not be construed to deny or disparage others, retained by the people.

ARTICLE X.
Of Powers Reserved to the States.

The powers not delegated to the United States by the Constitution, nor prohibited by it to the States, are reserved to the States respectively, or to the people. [*See 1 Wheat.*, 325.]

ARTICLE XI.
THIRD CONGRESS, SECOND SESSION, DECEMBER 2D, 1793.
Of the Judicial Power—See Art. 3, Sec. 2.

The judicial power of the United States shall not be construed to extend to any suit, in law or equity, commenced or prosecuted against one of the United States, by citizens of another State, or by citizens or subjects of any foreign State. [*See 6 Wheat.*, 405; *1 Pet.*, 110; *7 Pet.*, 627.]

ARTICLE XII.
EIGHTH CONGRESS, FIRST SESSION, OCTOBER 17, 1803.
Manner of Electing the President and Vice-President.

The electors shall meet in their respective States,* and vote by ballot for President and Vice-President, one of whom, at least, shall not be an inhabitant of the same State with themselves; they shall name, in their ballots, the person voted for as President, and in distinct ballots the person voted for as Vice-President; and they shall make distinct lists of all persons voted for as President, and of all persons voted for as Vice-President, and of the number of votes for each; which lists they shall sign and certify, and transmit, sealed,† to the seat of the Government of the United States, directed to the President of the Senate; the President of the Senate shall, in the presence of the Senate and House of Representatives, open all the certificates,‡ and the votes shall then be counted; the person having the greatest number of votes for President shall be the President, if such number be a majority of the whole number of electors appointed. And if no person have such a majority, then from the persons having the highest number, not exceeding three, on the list of those voted for as President, the House of Representatives shall choose immediately, by ballot, the President; but in choosing the President, the votes shall be taken by States, the representation from each State having one vote; a quorum for this purpose shall consist of a member or members from two-thirds of the States, and a majority of all the States shall be necessary to a choice; and if the House of Representatives shall not choose a President whenever the right of a choice shall devolve upon them, before the fourth day of March next following, then the Vice-President shall act as President, as in the case of the death or other constitutional disability of the President. The person having the greatest number of votes as Vice-President shall be the Vice-President, if such number be a majority of the whole number of electors appointed; and if no person have a majority, then from the two highest numbers on the list, the Senate shall choose the Vice-President; a quorum for the purpose shall consist of two-thirds of the whole number of Senators, and a majority of the whole number shall be necessary to a choice. But no person constitutionally ineligible to the office of President, shall be eligible to that of Vice-President of the United States.

ARTICLE XIII.
Slavery Prohibited—Thirteenth Amendment, Passed 1865.

SECTION I. Neither slavery nor involuntary servitude, except as a punishment for crime, whereof the party shall have been duly convicted, shall exist within the United States, or any place subject to their jurisdiction.

SECT. II. Congress shall have power to enforce this article by appropriate legislation.

---
* On the first Wednesday in December, by act of Congress, 1st March, 1792.
† Before the first Wednesday in January, by act of Congress, 1st March, 1792.
‡ On the second Wednesday in February, by the same act.

Fourteenth Amendment.

SECTION I. All persons born or naturalized in the United States, and subject to the jurisdiction thereof are citizens of the United States, and of the State wherein they reside. No State shall make or enforce any law which shall abridge the privileges or immunities of citizens of the United States. Nor shall any State deprive any person of life, liberty, or property, without due process of law, nor deny to any person within its jurisdiction the equal protection of the laws

SECT. II. Representatives shall be apportioned among the several States according to their respective numbers, counting the whole number of persons in each State, excluding Indians not taxed; but whenever the right to vote at any election for electors of President and Vice-President, or for United States Representatives in Congress, executive and judicial officers, or the members of the Legislature thereof, is denied to any of the male inhabitants of such State, being twenty-one years of age and citizens of the United States, or in any way abridged, except for participation in rebellion or other crime, the basis of representation therein shall be reduced in the proportion which the number of such male citizens shall bear to the whole number of male citizens twenty-one years of age in such State.

SECT. III. No person shall be a Senator or Representative in Congress, elector of President and Vice-President, or hold any office, civil or military, under the United States, or under any State, who having previously taken an oath as a member of Congress, or as an officer of the United States, or as a member of any State Legislature, or as an executive or judicial officer of any State, to support the Constitution of the United States, shall have engaged in insurrection or rebellion against the same, or given aid or comfort to the enemies thereof; but Congress may, by a vote of two-thirds of each House, remove such disability.

SECT. IV. The validity of the public debt of the United States authorized by law, including debts incurred for the payment of pensions and bounties for service in suppressing insurrection or rebellion, shall not be questioned, but neither the United States nor any State shall assume or pay any debt or obligation incurred in aid of insurrection or rebellion against the United States, or claim for the loss or emancipation of any slave, but all such debts, obligations and claims shall be held illegal and void.

SECT. V. The Congress shall have power to enforce, by appropriate legislation, the provisions of this article.

Fifteenth Amendment to the Constitution of the United States, Passed by the Fortieth Congress.

Be it resolved, etc., Two-thirds of both Houses concurring, that the following amendment to the Constitution of the United States be submitted to the Legislatures of the several States, and when ratified by three-fourths thereof, it shall be a part of said Constitution.

ARTICLE XV.

SECTION I. The right of citizens of the United States to vote shall not be denied or abridged by the United States, or by any State, on account of race, color, or previous conditions of servitude.

SECT. II. The Congress shall have power to enforce this article by appropriate legislation

Origin, Settlement and Population of United States and Territories.

State or Territory	Popular name	Settled	Territory from which derived
Alabama	Cotton	1713	District of Louisiana, Ga., Fla., Miss. Ter.
Alaska Territory			Bought from Russia.
Arizona Territory		1590	New Mexico.
Arkansas	Bear	1685	Dist. of Louisiana, Miss, and Ark. Ter.
California	Golden	1769	New Albion, Upper California.
Colorado	Centennial	1540	Dist. of Louisiana and Mexican Cession.
a Connecticut	Nutmeg	1633	North Virginia and New England.
a Delaware	Blue Hen	1627	New Netherlands.
District Columbia		1669	Maryland and Virginia.
Florida	Peninsular	1565	Florida Territory.
a Georgia	Cracker	1733	North Virginia and New England.
Idaho		1842	Idaho Territory.
Illinois	Sucker	1720	Northwest and Illinois Territory.
Indian Territory		1832	Louisiana.
Indiana	Hoosier	1730	Northwest and Indiana Territory.
Iowa	Hawkeye	1835	Dist. La., La. Ter., Mo., Mich., Wis. Ter.
Kansas	Sunflower	1850	Dist. Louisiana and Kansas Territory.
Kentucky	Bluegrass	1775	Virginia.
Louisiana	Pelican	1699	Dist. Louisiana, Territory of New Orleans.
Maine	Pine Tree	1630	New England, Laconia, Massachusetts.
a Maryland	Old Line	1634	
a Massachusetts	Bay	1620	North Virginia and New England.
Michigan	Wolverine	1670	Northwest, Indiana and Michigan Ter.
Minnesota	Gopher	1819	Dist. of Louisiana, Minnesota Territory.
Mississippi	Bayou	1716	Dist. of Louisiana, Ga. and Miss. Ter.
Missouri		1735	Dist. of Louisiana, Missouri Territory.
Montana	Stubtoe	1852	Montana Territory.
Nebraska	Black-water	1850	Dist. of Louisiana, Nebraska Territory.
Nevada	Silver	1850	Upper California.
a New Hampshire	Granite	1623	North Virginia, Laconia, New England.
a New Jersey		1627	New Netherlands.
New Mexico Ter		1582	Mexico.
a New York	Empire	1623	North Virginia, New Netherlands.
a North Carolina	Old North	1585	Albemarle Colony.
North Dakota	Flickertail	1859	Dakota Territory.
Ohio	Buckeye	1768	Northwest Territory.
Oklahoma Territory		1889	Indian Territory.
Oregon	Beaver	1811	Dist. of Louisiana, Oregon Territory.
a Pennsylvania	Keystone	1648	
a Rhode Island	Little Rhody	1636	No. Va., N. E., Aquiday, Prov., R. I. Plan.
a South Carolina	Palmetto	1562	Cartaret Colony.
South Dakota	Swingecat	1859	Dakota Territory.
Tennessee	Volunteer	1765	Kentucky Territory.
Texas	Lone Star	1690	New Philippines.
Utah		1847	Upper California.
Vermont	Green Mountain	1763	New Netherlands, New Hampshire Grants.
a Virginia	Old Dominion	1607	South Virginia.
Washington	Chinook	1845	Washington Territory.
West Virginia	Little Mountain	1607	South Virginia, Virginia.
Wisconsin	Badger	1715	Dist. Louisiana, Illinois Ter., Michigan Ter.
Wyoming		1867	Wyoming Territory.

a The thirteen original States.

State or Territory.	By Whom Settled.	Date of Admission or Ter. Organization.	bPopulation at Time of Adm'n.	cPresent Population.
Alabama	French	December 14, 1819	127,901	1,513,017
Alaska Territory		July 27, 1868		38,000
Arizona Territory	Spanish	February 24, 1863		59,620
Arkansas	French	June 15, 1836	52,240	1,128,179
California	Spanish	September 9, 1850	92,597	1,208,130
Colorado	French	August 1, 1876	150,000	412,198
aConnecticut	Em. from Mass	January 9, 1788	237,496	746,258
aDelaware	Swedes and Finns	December 7, 1787	59,096	168,493
District Columbia	English	July, 1791		230,392
Florida	Spanish	March 3, 1845	58,680	391,132
aGeorgia	English	January 2, 1788	82,548	1,837,353
Idaho	Emigrants	July 3, 1890	84,229	84,385
Illinois	French	December 3, 1818	34,620	3,826,351
Indian Territory	Spanish	June 30, 1834		345,000
Indiana	French	December 11, 1816	63,805	2,132,404
Iowa	Em. from N. E.	December 28, 1816	81,920	1,911,896
Kansas	Em. from West. St.	January 29, 1861	107,206	1,427,096
Kentucky	Em. from Virginia	June 1, 1792	73,677	1,858,635
Louisiana	French	April 30, 1812	76,566	1,118,587
dMaine	English	March 15, 1820	298,269	660,086
aMaryland	English	April 28, 1788	319,728	1,043,380
aMassachusetts	English Puritans	February 6, 1788	378,787	2,238,943
Michigan	French	January 26, 1837	212,267	2,086,889
Minnesota	Em. from N. E.	May 11, 1858	172,023	1,301,826
Mississippi	French	December 10, 1817	75,512	1,289,600
Missouri	French	August 10, 1821	66,586	2,679,184
Montana	Em. from South	November 8, 1889	131,769	132,159
Nebraska	Emigrants	March 1, 1867	60,000	1,058,910
Nevada	Em. from Cal	October 31, 1864	40,000	45,000
aNew Hampshire	English	June 21, 1788	141,885	376,530
aNew Jersey	Dutch and Danes	December 18, 1787	184,139	1,444,933
New Mexico Ter.	Spanish	September 9, 1850		153,593
aNew York	Dutch	July 26, 1788	340,120	5,997,853
aNorth Carolina	English	November 21, 1789	393,751	1,617,947
North Dakota	Em. from Mid. St's	November 2, 1889	182,425	182,719
Ohio	Em. from N. E.	November 29, 1802	41,915	3,672,316
Oklahoma Territory	Emigrants	April 22, 1889		61,834
Oregon	Em. from N. Y.	February 11, 1859	52,465	313,767
aPennsylvania	Swedes	December 12, 1787	434,373	5,258,014
aRhode Island	English	May 29, 1790	68,825	345,506
aSouth Carolina	French	May 23, 1788	249,073	1,144,149
South Dakota	Em. from Mid. St's	November 2, 1889	327,848	328,808
Tennessee	Em. from N. C.	June 1, 1796	77,262	1,767,518
Texas	Spanish	December 29, 1845	212,592	2,235,523
Utah	Spanish	{ Ter., Sept. 9, 1850 } { state, 1891 }		207,905
Vermont	Em. from Mass	March 4, 1791	85,339	332,422
aVirginia	English	June 25, 1788	747,610	1,655,980
Washington	Em. from Cal	November 11, 1889		349,390
West Virginia	English	June 19, 1863	442,014	762,794
Wisconsin	French	May 29, 1848	305,391	1,686,880
Wyoming	Em. from Mid. St's	July 10, 1889	60,589	60,705

The thirteen original States. b According to nearest census. c Census of 1890. d Previously a part of Massachusetts.

POPULATION OF THE UNITED STATES.

AT EACH CENSUS FROM 1790 TO 1890.

(Compiled from the Reports of the Superintendents of the Census.)

STATES AND TERRITORIES.	1810.	1820.	1830.	1840.	1850.	1860.	1870.	1880.	1890.
Alabama		127,901	309,527	590,756	771,623	964,201	996,992	1,262,505	1,513,017
Arizona							9,658	40,440	59,620
Arkansas		14,255	30,388	97,574	209,897	435,450	484,471	802,525	1,128,179
California					92,597	379,994	560,247	864,694	1,208,130
Colorado						34,277	39,864	194,327	412,198
Connecticut	261,942	275,148	297,675	309,978	370,792	460,147	537,454	622,700	746,258
Dakota						4,837	14,181	135,177	
Delaware	72,674	72,749	76,748	78,085	91,532	112,216	125,015	146,608	168,493
D. of Columbia	24,023	32,039	39,834	43,712	51,687	75,080	131,700	177,624	230,392
Florida			34,730	54,477	87,445	140,424	187,748	269,493	391,422
Georgia	252,433	340,985	516,823	691,392	906,185	1,057,286	1,184,109	1,542,180	1,837,353
Idaho							14,999	32,610	84,385
Illinois	12,282	55,162	157,445	476,183	851,470	1,711,951	2,539,891	3,077,871	3,826,351
Indiana	24,520	147,178	343,031	685,866	988,416	1,350,428	1,680,637	1,978,301	2,192,404
Iowa				43,112	192,214	674,913	1,194,020	1,624,615	1,911,896
Kansas						107,206	364,399	996,096	1,427,096
Kentucky	406,511	564,135	687,917	779,828	982,405	1,155,684	1,321,011	1,648,690	1,858,635
Louisiana	76,566	152,923	215,739	352,411	517,762	708,002	726,915	939,946	1,118,587
Maine	228,705	298,269	399,455	501,793	583,169	628,279	626,915	648,936	661,086
Maryland	380,546	407,350	447,040	470,019	583,031	687,049	780,894	934,943	1,012,390
Massachusetts	472,040	523,159	610,408	737,699	994,514	1,231,066	1,457,351	1,783,085	2,238,943
Michigan	4,762	8,765	31,639	212,267	397,654	749,113	1,184,059	1,636,937	2,093,889
Minnesota					6,077	172,023	439,706	780,773	1,301,826
Mississippi	40,352	75,148	136,621	375,651	606,526	791,305	827,922	1,131,597	1,289,600
Missouri	20,845	66,557	140,455	383,702	682,044	1,182,012	1,721,295	2,168,380	2,679,184
Montana							20,595	39,159	132,159
Nebraska						28,841	122,993	452,402	1,058,910
Nevada						6,857	42,491	62,266	45,761
New Hampshire	214,460	244,022	269,328	284,574	317,976	326,073	318,300	346,991	376,530
New Jersey	245,562	277,126	320,823	373,306	489,555	672,035	906,096	1,131,116	1,444,933
New Mexico					61,547	93,516	91,874	119,565	153,593
New York	959,049	1,372,111	1,918,608	2,428,921	3,097,394	3,880,735	4,382,759	5,082,871	5,997,853
North Carolina	555,500	638,829	737,987	753,419	869,039	992,622	1,071,361	1,399,750	1,617,947
North Dakota									182,719
Ohio	230,760	581,295	937,903	1,519,467	1,980,329	2,339,511	2,665,260	3,198,062	3,672,316
Oklahoma									61,834
Oregon					13,294	52,465	90,923	174,768	313,767
Pennsylvania	810,091	1,047,507	1,348,233	1,724,033	2,311,786	2,906,215	3,521,951	4,282,891	5,258,014
Rhode Island	76,931	83,015	97,199	108,830	147,545	174,620	217,353	276,531	345,506
South Carolina	415,115	502,741	581,185	594,398	668,507	703,708	705,606	995,577	1,151,149
South Dakota									328,808
Tennessee	261,727	422,771	681,904	829,210	1,002,717	1,109,801	1,258,520	1,542,359	1,767,518
Texas					212,592	604,215	818,579	1,591,749	2,235,523
Utah					11,380	40,273	86,786	143,963	207,905
Vermont	217,895	235,966	280,652	291,948	314,120	315,098	330,551	332,286	332,422
Virginia	974,600	1,065,116	1,211,405	1,239,797	1,421,661	1,596,318	1,225,163	1,512,565	1,655,980
Washington						11,594	23,955	75,116	349,390
West Virginia							442,014	618,457	762,794
Wisconsin				30,945	305,391	775,881	1,054,670	1,315,497	1,686,880
Wyoming							9,118	20,789	60,705
Total	7,239,881	9,633,822	12,866,020	17,069,453	23,191,876	31,443,321	38,558,371	50,155,783	62,622,250

The inhabitants of Alaska and the Indian Territory are not included in the above. The population of Alaska, in 1890, was 30,329; of the Indian Territory, 179,321. Total population of the United States in 1890, 62,831,900.

POPULATION: CENSUS OF 1790.—Connecticut, 237,916; Delaware, 59,096; Georgia, 82,548; Kentucky, 73,677; Maine,* 96,540; Maryland, 319,728; Massachusetts, 378,787; New Hampshire, 141,885; New Jersey, 184,139; New York, 393,751; Pennsylvania, 434,373; Rhode Island, 68,825; South Carolina, 249,072; Tennessee, 35,691; Vermont, 85,425; Virginia, 747,610. Total U. S., 3,589,063.

POPULATION: CENSUS OF 1800.—Connecticut, 251,002; Delaware, 64,273; District of Columbia, 14,093; Georgia, 162,686; Indiana, 5,641; Kentucky, 220,955; Maine,* 151,719; Maryland, 341,548; Massachusetts, 422,845; Mississippi, 8,850; New Hampshire, 183,858; New Jersey, 211,149; New York, 589,051; North Carolina, 478,103; Ohio, 45,365; Pennsylvania, 602,365; Rhode Island, 69,122; South Carolina, 345,591; Tennessee, 105,602; Vermont, 154,465; Virginia, 880,200; Total, U. S., 5,308,483.

POPULATION PRIOR TO 1790 (according to Bancroft): 1688, 200,000; 1714, 434,600; 1727, 580,000; 1750, 1,260,000; 1754, 1,425,000; 1760, 1,695,000; 1770, 2,312,000; 1780, 2,945,000 (2,383,000 white, 562,000 colored).

WHITE AND NEGRO POPULATION OF THE SOUTH.

The following shows the growth of the population by decades in the territory now covered by the sixteen Southern States—Alabama, Arkansas, Delaware, Florida, Georgia, Kentucky, Louisiana, Maryland, Mississippi, Missouri, North Carolina, South Carolina, Tennessee, Texas, Virginia and West Virginia, and the District of Columbia:

In 1790, the white population was 1,271,488; 1800, 1,702,980; 1810, 2,208,785; 1820, 2,831,560; 1830, 3,660,758; 1840, 4,632,530; 1850, 6,222,418; 1860, 8,097,462; 1870, 9,466,353; 1880, 12,578,253; 1890, 15,549,358.

In 1790, the colored population was 689,884; 1800, 918,336; 1810, 1,272,-119; 1820, 1,653,240; 1830, 2,187,545; 1840, 2,701,901; 1850, 3,442,238; 1860, 4,215,614; 1870, 4,538,883; 1880, 6,099,253; 1890, 6,898,806.

From the above it will be seen that in the above Southern States and the District of Columbia the colored population increased from 1880 to 1890, at the rate of 13.1 per cent., and the white at the rate of 23.6 per cent.

* Maine was a part of Massachusetts until its admission into the Union in 1820.

POPULATION OF THE UNITED STATES ACCORDING TO NATIONALITY.

(Compiled from the reports of the census of 1890.)

STATES AND TERRITORIES.	German Born.	Irish Born.	English Born.*	Scotch Born.	British American Born.	Scandinavian Born.	Russian and Polish Born.	French Born.	Italian Born.
Alabama	3,945	2,604	2,945	1,391	628	412	328	592	323
Arizona	1,188	1,171	1,117	318	722	407	66	296	207
Arkansas	6,225	2,021	1,570	439	947	518	364	428	187
California	61,472	63,138	35,566	9,296	26,028	22,389	1,054	11,855	15,495
Colorado	15,151	12,352	14,107	4,339	9,112	12,202	1,578	1,328	3,882
Connecticut	28,176	77,880	20,573	5,992	21,231	12,018	4,351	2,018	5,285
Delaware	2,469	6,121	1,917	432	399	301	731	181	459
Dist. of Columbia	5,778	7,224	2,128	578	655	270	309	383	467
Florida	1,855	1,056	2,705	570	1,151	843	118	275	108
Georgia	3,679	3,374	1,585	619	609	340	320	306	179
Idaho	1,939	1,917	3,138	645	1,791	3,506	128	178	509
Illinois	338,382	124,498	70,510	20,165	39,523	128,897	37,285	8,540	8,035
Indiana	84,900	20,819	11,290	2,948	4,854	5,515	3,620	3,297	468
Iowa	127,246	37,353	26,228	7,701	17,465	72,872	1,295	2,387	399
Kansas	46,123	15,879	18,086	5,546	11,871	22,018	10,195	2,236	616
Kentucky	32,620	13,926	4,162	1,040	1,173	396	566	1,168	707
Louisiana	11,625	9,236	2,457	465	762	626	445	8,137	7,767
Maine	1,104	11,144	7,286	2,285	52,076	2,711	174	111	253
Maryland	52,136	18,755	5,591	2,323	1,020	599	6,655	623	1,116
Massachusetts	28,034	259,902	76,513	21,909	207,601	22,658	10,466	3,273	8,066
Michigan	135,569	39,065	55,388	12,068	181,416	41,496	27,558	5,182	3,008
Minnesota	116,555	28,011	14,715	5,315	43,580	215,215	14,736	1,869	828
Mississippi	2,284	1,865	887	203	315	449	191	149	425
Missouri	123,464	40,366	18,675	1,604	8,525	7,461	4,065	4,175	2,416
Montana	5,089	6,618	6,481	1,588	9,040	6,411	842	478	734
Nebraska	72,618	15,963	11,172	3,830	12,105	46,311	7,786	1,256	717
Nevada	1,563	2,616	2,149	960	1,662	715	78	226	1,129
New Hampshire	1,631	11,800	4,763	1,906	46,321	1,525	218	222	312
New Jersey	106,181	101,059	43,785	13,163	4,698	8,467	8,935	4,711	12,989
New Mexico	1,413	966	1,258	436	681	215	97	284	355
New York	498,602	483,375	114,422	35,572	93,186	43,270	81,184	20,443	64,141
North Carolina	1,077	451	882	341	355	90	97	55	28
North Dakota	8,963	2,987	3,321	1,788	23,045	34,216	4,335	208	21
Ohio	235,668	70,127	51,027	10,275	16,515	1,269	10,513	7,171	3,857
Oklahoma	739	329	280	118	420	211	64	82	11
Oregon	12,475	4,891	5,079	2,242	6,460	7,354	2,679	842	589
Pennsylvania	230,516	243,836	125,115	32,084	12,171	23,584	42,306	20,033	21,662
Rhode Island	3,200	38,920	20,913	4,984	27,934	3,831	861	460	2,408
South Carolina	2,702	1,695	597	293	159	119	241	138	106
South Dakota	18,188	4,774	5,113	1,579	9,493	34,372	12,674	350	209
Tennessee	5,364	5,016	2,857	704	1,020	465	645	490	788
Texas	48,843	8,201	9,443	2,172	2,866	4,768	2,568	2,730	2,107
Utah	2,121	2,015	20,906	3,474	1,222	16,863	310	205	347
Vermont	877	9,840	3,519	1,730	25,004	966	212	175	445
Virginia	4,361	4,578	3,355	1,051	780	125	171	331	1,219
Washington	15,399	7,799	9,857	3,544	17,442	21,163	2,327	1,046	1,108
West Virginia	7,202	4,799	2,700	914	374	123	195	213	632
Wisconsin	259,819	33,306	23,633	5,494	33,463	99,738	19,969	2,909	1,123
Wyoming	2,037	1,900	3,148	1,380	1,134	2,382	812	127	259
Totals	2,784,894	1,871,509	909,092	242,231	980,938	933,249	330,084	113,174	182,580

* Includes natives of Great Britain not specified.

The following are the total number of foreign born inhabitants in the United States, according to nationality: From Germany, 2,784,894; Ireland, 1,871,509; British America including Newfoundland, 980,938; England, 909,092; Sweden, 478,041; Norway, 322,665; Scotland, 242,231; Russia, 182,644; Italy, 182,580; Poland, 147,440; Denmark, 132,543; Austria, 123,271; Bohemia, 118,106; France, 113,174; China, 106,688; Switzerland, 104,069; Wales, 100,079; Netherlands, 81,828; Mexico, 77,853; Hungary, 62,435; Belgium and Luxembourg, 25,521; Cuba and West Indies, 23,256; Portugal, 15,996; Central and South America, 6,198; Spain, 6,185; India, including Asia, not specified, 4,403; Japan, 2,292; Greece, 1,887; all others, 11,729. Total foreign born, 9,249,547.

The number of persons in the United States of foreign parentage (1890) is 20,676,046, being 33.02 per cent. of the population. The percentage in 1880 was 29.75; in 1870 was 28.25. The total number of foreign born and born of foreign parentage, 29,925,593. Total number of native born and born of native parentage, 32,696,657.

Percentage of increase of foreign born inhabitants from 1880 to 1890, specified according to nationality: Hungarians, 441.7; Russians, 411.3; Italians, 312.8; Austrians, 248.8; Poles, 203.6; Swedes, 146.0; Danes, 106.4; Portuguese, 86.5; Norwegians, 77.5; Belgians, 45.7; Scotch, 42.3; Cubans and West Indians, 41.8; Germans, 41.6; Dutch, 40.8; Bohemians, 38.3; British-Americans, 36.7; English, 36.8; Spaniards, 29.7; Welsh, 20.1; Swiss, 17.4; Mexicans, 13.8; South Americans, 9.6; French, 5.8; Chinese, 2.4; Irish, 0.9.

POPULATION OF THE UNITED STATES.

(Compiled from the Census Report of 1890.)

NUMBER OF DWELLINGS AND FAMILIES IN EACH OF THE STATES.

STATES AND TERRITORIES.	Number of Dwellings.	Persons to a Dwelling.	Number of Families.	Persons to a Family.	STATES AND TERRITORIES.	Number of Dwellings.	Persons to a Dwelling.	Number of Families.	Persons to a Family.
Alabama	284,692	5.37	287,292	5.27	Nevada	10,066	4.55	10,170	4.50
Arizona	13,358	4.47	13,195	4.42	N. Hampshire	76,665	4.91	87,548	4.31
Arkansas	209,190	5.39	213,620	5.28	New Jersey	247,332	5.84	308,539	4.69
California	235,925	5.12	245,710	4.92	New Mexico	34,671	4.43	35,504	4.33
Colorado	81,127	5.08	84,276	4.89	New York	895,593	6.70	1,308,015	4.59
Connecticut	130,779	5.71	165,890	4.50	N'rth Carolina	304,571	5.37	306,952	5.27
Delaware	33,882	4.97	34,578	4.87	North Dakota	37,918	4.82	38,478	4.75
Dist. of Col.	38,798	5.94	43,967	5.24	Ohio	720,414	5.10	785,291	4.68
Florida	78,816	4.97	80,050	4.89	Oklahoma	14,992	4.14	15,049	4.11
Georgia	342,871	5.36	352,059	5.22	Oregon	61,925	5.07	63,791	4.92
Idaho	17,882	4.73	18,113	4.66	Pennsylvania	999,364	5.26	1,061,626	4.95
Illinois	669,842	5.71	778,015	4.92	Rhode Island	72,250	6.51	75,010	4.64
Indiana	452,043	4.85	467,146	4.69	S'th Caro ina	217,195	5.30	222,941	5.16
Iowa	379,318	5.04	388,517	4.92	South Dakota	68,894	4.77	70,250	4.68
Kansas	292,086	4.89	297,358	4.80	Tennessee	323,136	5.47	334,194	5.29
Kentucky	335,900	5.53	351,193	5.24	Texas	402,422	5.56	411,251	5.44
Louisiana	244,344	5.47	244,128	5.22	Utah	37,285	5.58	38,815	5.36
Maine	135,255	4.89	150,355	4.40	Vermont	49,817	4.76	75,896	4.38
Maryland	184,204	5.66	202,179	5.16	Virginia	292,654	5.66	304,673	5.44
Massachusetts	355,290	6.30	479,790	4.67	Washington	68,853	5.08	70,977	4.92
Michigan	434,370	4.82	455,004	4.60	West Virginia	136,378	5.59	140,359	5.43
Minnesota	229,678	5.67	247,975	5.25	Wisconsin	346,163	5.34	365,456	5.03
Mississippi	235,656	5.47	241,148	5.35	Wyoming	11,880	5.11	12,065	5.03
Missouri	485,320	5.52	528,295	5.07					
Montana	26,934	4.94	27,501	4.84	Total	11,483,318	5.45	12,690,152	4.93
Nebraska	201,470	5.26	208,820	5.12					

NATIONALITY OF INHABITANTS OF LARGEST CITIES—1890.

CITIES.	Total Foreign Born.	British Americans	Irish.	English.	Scotch.	Germans.	Austrians	French.	Italians.
New York	639,943	8,398	190,418	35,907	11,242	210,723	27,193	10,535	39,951
Chicago, Ill	450,666	24,297	70,028	28,337	9,217	161,039	6,043	2,502	5,685
Philadelphia, Pa	269,180	2,584	110,935	38,926	8,772	74,971	2,003	2,550	6,799
Brooklyn, N. Y	261,700	5,897	84,738	26,493	7,417	94,798	1,493	2,102	9,563
St. Louis, Mo	114,876	2,008	24,270	6,507	1,370	66,000	1,586	1,717	1,295
Boston, Mass	158,172	38,294	71,441	13,454	4,190	10,362	391	875	4,718
Baltimore, Md	69,003	521	13,389	3,089	666	40,709	1,221	424	824
San Francisco, Cal	126,811	4,371	30,718	9,828	3,184	26,422	1,263	4,643	5,212
Cincinnati, O	71,408	915	12,923	2,950	621	49,415	389	899	738
Cleveland, O	97,095	5,157	13,512	10,950	2,660	39,893	2,584	123	635
Buffalo, N. Y	89,485	10,610	11,664	7,098	1,625	42,660	1,036	975	1,832
New Orleans, La	34,369	346	7,923	1,509	270	11,338	268	5,710	3,622
Pittsburg, Pa	73,229	630	21,105	10,143	2,157	25,363	1,196	660	1,899
Washington, D. C	18,770	655	7,224	2,126	578	5,778	130	385	467
Detroit, Mich	81,709	18,791	7,447	7,168	2,459	35,481	658	864	338
Milwaukee, Wis	79,776	1,249	3,136	2,109	686	54,776	928	206	157
Newark, N. J	55,571	529	13,234	5,625	1,570	26,520	941	589	2,921
Minneapolis, Minn	60,358	7,773	3,746	2,487	950	7,719	571	232	140
Jersey City, N. J	53,358	922	22,159	5,442	1,849	16,086	345	618	1,195
Louisville, Ky	23,510	390	5,263	987	276	14,094	91	412	264

	Russians.	Hungarians.	Bohemians.	Poles.	Norwegians.	Swedes.	Danes.	Spaniards.	Chinese.
New York	48,790	12,222	8,099	6,759	1,575	7,069	1,495	887	2,048
Chicago, Ill	7,483	1,818	25,105	24,086	21,835	43,032	7,987	120	584
Philadelphia, Pa	7,879	1,354	189	2,189	1,500	1,626	704	136	785
Brooklyn, N. Y	3,397	663	143	1,887	4,873	9,325	1,839	526	600
St. Louis, Mo	1,638	253	2,301	875	134	876	25	45	177
Boston, Mass	4,805	188	104	954	861	3,113	353	149	497
Baltimore, Md	4,057	162	1,568	935	139	213	81	40	190
San Francisco, Cal	1,064	167	82	501	1,396	3,594	1,785	230	21,613
Cincinnati, O	978	120	28	227	9	90	41	16	21
Cleveland, O	1,482	3,210	10,287	2,848	129	464	24	10	38
Buffalo, N. Y	610	80	15	8,879	132	515	128	23	19
New Orleans, La	146	25	9	36	63	163	115	693	152
Pittsburg, Pa	2,279	794	95	2,750	31	656	37	10	96
Washington, D. C	244	41	10	65	70	128	72	41	95
Detroit, Mich	699	112	513	5,351	77	196	162	13	10
Milwaukee, Wis	548	197	1,060	9,229	1,521	320	311	5	18
Newark, N. J	1,285	430	69	463	39	211	186	9	137
Minneapolis, Minn	994	269	293	381	12,624	19,398	1,592	6	22
Jersey City, N. J	576	78	11	1,206	316	558	195	49	140
Louisville, Ky	274	13	7	126	95	66	41	21	9

REQUIREMENTS REGARDING THE REGISTRATION OF VOTERS.

The registration of voters is required in the States of Alabama, California, Colorado, Connecticut, Florida, Idaho, Illinois, Louisiana, Maryland, Massachusetts, Michigan, Minnesota, Montana, Mississippi, Nevada, New Hampshire, New Jersey, North Carolina, Ohio, Pennsylvania, South Carolina, Vermont, Virginia and Wyoming, and the Territories of Arizona, New Mexico and Utah.

In Georgia, registration is required in some counties by local law.

In Kentucky, registration is required in cities; in Kansas, in cities of the first and second class; in Iowa and Nebraska, in cities of and over 2,500 inhabitants; in North Dakota, in cities of over 3,000 inhabitants; in Ohio, in cities of not less than 9,000 inhabitants; in Maine, in all cities and in towns having 500 or more voters; in South Dakota, in cities and towns having over 1,000 voters and in counties where registration has been adopted by popular vote, and in Tennessee, in all counties having 50,000 inhabitants and over.

In Missouri, it is required in cities of 100,000 inhabitants, and in Wisconsin, in cities having 3,000 inhabitants and over. In New York, it is required in all cities and in all incorporated villages of over 7,000 inhabitants. In Rhode Island, non-taxpayers are required to register yearly before December 31st. In Texas, cities of 10,000 or over may require registration.

The registration of voters is not required in the State of Oregon. It is prohibited in Arkansas and West Virginia by constitutional provision.

WOMAN SUFFRAGE.

The Legislatures of Connecticut and New York, in their sessions of 1893, passed laws permitting women to vote for school officers. The privilege was used to a limited extend in both States, but in the November election a Supreme Court Judge in New York decided that the act of that State was unconstitutional. Notwithstanding this, the Attorney-General of the State advised all election officers to treat the law as constitutional until the question could be adjudicated by the highest tribunal. The Iowa and Ohio Legislatures in 1894, granted suffrage in school elections to women.

In the New York State Convention in 1894, to revise the Constitution, a woman suffrage amendment was defeated by a vote of 97 to 58.

The Michigan Legislature of 1893, adopted a law authorizing women to vote at municipal elections. In October the Supreme Court of the State declared the law unconstitutional.

In Wyoming, women have full suffrage and vote for all officers, including Presidential electors. The woman suffrage law was adopted in 1870.

In the State election in Colorado in 1893, the people voted in favor of general woman suffrage.

In Kansas, women exercise the suffrage largely in municipal elections. In November, 1894, the people voted upon a constitutional amendment providing for woman suffrage.

Women formerly voted in the Territory of Washington, and until they were excluded by a decision of the Territorial Supreme Court. In adopting a State Constitution, the question of allowing women to use the ballot was submitted to a separate vote of the electors, and was defeated. Women voted in the Territory of Utah until excluded by the Edmunds law.

But in some form, mainly as to taxation or the selection of school officers, woman suffrage exists in a limited way in Arizona, Colorado, Delaware, Idaho, Illinois, Indiana, Iowa, Kentucky, Massachusetts, Michigan, Minnesota, Montana, Nebraska, New Hampshire, New Jersey, North Dakota, Ohio, Oklahoma, Oregon, South Dakota, Texas, Vermont, Washington and Wisconsin.

In many European countries, in Australia and New Zealand, in Cape Colony, in Canada, and in parts of India, women vote on various terms for municipal or school officers.

THE BALLOT REFORM MOVEMENT.

The following is a list of the States and Territories which have adopted new ballot laws, based more or less on the Australian system :

1888—Kentucky (applying only to Louisville), Massachusetts.

1889—Connecticut, Indiana, Michigan, Minnesota, Missouri, Montana, Rhode Island, Tennessee, Wisconsin.

1890—Maryland (applying to Baltimore), New Jersey, New York, Oklahoma, Vermont, Washington, Wyoming.

1891—Arkansas, California, Delaware, Idaho, Illinois, Maine, Nebraska, New Hampshire, North Dakota, Ohio, Pennsylvania, South Dakota, Oregon, West Virginia, Colorado.

1892—Iowa, Maryland (whole State), Mississippi.

1893—Alabama, Kansas, Kentucky, Nevada, Texas, and in Florida for the city of Jacksonville.

1894—Virginia.

The only States in which some form of reformed balloting does not yet exist are : Georgia, Louisiana, North Carolina, South Carolina.

FORM OF BALLOT.

The distinctive feature of the ballot practice in New South Wales is that the names of all the candidates being on one ticket, the names of persons for whom the voter does not wish to vote must be crossed off, a blue lead pencil being provided for the purpose by the authorities, while there are clearly printed on the ticket, in red ink, directions as to how many candidates must be voted for.

Under the New York and New Jersey laws each party ticket is printed on a separate ballot. For straight voting, therefore, no marking is required. For the benefit mainly of the illiterate or blind, as claimed, the paster ballot is permitted in New York.

In all the other States which have adopted the reform system of voting, the single or "blanket" ballot is used. All the names in nomination are printed on one sheet, the voter's choice to be indicated by marking. There are two methods used of grouping the names of the candidates. The Australian plan arranges the titles of the offices alphabetically, the names of the candidates, and usually their party connection being attached.

The States which follow this plan with more or less variation in the form but preserving the feature of alphabetical arrangement of titles of offices to be voted for, are California, Kentucky, Massachusetts, Minnesota, Montana, Nebraska, New Hampshire, Oregon, Rhode Island, Tennessee, Vermont, Virginia, Washington and Wyoming.

The other form groups all names and offices by parties. The voter of a straight ticket marks a cross in the circle at the head of his ticket. The voter who scatters, marks squares opposite the names of all the candidates on the tickets.

The States and Territories which use this plan, with or without immaterial variations, are Delaware, Illinois, Indiana, Kansas, Maine, Maryland, Missouri, Ohio, Wisconsin and Oklahoma.

www.ingramcontent.com/pod-product-compliance
Lightning Source LLC
Chambersburg PA
CBHW032138160426
43197CB00008B/693